In My Skin

In My Skin

A NOVEL

ERIN LODES

For my younger self and everyone who's ever felt guilty for struggling.

TRIGGER WARNING

This book contains descriptions of depression, self-harm, sexual assault, and attempted suicide. The main character's struggles with mental health and self-harm are based on my own experiences, and I am hoping this book will be to you what so many books have been to me over the years: a friend in the dark. Proof that someone else has felt and thought the same things I have, things I kept secret for so long.

I have included trigger warnings before particularly difficult scenes and chapters in an effort to help readers who might be struggling still find some solace in this story without worrying about stumbling across a particularly triggering scene in a moment when you're not on solid ground.

Resources can be found at the back of this book.

You're not alone. Take care of yourselves.

ONE

I'm not here.

"Kara I know you're in there. You can't avoid me forever."

The voice is muffled through my dorm room door. I'd locked it. I must have. I always lock it now. But dragons break down doors in all the stories. I'm not safe. I don't feel safe. Which means I should feel scared. Except I don't.

I don't feel anything.

I don't feel the floor underneath me or the wall at my back. I don't feel like I should run. I don't feel like I should hide. Because I'm not here. It isn't me.

That isn't my body, still tucked inside my thick winter coat, sitting on the floor against the wall with my knees pulled up to my chest. Those aren't my eyes, staring at my door like it's a thousand miles away. Those aren't my fingers, curled so tightly into fists that I—

Oh.

Deliberately, I unclench my fingers. They ache, stiff, as I stretch them out. I rest them palms up on my knees. How long have I been sitting here? How long has it been since it happened?

We can't do this anymore.

"Kara? It's me."

I don't need to see the person talking to know who it is.

I'd know that voice anywhere. Shush is a presence. A force of nature. You'd remember her physical appearance for sure with her large black curls and piercing gaze, but it's her voice that really sets her apart. Rising above the rest of the world's noise, making sure you hear her.

"Kara come on, open the door."

There's a slight pleading tone to her voice I recognize. She used it the last time I spoke with her. Three weeks ago. Quick passing words in a cold parking lot.

Eventually you'll forgive me.

I stare at my palms, where my nails have carved little white open-mouths into the soft flesh. I hadn't noticed.

"Kara?"

She knocks. Two soft raps. Hesitant, which isn't like Shush at all.

When she knocks, she announces her arrival like you were not only expecting her but will be delighted to discover she's finally appeared. She knocks and then just walks right in, confident you'll be happy to see her.

That's what started this whole mess.

"You have to let me in."

I don't move. If I open the door, all her loud words are going to come screaming out and they'll be so heavy. Weights on my shoulders, wrapped around my wrists, my ankles. I lean my head back against the wall and close my eyes. None of it matters anyway. I'm not moving. Whatever happens, happens. I don't care.

She stops knocking, stops talking, and in the silence I hear Eric.

We can't do this anymore.

And even though it just happened, I don't feel it. I don't feel like it *really* happened. Not to me. It happened to some other girl. Some other girl with blond hair and a face that looks like mine.

It's over.

I hadn't seen it coming. The break-up. The end. Of us. Of our story.

We hadn't seen each other over Winter Break. But we'd texted and talked on the phone and in three weeks I hadn't caught the edges of anything amiss.

It's over.

It's like a book ending in the middle. The last half nothing but blank pages when I thought there was so much story left.

I didn't cry when he did it. And I'm not crying now.

Because it didn't happen. Not really. Not to me. It happened to that other girl. The one wearing my face. The one who nodded and slipped away without a fuss.

I'm fine. I mouth the words silently, focusing on the way they feel on my lips.

Call me Eric.

I'm fine.

You're magic.

I'm fine.

It's all going to be okay.

I'm fine I'm fine I'm fine.

When he did it I walked out like nothing happened. As if the rug of my world hadn't just been ripped out from under me. As if I could still feel the ground beneath my feet.

You're magic.

None of it makes any sense. I should feel devastated. I should be sobbing. I should be breaking into pieces. Which means this can't be me. Sitting here existing and breathing like nothing has happened. It can't be me.

I'm not here.

A month ago, I would have gone straight to Shush after Eric broke up with me. I would have asked her for answers to my questions.

What do I do now?
But I'm not speaking to her anymore.
Kara you have to tell someone.
When I first met Shush, I'd just arrived at college, ready
to start my freshman year and trying to feel like I knew
what I was doing, trying to feel like—what's the expression?—a bright and shiny newly minted penny.

Having apparently made it through the heat and pressure of high school, I was supposed to arrive at college
with a clear picture of a head and a date. Instead, I felt like
currency from a country no one had ever heard of. I'm good
enough at pretending that you think I'm the right size and
weight to fit through the slot and get you that candy bar you
were craving but I slip right through, clanging uselessly into
the change cup for you to pick up and look at with confused
disappointment.

Not like Shush. Shush is the type of person who can be a
penny and also be a quarter at the exact same time and who
the hell are you to tell her otherwise.

The first words she ever said to me were an interruption.
It was a Friday afternoon, the day I moved to campus. I'd
finally managed to usher my parents out of my new dorm
room—they'd been helping me unpack. I got my own
room. Which, as an only child used to having space, I was
grateful for.

After my parents left, I'd debated closing the door but all
the other new students had their doors open and I didn't
want everyone to think I was an antisocial loner, so I left the
door open while I finished unpacking. I threw my clothes
in the small wardrobe and organized my new books on the
desk, tucked under the single window in the small room.
Then I curled up on my bed with a book.

I was lost in the deep, dark woods of an enchanted forest

when I was wrenched back to reality by a loud knock and a louder, "Hi."

I looked up and was nearly blinded by a bright smile.

"I'm Shush," she said, taking an uninvited step into my room. "I'm your new RA and I'm in charge of our orientation activities this weekend."

"Nice to meet you," I said. I didn't move to get up from my bed. She was just introducing herself. She'd soon disappear back the way she came. I should have known better. Dragons don't ever just disappear.

"Kara, right?" She was still smiling. It must hurt her face to smile that wide.

"Yeah, sorry. Kara." My face flamed slightly at my misstep. There were simple rules to an introduction, stage instructions I'd known since I was a child, but still somehow I had failed to follow the lines. Give the stranger your name. Duh. I'm always making mistakes like that.

"You settled in okay?"

"Yeah I'm good."

"Great. I'm just getting our floor together for the first part of orientation."

I wasn't sure what to say. I definitely didn't want to go but an outright dismissal seemed rude so I settled on, "Cool."

Don't say it. My body stilled, as if she was a dragon who only sensed movement. If I didn't move, she wouldn't see me, she'd just leave. Don't say it. Don't say it. Don't say—

"You coming?" she said.

No.

"Everyone else is heading downstairs for the first meet-up."

I swallowed a sigh. Apparently she was not the type of dragon who only sensed movement. Or the type of person who took hints.

"Yeah," I said, closing my book and getting up. "I'm coming."

You know those quizzes you take online? Answer some questions and they'll tell you what Hogwarts house you belong in or what character from *Friends* you're most like. Everyone seems to find them so easy, fun even. Whenever I take them, I feel like they're a test I fail. Like I answer the individual questions wrong, so I can't trust the result.

It's the same with the kinds of games you play at the start of every single team-building event you can think of. Get-to-know-each-other games. I've always hated them. They seem so simple. Tell your name and your favorite flavor of ice cream. But what if you aren't sure what flavor is your favorite? What if you don't know your favorite color or your favorite song? What if you find mysteries where everyone else finds simple answers? What do you say then?

There were fourteen of us there, sitting on cheap folding chairs in a semicircle. If I was in Shush's position, I would have been terrified. Getting up in front of people makes my fingers tremble. But Shush seemed entirely at ease. She stood in front of us, spinning a beach ball in her hands, obviously in her element.

"Call me Shush. You know, like 'shush be quiet.' My full name's Precious but like, really, call me Shush."

She didn't explain it then, but one night when we were up late studying, I'd finally asked her about the nickname.

"It's something my parents started to call me," she'd said. "I'm not sure when but probably as soon as I could form words they started calling me that. You can probably tell I really like to talk—it's something people notice about me right away and I'm not ashamed of it so that's fine and if I talk too much just tell me to shut up but anyway they told me when I got older and started talking that they used to tell me to 'shush' like 'Precious shush' and eventually it just turned into a nickname and it kind of stuck."

She seemed to say it all in one breath. She always talked that way, as if the words were running away from her and she had to tackle them before they could escape. It suited me. I'm not much of a talker and I found it relaxing to listen to her. Her voice, running like a river, could drown out the words inside my own head, the ones I didn't want to listen to.

Standing up in front of our orientation group for the first time, she smiled brightly—always brightly. "Here's the deal, catch the ball, say hello to the person who threw it to you— say their name—and then tell us your name, your favorite TV show, and your major. I'm an English major and I'm calling *The Newsroom*."

When she tossed the ball to me, I did the best I could.

"Kara," I said. "Hi Shush." I knew that much. But the rest… "I'm undecided."

And then I tossed the ball to someone else.

In the distance, a bell rings, pulling me out of the memory.

I open my eyes. Force air into and out of my lungs. Focus on my dorm room door.

Is Shush still here? Slowly, I get to my feet, careful not to make a sound. I make my way across the room and press my ear to the door, listening. It sounds like she's gone. At least for now. Shush isn't the type of person who gives up.

The bell rings again. Faint, but familiar. Sunday evening mass. A Catholic church sits a few blocks away from my dorm building, right on the edge of campus. My family isn't religious but I've been to mass a few times with my grandparents. It fascinates me. The elaborate costume the priest wears. All the different holy items he uses and the specific way he uses them. The dance of standing up and sitting down at points that seem random to me but make sense to everyone else. The song of call outs and responses. Rituals so practiced the whole church moves in unison.

I'm not sure how I feel about god or religion, but ritual is something I understand. How it's nice to wrap yourself up in repetition. To not have to think, to not have to work to create your reality. It's simple, easy, to follow along in the path that's already been made rather than forge a new one. It's comforting to be somewhere familiar. Somewhere you know what to say, what to do. It's like coming home.

I know all about rituals. I've spent years developing my own.

I'm moving before I realize I've decided to. I go to my desk first, grabbing a small black box hidden behind my books. Then I go into my bathroom and turn on the shower. My costume is much simpler than the robes the priest wears. Mine is just skin. Starting with my coat and boots, I remove all my clothing bit by bit, and step into the hot water. My cathedral doesn't have stained glass windows and holy paintings. It's decorated with a bar of soap, bottles of shampoo and conditioner. Instead of chandeliers and candles, I have a shower head.

Everything I need to make myself clean.

TWO

7:36 a.m.

When I step outside the next morning, the cold air is a shock. I take deep breaths, feeling it stab the soft tissue of my lungs like ice, sharpening my senses as I walk to class. I'm only halfway there when my phone rings. Hope explodes in my chest only to die when I see the caller ID. It's not Eric.

"Hi Mom." I answer my phone with a forced smile so she'll hear it in my voice. Last semester, my mom called me maybe once a week. I've been back on campus for three days and this is the fourth time she's called. Maybe this is how it's going to be now.

All because of Shush.

In some stories, dragons bring ill luck on the towns-people. It isn't just them taking all your gold, eating your friends, and burning down your house. It's trying to rebuild and finding nails no longer hold in the wood. Rains that are supposed to make your crops grow tall don't come and when they do, they wash away all the good soil. Sometimes dragons disrupt the natural balance of your environment, throw everything off course. The world you have to survive in is different now.

"Morning sweetheart," my mom says. "How are you?"

"I'm good." I turn off the sidewalk and walk down the edge of a road. "Just on my way to class."

"Do you have class with Shush today?"

I flinch at her name. Like saying it will summon her. "Yup. Biology."

"How is she? How are you two doing? I know you've been having some... some problems."

Problems. This is the way she's found to say it.

My parents love Shush. They think she's a good influence on me. I think they're hoping some of her outspoken confidence will rub off on me, and I can't even blame them. Once upon a time I'd hoped the same thing. I haven't told them we're not on speaking terms any longer. They're already far too worried about me and I don't want them to worry more. Their world is different now too.

"She's good. We're good. I think we've worked everything out." The lies, words broken in half to release their meaning, cut my tongue on the way out of my mouth. By now the pain is as familiar as the feel of my tongue against my teeth, holding back certain words so they can't escape, holding them until I can swallow them back down, force them back deep inside me where they belong.

"Oh that's great honey. That's just great. I'm so glad. It's important not to let little fights get in the way of friendships. You know she was just trying to do the right thing."

I do know. She was trying to do what *she* thought was the right thing. But just because she thought she was right—and she always, always, always thinks she's right—doesn't mean what she did was actually the right thing to do.

Kara you have to tell someone.

I bite my tongue, swallowing my protests. There's silence coming from the other end of the line and I can almost hear her mind working, trying to figure out how to say the thing she doesn't know how to say. I hug the edge of the road, letting faster-moving students go past me. Her hesitation is painful. I can feel the claws of her uncertainty in my chest.

"What's up?" I ask.

"Well…" She lets out this great big sigh. "We got a letter from the college."

My mind goes to Eric. To Shush. What's she done now?

"About what?"

"You failed a class last semester?" She's hiding it well but I can still hear the disappointment in her tone. The worry. With my good grades and tendency to stay at home and read rather than go out and party, she's rarely had a chance to be disappointed or worry about me. Now, everything is different. Both of those have become constant undertones whenever she talks to me. It's exhausting.

"Yeah… Calculus. Didn't I tell you?" Liar. I hate lying to my parents. I hate that Shush has turned me into a liar. "I'm retaking it this semester. It'll be fine."

"It's just… the letter said you could lose your scholarship."

I stop walking. "What?"

"Because of your GPA. If it goes under a three-point-five, you lose it. Honey… we can't afford—"

"I know. I know Mom. I know." The only reason I can be here is because of that scholarship. People brush past me, trying to avoid the cars on the road. I step into the snow to give them space. My feet sink into the bank that's been pushed up by snow plows. It comes up over the tops of my boots. I can feel it sliding inside at the edges. "Calc was just harder than I was expecting," I say. "I'll make sure I don't fail it this time, promise."

"I'm not pressuring you or anything. I know college is hard. I know you're a fully capable adult. I just don't want—"

"I know Mom. It's okay."

There's a beat of silence. Time to escape.

"Well I've got to go Mom. I've got class."

"Okay, okay. I umm… And you're okay? You're… you're doing okay? With… with everything?"

My throat tightens. I want the snow to keep coming up my legs, up my torso, until it swallows me whole, blocking out everything. Maybe if I sit down the next pass of the snow plow will bury me. Then all of this will go away.

"Yeah Mom. I'm good. I promise."

"Okay, well… I love you. We're here if you need anything, okay?"

"I know. Love you too. Bye Mom."

I hang up before she can say anything else, shoving my phone back in my pocket and hurrying towards class with the rest of the students.

I don't need the weight of losing my scholarship pushing down on me right now. Not with everything else going on. I've never failed anything before. I've never even gotten a C. I'm smart enough that I got through high school without working too hard, and I figured college would be like that too. But apparently I'm not as smart as I think I am. Something else to add to the infinite list of what I don't know.

I want to go back to my dorm room. I want to be alone. I need a few minutes to breathe. My fingers itch to perform my ritual again. But I can't miss class. Not when I'm apparently on the verge of losing my scholarship. I push into the science building and head not for the classroom, but for the bathroom.

7:46 a.m.

Fourteen minutes until Biology starts. Fourteen minutes until I see Shush, face to face, for the first time since she tried to tear everything in my life apart. I hide in a bathroom stall, trying to pull myself together.

I should feel claustrophobic, like the four metal walls of the bathroom stall are closing in around me. But instead it all feels far away. Like I could reach out and not touch the edges of anything. I stretch out my hand, trying to connect to something, trying to feel like I'm here. Press my palm against the stall wall, trying to feel the world around me, trying to feel my own flesh, trying to make sure I am solid and substantial and real.

I'm here.

The wall doesn't feel cold like I expected. And it doesn't feel solid like I want it to. It feels hollow. Like it might fall down if I push just a little harder.

Call me Eric.

Eric. Eric. Eric.

My fingers are surrounded by graffiti. Some in marker, some in pen, some carved into the paint.

Violet loves Greg
This place sux
B+D 4ever
Fuck this place

I trace over the words with my fingers, feeling my lungs expand, collapse, expand, collapse. The campus newsletter shouts at me from the back of the stall door, headlines in bold. I try to focus on the words, try to use them as a tether to keep me from slipping under.

Protest March Scheduled for January 21st.
Need help declaring a major?
It's not too late! Find your group!
Join a student club today!

I focus on taking deep breaths. In. Out. In. Out. All without a sound. Which only makes the words louder. Whispering and talking and *screaming* inside my head.

You're safe with me.

I'm here.

It's over.

Let me in.

You can't avoid me forever.

Kara you have to tell someone.

I'm fine.

I don't need her.

I don't need to tell anyone anything. I dig my fingernail into a crack in the paint on the stall wall until a small sliver chips away.

I'm fine.

7:52 a.m.

I pick at the paint, chipping away at it, trying to ignore the exhaustion pulling me down. The sleepless hours of last night are catching up with me. Facing Shush with such weak, sleep-deprived armor seems like a terrible idea and for the millionth time, I remind myself why I can't go see Eric. He would know the right thing to say to get me through class with Shush.

You're safe with me.

But the princess waits.

Once upon a time…

I know how the stories go. I grew up learning these lines, from bedtime stories and Disney movies and romantic comedies. I'm the princess and he's the prince. That's our story. He has to see me in the tower, in the forest, at the ball, and come to me. I can't go seek him out. That isn't how it works. If I don't keep my role as the princess-in-waiting, everything will be ruined. I just know it. But it's okay. It's okay. I can wait. I can do this.

7:58 a.m.

I get up and leave the bathroom. I climb the stairs to the second floor and slip into my classroom just as the professor starts talking.

"Good morning class, I'm Dr. Nelson. Welcome to Intro to Biology."

I take in the large lecture hall, a big amphitheater type room with sloping floors and stairs on either side. I come in at the top, at the back, because down near the front—where I knew she would be because she always wants to be front and center—is Shush.

You can't avoid me forever.

Shush is a junior, a year ahead of me, but she'd talked me into signing up for this class with her. She's an English major and I'm undecided, but everyone needs a GenEd science credit. So here I am.

"Alright, let's get started with attendance." Dr. Nelson starts calling out names and I focus on taking out my textbook, my notebook, my pen. Just breathe, I tell myself. Just breathe. I'd forgotten about attendance. When I'd have to announce my presence and exact location to the whole class.

"Sandra Lee."

"Here."

"Nicholas—Nick?—Howard."

"Nick. Right here."

An inane but necessary scripted ritual for the first day of classes. I hate it. It makes it seem so easy. Identify yourself with your name. A few syllables given to you at birth before anyone knew anything about you. As if it's that easy. As if a title is all there is to a story. As if it means anything at all.

"Kara Winterson."

She's going to see me now. She's already turning in her

seat, scanning the faces of the other students, looking for me.

I slip my hand silently into the air.

Shush locks eyes with me. Dr. Nelson keeps going down her list but all I can see is Shush, staring at me. I drop my raised hand and clench it into a fist in my lap. I can't look away from her. My fingers itch to find the edges of my skin, to force themselves underneath and peel it from my body. I want to slip into a different one, find one that fits better, that feels better, that feels more like mine. It's her expression, the way she's looking at me. Her brow furrowed, her eyes slightly wider than usual, her mouth pulled down at the corners. She's looking at me like I'm someone else. Someone I don't want to be. Someone I refuse to be.

She's wrong.

She's wrong she's wrong she's wrong.

I'm not that person.

It's pulling me in, forcing the air from my lungs, a black hole at the center of her dark eyes.

Pity.

I can't breathe. I can't breathe. I can't—

Shush turns back to face the front and I slouch in my seat, even more exhausted than I already was. I close my eyes, just for a second. I can do this. I just have to make it to tomorrow afternoon. Through this class and the writing class I have after it. Through math class in the morning, work after that, and then I'll see Eric. And it will all be fine.

It's all going to be okay.

I open my eyes just in time to reach over the row in front of me, down to where another student is stretching back with a stack of papers. I take one packet off the stack and pass the rest down my row to another student. The syllabus. I give it a quick glance, looking through the chapters we'll be studying, noting the big assignments: the midterm, the final, and a final project we'll need to complete with a partner. Oh great. Dr. Nelson is starting up a presentation for her lecture and I take out my notebook, glad for something else to concentrate on.

Class goes much faster than I'd anticipated and soon it's over. I'm out in the hallway as soon as Dr. Nelson dismisses the class, and still somehow Shush is behind me, shouting my name.

"Kara wait!"

Ignoring her, I pick up my pace, weaving in and out of students, mumbling apologies as I go. A hard grip on my arm stops me. I spin around and somehow there she is, a dragon waiting to consume me alive.

THREE

I've been awake for ages. I'm waiting for the sun to rise. I stopped waiting to fall asleep a while ago.

I'm intimately familiar with the never-ending series of insomnia. I know the feeling of exhaustion in my bones, how it writes the story of the sleepless, not in bold black letters but in thin invasive lines of cursive. They have a life of their own; I have no control. They sneak in one letter, one moment, at a time, until the clock reads four in the morning and it's too late.

I can't make it stop. At first I tried to distract myself with TV and books, with other people's stories. But now I'm too tired to fight my brain. Too tired to try and make it stop. Shush ambushing me after Biology plays over and over in my head.

My fight or flight response has always been faulty. Instead of taking some sort of action, I freeze. No fight. No flight. I can't do anything. My brain starts going a million miles a minute but I can't hang on to any one thought long enough to get it to tell my body to do something.

When she grabbed my arm after Biology, I couldn't move. I just stared at her hand on my arm, unable to say anything, unable to do anything.

"I'm sorry," she said, letting me go.

I flinched away as if she'd burned me.

She held her hands up, palms out, trying not to spook me.

"Kara," she said, keeping her voice low as she closed the distance between us. "Kara please you have to listen to me."

I needed to say something. To tell her I didn't have to listen to anything she said, not ever again. I needed to tell her to leave me alone. To get out of my way. *Something.*

"I'm sorry," she said. "I'm really, really sorry."

Eventually you'll forgive me.

I wanted to ask her what she was apologizing for exactly. For some individual thing she had done—and there were many—or for all of it? For trying to ruin my life. I wanted to ask her why she was apologizing if she wasn't really sorry. Because she wasn't. She thought she'd done the right thing. She thought she was *still doing* the right thing. I could see it in the grim line of her mouth as she looked at me, realizing I wasn't going to respond. She was still on her mission. Apologizing even as she opened her mouth to breathe more fire.

"You need to stay away from him," she said, voice hard. "You don't understand. Just let me explain—" She took a step closer to me. I couldn't help but take a step back and a look of hurt flashed across her features.

"Talk to me Kara. Please. Just say something. Anything."

Laying in bed now, I press the heels of my hands into my eyes so hard it hurts, trying to erase the memory of her expression. She'd looked at me like I knew the magic words to fix what she'd broken between us. Like it was my fault. But it was her. It was *all* her.

I left then, walking away without a word and leaving her there in the hallway.

Her hurt and still somehow hopeful expression is burned into my brain and even though I'd done nothing, guilt keeps stabbing me in the chest. I have to get out of here. It's four a.m. and I should definitely be in bed but I can't stay here. I'm up and throwing on my coat and boots without another thought.

I step outside and fill my lungs with crisp Michigan-in-January air. I start walking without a destination in mind. I walk down empty streets I've walked many times before. Campus is spread out in a sprawling kind of way that makes it clear it started so much smaller than it ended up. The roads and sidewalks link together in nonsensical ways, designed to go around whatever had already been there upon their creation.

Makes sense to me. It's so much easier to wrap yourself around something sturdier, letting it give you shape.

Call me Eric.

I shove my hands deeper into my pockets, walking a little faster. Like I can outrun what happened.

It's over.

Even with my increased pace, I make no sound, moving silently over the thin layer of snow on the pavement. I'm so quiet I might not exist at all. I learned a long time ago how to operate as a ghost, making as little imprint on the world as possible. It came easily, naturally. I'm not a force of nature, not like Shush. I'm not a presence. I'm an absence.

I've always been thin. It's not something I work towards, I've just always been composed more of bone than of flesh. My shoulders stick out like corners, my elbows can be dangerous, and my knees wear holes in all my jeans. When I was a kid I decided I had bird bones, hollow, ready to be carried away in a stiff wind. I used to wait for it. Wait to disappear. Here one second, gone the next.

And then he saw me.

Do you know the fairy tale behind the invention of the kiss?

I stop walking.

Breathe Kara. Just breathe.

It still hasn't hit me yet.

Not really.

A whole day has passed and it still feels like it's something that happened to someone else.

It's over.

I look up, inhaling the bitter cold air, and something soft grazes my cheek. It's starting to snow. It isn't windy, this isn't the kind of snow that assaults your face so you have to bend your head down and stare at your feet, hoping you don't run into something. This is the kind of snow that makes you stop and stare, the kind you watch as it slowly floats its way to the ground, and suddenly you're noticing how quiet everything is. No insect noises, no animal noises, no people noises. No knocking. Everyone is hibernating, waiting until it's warm to come out again.

I take another deep breath and revel in the silence. The calm, peaceful, comforting silence.

"Oh my god it's so fucking cold Hannah. Why the hell did we come out in this?"

Two girls burst out of the trees ahead of me, coming onto my sidewalk and hurrying down it, kicking up snow as they go.

"Get over it already. Welcome to Michigan." She passes a bottle of some kind to the other girl, who takes it with gloved hands and brings it to her lips.

"Swear to god if you say that one more time I'll murder you with my freezing hands."

"No you won't." The girl takes the bottle back and takes her own drink. "If I hadn't made you go to that party with me, you never would have kissed Kali."

Their voices are already starting to fade as they get farther away, but I can still hear the hope in her voice as she says, "She's amazing isn't she?"

"You're so in love with her."

"Shut up."

"I'm going to write your love story. And I'm starting it tonight, with you drunkenly going up and asking her to dance, you brave, brave fool."

"Shut *up*."

"Once upon a time…"

I press the sharp ridges of my teeth into the soft flesh of my tongue.

I can't tell what she's saying anymore and in another minute, I can't hear them at all.

Once upon a time…

Breathe Kara. Breathe.

I'm fine.

I'm fine I'm fine I'm fine.

I am so. Freaking. Tired.

It hits me all of a sudden. Bone-deep exhaustion. Like I've been running a marathon.

I start walking, heading for the break in the trees where the girls appeared. I discovered this trail halfway through last year, more of a deer path than anything else. Tonight's the first time I've ever seen other people use it.

I follow the footprints the girls had made in the snow at first. If I keep following them, they'll come out on the other main road on the opposite side of campus. But part way I turn off their path and follow my own. Soon I reach a break in the trees and pause. I'm at the crest of a hill, looking down at what I know is a small pond, although I can't see it.

The water's been frozen over since the start of December, back when I was still talking to Shush and Eric still wanted to talk to me. But I'd always been able to see the pond's outline through the snow, a depression where the snow wasn't quite as thick. Now the snow has drifted in such a way that it's erased any recognizable shape from the small clearing.

And I know I'm all alone. There aren't any footprints from animals or other people. There's no sign of another living soul here. I know no one is talking. But as I head down the hill, I hear Eric all the same.

You're safe with me.

He'd said it easily, as if he understood immediately that I was afraid.

I thought he could put words to it. To the unsteady feeling the ground always has beneath my feet, as if it might swallow me whole without warning.

Can you tell me what I say?

I have to talk to him. He has to have the answers. He's always so sure of himself, his voice solid and steady, syllables spoken with such easy confidence. As if he's been around the world and could lead you on the journey with the way he strings his sentences together. As if he could hold you up with the way he answers a question.

What do I do now?

I walk to what I think might be the edge of the pond, my breath fogging the air in front of my face.

The riddle that needs solving now is how I get him to talk to me again, really talk to me, the way he used to. Telling stories in a way that seemed so much more like casting spells. I need that magic back, I need the protective coating of his words.

You're magic.

With Eric, I always knew my role. The princess waits in the tower for the prince to come rescue her. She waits until he calls. Our relationship had always been like that. He took the lead and I was more than happy to follow. If I want him to take me back as his princess, I have to follow that role. I have class with him this afternoon. I have that long to figure out a plan. I can do that. I can survive that long without him. I already made it through all of yesterday.

I take a deep breath of frigid air.

I can do this.

I can.

I'm fine.

The snow is slowing down. It's quiet. Peaceful. I try to use that to prop myself up. I still have a few hours until I need to be strong again. It should be easy now, after making it through Biology with Shush.

You can't avoid me forever.

I take a step forward.

Let me in.

Maybe, if I keep walking, I can walk across the pond. It's been pretty cold all winter. It'll hold me up. I wonder if I'll know when I leave solid ground, when I step onto ice. If I'll feel that beneath what seems solid, ready to support me, there is something unsteady, waiting to drown me.

Kara you have to tell someone.

I take another step.

A slight cracking sound shoots a lightning bolt of fear through my body and I stop. I can't take another step forward. Instead, I take a step back, moving onto familiar ground.

Turning, I climb back up the hill.

I just have to make it through math class, through work, and then I have class with Eric. I can make it that long. And then everything will be fine. I'll be fine. Because Eric will know what to say to give me the armor I need to survive now. He always knows what to say.

It's all going to be okay.

It's calling to me. The ritual.

I walk towards my dorm room with purpose. I need to pray.

TRIGGER WARNING

The following section contains graphic depictions of self-harm. If you are not in a place where you feel up to reading that, please skip to the next section.

Remember, you're not alone. Mental health resources can be found at the back of this book. Take care of yourself.

FOUR

A priest uses many different holy items. In addition to the Bible he has a sacramentary, a book of gospels, a lectionary, a hymnal. For communion there's the paten for the bread, the chalice for the wine, and a variety of cloths. I'm not sure how long it took the Catholic church to come up with their rituals and holy items, but mine only took a couple years to perfect.

The first time I walked the hallowed halls of my body cathedral, years and years earlier, my only holy item was the needle of a safety pin. My prayer was simple: dragging its point across the fleshy skin of my thigh, raising a red line on my skin. It looked like something bursting at a seam, struggling to get out.

It wasn't enough.

It took me time to learn, to perfect each part. Catholics say the same prayers every Sunday, so I followed their example. The next time, I ran the point across the same line over and over, until the repetition of my prayer resulted in the release of red, coming up hesitantly from beneath my skin.

I just hadn't prayed hard enough. The next time I needed to be more devout. The next time I tried scissors.

I've brought my tabernacle into the shower with me, setting it on the ledge farthest from the spray so it won't get wet. A small black plastic box the length of my thumb. First, I stand in the hot water, let it wash over me, warm my skin, preparing me. Then, I begin.

Open the catch on my tabernacle, reach in for a razor blade, pick it up delicately between my fingers. I always examine it first, the dull gray body, the gleaming silver edge. I check for rust, for signs it needs replacing. Then comes the selection of skin. Most days I choose a patch already crisscrossed with thin white scars, the evidence of my previous devotions. Tonight I choose my upper thigh, right below my hip.

Then, my call and response.

Call.

The pressing of blade to skin, to flesh, gradually increasing the pressure until there is a sharp biting pain, until I *feel*. Drag the blade sideways. Lift the blade from the skin and—

Response.

Rich, red blood wells up, bright on my skin.

Breathe.

And again.

Press the blade to my skin, my index finger on top for leverage, my thumb and middle finger holding the sides for stability. Pressure, pressure. Pain. Gritting teeth. I go slowly, the pressure on the point of the blade opening my closed skin. I'm careful to make the cut uniform to the one above it, small, an inch across.

Breathe.

Wait for the blood to make its way to the surface. The deeper the cut, the quicker it is. Today I don't press very hard, using just enough pressure to break the skin. It takes a second after each cut for the blood to appear.

Again.

Pressure. Pain. Blood. Breathe.

Three cuts, three red lines on my skin.

Carefully, I place the razor blade onto the ledge of the shower, next to the shampoo. After, I'll dry it and return it to my tabernacle where it will be safe until I need it again. I watch the blood well up on my thigh until it collects into a drop heavy enough to slip and fall down the length of my leg, paling as it goes. Then I step into the spray of the shower, bracing for the stinging pain of the water hitting my open flesh. It's slight, not as sharp as the beginning of the ritual, but still necessary. The ending of the prayer.

Amen.

It's like coming home.

Something tight and tense in my body releases and I take a breath.

I get out of the shower.

I'm fine.

Climb into bed.

It's fine.

Close my eyes.

I'm fine.

And breathe.

It's all going to be okay.

FIVE

Only a few hours after I managed to fall asleep last night, I yank open the door to the Math and Science Building and head inside, trying not to panic about my Calc class.

I can't fail college. What would I do? Move back in with my parents? Be labeled a failure forever? Never see Eric again?

Stop.

Breathe.

I'm fine.

It's all going to be okay.

Five more hours until I see Eric.

Math. Work. Eric.

I can do this. I can make it.

It'll be fine.

I'm fine.

I walk into the familiar classroom, the same one we used last semester, and grab a seat by the window in the back corner. It's okay. I'll be fine. I won't fail. I won't be a failure. That can't be who I am. I'll have to work harder. I can do that. I'm sure once I'm back with Eric, he'll—

"Kara," exclaims a familiar voice. I look up to find a short girl with brown hair, pulled back in a ponytail. A freshman. It's obvious from her slightly nervous smile and the way she's looking at me with her big freshman eyes. Hope, with just a hint of desperation. Like a kite looking for someone to hold its string.

I must have looked that way to Shush last year. And to Eric.

It takes me a second to place her. "Hi Ella," I say. She works in the campus coffee shop, *Spill the Beans*. Thanks to my regular bouts of insomnia, I'm a frequent customer.

She points to the seat next to me. "Anyone sitting here?"

I shake my head and force a polite smile onto my face, even though I can't do a conversation with a stranger right now. I don't have the energy.

Eventually you'll forgive me.

Or the brain space.

It's over.

When the words in my head get like this, I find it hard to make conversation, which makes me even quieter than usual. Sometimes people notice and ask me what's wrong. They always want an explanation. *I'm just tired* usually works but what if she's the type of person who wants a real answer? One of the *No really tell me how you're doing* very-well-meaning people who want your life story. I'm not prepared to give any explanations to anyone for anything. Which is, of course, one of the reasons I'm no longer speaking to Shush, who demands detailed explanations for every single action, every single thought. She digs. Poking and prodding and needling, dissecting every little thing with a razor-sharp scalpel until she thinks she has all the facts.

Just thinking about it is exhausting.

Ella meets my gaze, still wearing her big freshman eyes and the smile so wide it hurts my face. I can't do this right now. I can't be friendly right now. I can't even be *human* right now. I have to not fail this class. I still have to figure out what I'm going to say to Eric.

She takes a breath, opens her mouth, and I brace myself.

Some people don't like questions with obvious answers. They think the people who ask them are stupid or not thinking. They think those kinds of questions are a waste of time. Not me. I think those questions are a breath of fresh air. They're simple. Easy. I spend so much time trying to answer difficult questions that when someone asks a simple one, it feels like a rest in the middle of a marathon. So when Ella asks, "You're taking Calc too?" I let out a sigh of relief.

"Yeah," I answer.

"That's awesome." Her ponytail whips around as she plops down into the seat next to mine. "I was worried I wouldn't know anyone."

Know anyone. I stiffen at the phrase. People use that word so carelessly. Know. There's no way Ella really *knows* me. We've barely had a conversation. The only one who knows me is Eric.

I need to say something, respond to her, but I can't think of anything. I'm saved from the awkward silence by the next student that walks in.

His name is Jake Edwards and he lives in my building. That's all I know about him. Shush introduced us. I've never said more than a handful of empty words to him, passing hellos and how are yous. He gives me a nod of greeting before grabbing a seat near the front and Ella immediately takes control of the conversation.

"He's *cute*," she whispers, a new edge of excitement in her tone. "You know him?"

"Kind of," I say. "He lives in my building."

"Really? You think you could introduce us?"

There's so much hope in her voice. She's looking at me like I might be her fairy godmother, come to enchant her dress and take her to the ball to meet her prince.

Once upon a time…

Always with the ellipses. Once upon a time dot dot dot. So much in those three little dots. That brief pause. A tiny and somehow still infinite amount of possibility. She can see it. This could be the start to their story, to a fairy tale. To her fairy tale.

"I don't know," I say. "We're not really friends or anything."

"Oh…" Her face falls. It's like watching a kite crash to earth. I have to try to save it.

"I mean, I can try."

"Yeah?" There she goes, catching a current of wind, soaring up again.

I'm saved from having to respond by the professor walking in.

"Sorry I'm late everyone, let's get started."

Dr. Howards moves through the whole first-day-of-class routine, making me raise my hand. It doesn't feel any less forced than all the other times I've had to identify myself solely by my title, but at least there's no judgment in her gaze when it falls on me, just a simple recognition. She moves smoothly into her lecture and Ella and I don't have a chance to say anything else until class is over.

When Dr. Howards dismisses us, and we start packing our things, I look for a way to head off the impending conversation with Ella about how to choreograph a meet-cute with her and Jake.

"You didn't take any notes," I say. She just sat there. The whole class. Listening and attentive, but not writing anything down. I was scrambling to get everything I thought might be helpful down on paper, driven not only by a slight desperation to get a decent grade, but also because continuous note-taking is one of the few things I've found that keeps thoughts of Eric from sneaking in and distracting me.

Ella shrugs. "We haven't really gotten into anything hard yet. I'm good with math. This was all really basic stuff."

"Seriously?" I recognized it all from last year, but that didn't mean I fully understood it. "That all seemed pretty confusing."

"Numbers just make sense to me."

Her gaze follows Jake as he leaves the classroom. Something in her deflates, but she turns to me with yet more hope in her expression. "I'm headed to the café. Want to come? I can help you with the math homework."

I stand up and sling my bag over my shoulder. "Sorry. I've got work."

"Oh. Where do you work?"

I hesitate because I know if I tell her, she'll want to come with me. But if there's an easy way to extricate myself from this situation, I can't think of it. So I say, "The library."

"That's awesome. I'll come with you!"

I clench my fingers around the strap of my bag. Math is over. Just work. And then Eric.

"Okay, sure."

Work. Eric.

I can do this.

I'm fine.

SIX

Sitting at the front desk of the library, I peek from behind my computer monitor, trying to stay hidden as I scope out people walking in. The library used to be a haven for me. I love working here, studying here, reading here. I know who I am here. Someone simple. A cardboard cutout. The stock character in the background while the two main characters have their meet-cute. Behind this desk, I don't have to make decisions about which character to be, who I should present to the world.

I feel good here.

Or I used to. Now I can't seem to relax.

I was so happy to get this job. Even with my scholarship I need a paycheck to keep my head above water, and I ended up in the best place to work on campus. I actually used to look forward to my shifts working here. But now I can't stop looking for Shush. Even before our encounter in Biology yesterday, I worried she'd try to hunt me down here. The front desk is right by the main entrance; it's such an easy place to corner me.

I've been at work a half hour and every time someone walks in, my heart rate picks up. There hasn't been any sign of her yet, but I still have two hours left on my shift.

I take a breath and force my attention back to my homework.

All you have to do is write one true sentence.
Write the truest sentence that you know.

I write the Hemingway quote at the top of a blank page
in my notebook. Underline it twice. There's *something* there.
Something I can't let go. Something that keeps me turning
the words over and over in my head.

This happens all the time. I'll see something—a phrase,
a scene from a book or a movie, a music video or a dance
routine—and I won't be able to let it go. I'll stay up all night,
listening to the same song, watching the same movie, reading the same pages or the same sentence, over and over and
over again. Because something inside of it reached out and
hooked into something inside of me.

And I don't know why.

If I can just discover exactly what's gripping my insides,
then I'll know *something*, even if it's a small something,
about myself. I should do something about it, write something or tell someone—*get it out*—but all I can do is watch it
again, trying to decipher what it is about the movements of
the dancers, the facial expressions of the actors, the phras-
ing, the word choice, *something* that seems to have a piece of
me inside it. A piece of truth.

All you have to do is write one true sentence.

Yesterday afternoon I had my first Intro to Creative Writing class—another class I'm taking because Shush told me
to. My new writing professor, Dr. Leery, had the quote on the
whiteboard at the start of class. "Creative writing—no matter
if it's fiction, nonfiction, or poetry—is all about telling stories,"
she'd said. "It's about making the reader see what you see,
feel what you feel. And it's a lot harder than it sounds."

One true sentence.

In a few hours, I'll see Eric for the first time since the

break-up. And I have no idea what to say to him. What if what I say just confirms to him that he was right to break up with me?

Before him, my life might not have been a fairy tale but at least it was familiar. I knew the boundaries of my tower room. I knew the view, the places I looked at every day. When he broke me out of my tower, I went with him to places I'd never been because he knew where we were going and I trusted him to get us there safely.

But now he's gone. I'm down in the deep dark alone and I don't recognize where I am or how I got here. Without him, I'm lost.

I have to figure out the right thing to say.

Somehow, I thought attempting my writing homework would help. I thought figuring out the truth would help me figure out what to say. I stare at the page but when I put my pen to the paper, I only manage to repeat the quote.

One true sentence.

The first assignment is supposed to be easy. Write something.

"A feeling, a memory, a dream, a thought, anything as long as it's true," Dr. Leery had said.

One true sentence.

The blank page seems vast, intimidating.

Please take me back seems hollow. The words don't quite fit. *I miss you* feels better. But it's still lacking something. It has no direction, it's a map without a compass. *I don't know who I am without you* is the closest I've come to the truth.

But none of it feels *right.*

Maybe I'll try to tell him our story, show him I was listening, that I remember how amazing it was.

Once upon a time a princess met a prince.

A single sentence. A beginning. Mine and Eric's beginning.

The truth.

Kara he's not what you think.

Shush's voice in my head is a dragon's roar.

I rip the page out of my notebook and crumple it into a ball. I close my eyes, digging my fingernails into the palms of my hands. Breathe. Just breathe.

I can do this. I can figure this out.

I'm fine.

A guy sets down a few books on the counter in front of me, interrupting my train of thought. "Hi," he says.

"Hey." I straighten in my tall chair at the waist-high counter. "Find everything okay?"

"Yeah." He hands me his student ID card.

I pick up my handheld scanner and point it at the barcode on the back of the guy's ID. After his account comes up, I scan each of the books. Usually I hate talking to strangers. But I don't mind here. Here, I don't have to search for the words. There's a script.

"These are due back in three weeks. You can renew online or just ask someone here to renew them for you."

"Thanks," he says, taking the books and shoving them into his backpack before walking away.

As I watch him leave, there's a tugging sensation in my chest. The first time Eric ever spoke to me outside of class, it had been here. I knew then I had a… I don't want to call it a *crush*. That seems so juvenile. It felt more like a pull. A fascination. A hook inside my rib cage. Something that made me look for him first every time I walked into class, made me look for him as I walked around campus, made me think about him when he wasn't around. Something that, one day when I was reading at work and his familiar voice pulled me out of my book, made my whole body react.

"Kara, right?" he'd said, smiling at me over his stack of books.

"Umm, yeah." I sat up straight in my chair, every part of me entirely and completely *awake*. I was suddenly aware of the exact angle my body sat on the chair, the weight of the book in my hands, my cheeks turning red as I tried to follow my usual script. "How can I umm, how can I help you?"

I hoped he didn't hear the slight tremor in my voice. It was silly. My reaction to him. I knew it was but I still couldn't help it.

"Just need to check these out."

"No problem." Just be cool, I told myself. This is no big deal. This is your job. You do this all the time. I closed my book and started scanning his. I knew I should say something but small talk always seemed forced when it came out of my mouth.

"So are you enjoying class?" he asked, saving me from taking that first step. Introduction to Fairy Tales was where we'd met a month before, the start of spring semester my freshman year.

"Oh I love it." Hopefully he couldn't hear the relief in my voice at not having to pick a conversation topic. "It's the most interesting class I've ever had."

"It's such a fascinating subject."

I leaned towards him, as if he was going to start telling me exactly what he loved about fairy tales, but he picked up his books.

"I look forward to seeing you next class Kara."

And then he walked away, leaving me with his words burning like a small ember in the center of my chest.

I look forward to seeing you.

"What if we ask him for help with the homework?"

Ella's question pulls me out of the memory and I stifle the urge to sigh. Other than the fact that I'm surrounded by books, the main reason I like the library is because it's quiet.

People understand you don't have to speak here. Talking is actually *discouraged*. It's relaxing to not have words expected of me. Ella, with her chipper freshman energy, is ruining that. Not to mention she's distracting me from figuring out what to say to Eric.

She's doing her homework at a nearby table and every few minutes she pops over and proposes a new plan for introducing herself to Jake. The first had been to randomly bump into him, maybe drop her books so he would be obliged to help her pick them up. But that was dismissed because of course he would know it was on purpose and besides did she really want him to think of her as clumsy right from the start? The second had been a cold introduction. Us going up and me saying, "Hey Jake, have you met Ella?"

But the thought of doing something that bold had me starting to sweat with nerves. What if he just stared at me like I was crazy? I'd turned that idea down in a hurry.

And now the third plan. Help with homework. Which still seemed to have problems.

"I thought you were good at math?"

"I am." She leans on the counter, propping her chin up on one hand. "That doesn't mean I can't pretend not to know what I'm doing."

"Are you sure that's a good idea?" I ask.

"Why wouldn't it be?"

"Well… how long are you going to pretend? A week? A month? A year? Happily ever after?"

Ella frowns. "Good point." With a sigh, she goes back to her homework.

There's movement out of the corner of my eye—a head of black curls—and I whip my head around towards the entrance, tensing in my seat, preparing for a fight. But it isn't Shush. Closing my eyes, I grip the armrests of my chair and try to tell my body to relax. Breathe.

You can't avoid me forever.

I need to get out of here. I need a few minutes on my own.

"I'm going to do some re-shelving," I tell Tom, my coworker. He glances up from his computer screen as I grab a cart filled with books.

"Cool," he says. "I'll hold down the fort."

Pushing the cart out ahead of me, I move past Ella, seated at a table with books and notebooks sprawled around her. I wonder how much of it is homework and how much of it is her plotting how to get Jake's attention.

"I'll be back in a bit," I say.

She glances up. "Okay. I've got to get going in a few. I'll see you later?"

I don't want to feel grateful she won't be here when I get back because I know that's kind of mean, but still. At least it will be quiet. "Yeah," I say. "See you later."

"Text me if you think of anything for the plan."

I force a smile. "Will do."

Before she can say anything else, I put in headphones and put some music on my phone. I give her a little wave goodbye and try not to shake my head as I walk away, pushing the cart in front of me. There's no way I'll be able to think about her and Jake when I still haven't figured out what to do about Eric. And I've only got an hour and a half to come up with something.

I move past rows of shelves, past more tables with students studying. The music does its job. Gradually the words that won't stop circling around and around in my head fade into the background.

I feel less like climbing out of my skin.

Then I round a corner and stop, staring down the aisle at the group rooms. A row of doors with numbers, where students can study in groups and talk without disturbing the quiet of the library. I stare at group room three and tighten my grip on the book cart.

That room is the first place Eric spoke to me.

SEVEN

There are students in the group room now, gathered around the table studying. I can see them through the large window each group room has—a precaution against students getting up to things other than studying in the rooms. But I don't see them. I see Eric. I see me. I see *us*.

It wasn't the first time he said words to me, obviously that happened before, but it was the first time he *really* spoke to me. The first time he said something and I could hear something else underneath his words.

There had been a group of us there, going through the midterm study guide for class. We were wrapping up and the other students started trickling out of the room. Eric was the default leader of the group and as everyone left, I kept expecting him to end the study session. To announce he had to leave too. But he didn't. And one by one the other students left. Until it was only the two of us.

By the end, our study session had devolved to sharing our favorite books. I would have stayed there all night but then the announcement came over the intercom that the library was closing in fifteen minutes, which meant it was nearly midnight.

"Is it that late?" Eric asked, leaning back in his chair with a small smile, looking at me. "Time flies."

He was probably the best-looking guy who'd ever spoken to me in my entire life. And it wasn't just his thick black hair or the sharp cut of his stubble-covered jaw. It wasn't just how tall he was or the breadth of his shoulders or his ink-colored eyes. It was how he spoke; always with such passion in his voice. It was how his strong hands could hold a stack of books with ease or delicately turn the pages as if they might rip under his touch.

And when he looked at me like that, I didn't know what to do.

I'd been telling myself I was making it up. Why would he ever look at me like that? At *me*. Like *that*. It had to be all in my head. But sitting across from him in that moment, I couldn't have been imagining the way his black eyes danced over the lines of my face as if he couldn't get enough. As if I was a book he wanted to read. As if he couldn't wait to open me up, to read my words, to discover my story.

Part of me felt terrified. If he wanted to discover what type of story I had to tell, he was obviously expecting something spectacular. A sprawling landscape, a world full of adventure, shrouded in mystery, brimming with magic. And more than that, he was looking at me like he thought my story was a happy one.

I didn't want him to discover that none of that was true.

I've never been able to read my story. I do things that make no sense to me. I think things that seem so different to what everyone else is thinking. I don't know exactly who I am or what my story is, and I don't know how to figure it out. But I do know some things. I know I'm not a Tolkien world that will pull you in for years to come. I'm not an interesting story. And I'm not a story where the good guys win. I can't read the words written on my skin but I can feel what they mean. I've felt it my whole life. I know it isn't a story where the heroes beat the dragons. My story doesn't have a happy ending.

I'm a tragedy.

And still some part of me, deep down where I hardly wanted to let it out, felt hopeful. He knew so much. If he was looking at me that way, maybe there was something about me he could see that I couldn't. Maybe I do have a Gaiman adventure or a Schwab magical realm written on my skin. Maybe I've been reading my story wrong this whole time. And the more he looked at me like that, the more hopeful I became that he knew something I didn't.

"I guess it's time to go," Eric said, still staring at me. But he didn't move.

I pulled myself out of his gaze, out of the fantasy. "Yeah, I guess it is."

I needed to get a grip on my brain, stop letting it run away with me. I was the first to move, to start closing my books, putting everything into my bag. He followed suit, and then we were both getting to our feet. "Thanks for all your help," I said, slinging my bag over my shoulder.

"My pleasure."

There it was again. That look.

I felt my face heat up and I turned away, reaching for the door handle before he could see a blush light up my pale skin.

And then the door didn't open.

I tried a few times, twisting the handle, pulling and pushing, trying to get the thing to door like a door was supposed to.

"I think it's stuck or something," I said. Stupid, stupid. Obvious thing to say. Eric moved past me and tried the door himself.

"I think you're right."

"Wait what study room are we in?" I asked.

"Three I think."

"Well that explains it." I should have known.

Eric looked at me, a question quirking up the left corner of his mouth into a smirk.

I ran a hand through my hair. "The lock on this door is broken. Half the time it doesn't work. I've had to let students out of here plenty of times."

"Ah. Well that does explain things."

He was still looking at me. He didn't seem upset at this turn of events. If anything, he seemed happy about it, as if it was an unexpected twist in a book and he couldn't wait to see where it went. Our bodies were close, both near the door, and I felt like maybe I should step back, create some space. Except he hadn't. As if he didn't mind the closeness. As if he might want it.

I didn't think I'd ever been so aware of another person. Of their closeness to me, of the rise and fall of their chest as they breathed, as their weight shifted, bringing them even closer. My heart beat so hard in my chest, I was sure he could hear it.

"I umm… Someone will be up to check and make sure everyone's gone. Before they close up the library. It shouldn't be long."

"I don't mind," he said. And I believed it. I believed he really was looking at me the way I felt he was. I believed he wanted to know what story I had to tell. I believed my story, whatever it was, was worth telling. I believed it didn't have to be a tragedy.

"Anything else you want to ask me?" he asked. And I knew he was talking about the material for the test. But I knew all of that backwards and forwards. I only came to the study group because I knew he was going to be here. I wasn't worried about the midterm. I was worried about everything else. Like the way he was looking at me expectantly, waiting.

I wanted to make up a question. Something insightful, something to show I actually had a brain, to show I had something to offer. My fingers clenched around the strap of my bag, crossed over my chest like a shield.

"Anything at all?" He moved even closer to me and I couldn't speak because I couldn't breathe.

I could picture it. Like a scene from a story. I would hand him the book of me, something I had always carried but never known how to read.

I don't speak this language. Can you tell me what I say?

He would open it with the same reverence he treated all books. And then he would tell me everything I'd ever wanted to know. He would tell me if I really was a tragedy. Or if I was a fairy tale.

Forcing air into my lungs, I opened my mouth, unsure how to put that into words but sure no matter what I said, he'd understand.

And then the door opened.

"You guys get locked in here?" Tom asked.

The spell broke. We left the group room with Tom and headed to the exit. I spent the whole time trying to figure out how I could get back to that place, to that magical moment where I'd felt I could ask Eric everything I ever wanted to know.

Anything else you want to ask me?

But it was Eric who took the next step. We were about to part ways outside the library, and he stopped, looking at me that way again. As if he couldn't wait to read the next chapter of me.

"Have you chosen a topic for your final paper yet?"

I nodded and tried not to sound relieved that he hadn't

simply said goodnight and left. "Female archetypes in fairy tales."

"Perfect. I'd be happy to help you, if you want."

"That would be amazing." The words came out of my mouth before I could turn them into something less high-school-girl-with-a-crush-y. But Eric had smiled and said we could talk later about meeting up before walking away into the dark.

A girl brushes past me on her way down the row of books, startling me out of my memory.

"Sorry," she says.

My face feels hot, like it did that night. I take a deep breath and let it out, pick up a book off the cart and start searching for its place on the shelf. Focus. Focus. I'm fine. I need to calm down and usually re-shelving books helps me with that. But I can't stop thinking about how I'm going to see Eric soon. I can't stop reliving the time we had together. I don't want to.

After that night in group room three, we started meeting regularly outside class. I kept telling myself not to get my hopes up, not to let myself create some whole elaborate fairy tale. Kept telling myself he was just being nice. Just being friendly. He wasn't really interested in me. There was no way a guy like him, good-looking and smart and confident, would be interested in a quiet, shy girl like me. But that didn't stop me from over-thinking every look he gave me, every word he said.

I'd never been that girl before. The girl who can't stop thinking about a boy. I've never thought of myself as the type of person Ella seems to be. Boy-crazy. But with Eric, right from the start, it was different. I wanted to see if this was a skin I could belong in. A girl who really, really liked a boy. A girl whose whole world revolved around a boy.

Maybe it was a skin that could fit. The girl in the fairy tale. The princess.

I shelve the last book that needs to go on this floor and head for the elevator, for the second floor. When the elevator doors open, I make my way towards the English literature section, not just because there are books to re-shelve there, but because it's where Eric and I met for the first time to work on my final paper. We'd been here, in the far aisle, going through books for source material.

The first time he handed me a book, his fingertips brushed mine. The contact was so fleeting I thought it must be accidental. Innocent. Surely it couldn't be anything else.

Except then it happened again.

I was in the middle of a sentence and there was zero chance he hadn't noticed the hitch in my voice, the way I stumbled through the rest of my words. But the only indication he noticed was the ghost of a smile in the left corner of his mouth. I learned to watch that corner. It was the secret to unlocking what he was thinking. Which was why, the next time he touched my hand, I looked there. And saw the smile hiding on the edge of his mouth.

A smile tugs up the corners of my own lips now as I remember how easily he had flirted with me. Eric wasn't the first guy to ever flirt with me. There had been a few guys in high school. Guys in class, guys who asked me to school dances or asked me to wear their jersey on game days. I'd even had boyfriends.

But Eric was different.

Yes, I flirted with those boys. I studied the other girls, copying what they did. Asking questions like what the boy had said was terribly interesting even when I had no interest in it, laughing with a hand on the boy's arm, angling my body in such a way that the boy wouldn't be able to not think of how we might fit together.

I'd been able to act out those actions with the boys in high school, but it had always been just that—acting. I'd never felt *real* attraction. Curiosity, sure. But never that inexplicable pull that seemed to tug my body towards Eric's without him ever touching me. With Eric I wasn't pretending. What he said *was* interesting. What he said *did* make me laugh. My body *wanted* to see how it fit with his.

Forcefully, I push the cart of books past the fairy tale section. I have other books to put away. One last floor and—I check my phone—half an hour until my shift is over and I head back to class. Back to Eric. And I still have no freaking clue what I'm going to say.

When the elevator doors slide open on the third floor, I don't start re-shelving right away, instead I head to the windows. One wall of the third floor is made entirely of glass so you can see down over a maze of campus sidewalks and buildings. Right now the sun is shining, reflecting off the snow so the view is a dazzling bright white. I like to look down and watch the people, I like to create stories for them.

That was the first secret I ever told Eric about myself. I was taking a study break and standing at the window, watching the people below. He came up behind me, a surprise since I hadn't known he was in the library at all, his voice an intimate whisper of breath that made all the hairs on the back of my neck stand up.

"Hello Kara."

"Hi." My body leaned slightly back towards his. One more inch and we would have been touching. Then he moved, coming to stand beside me.

"What are you doing?"

I could have told him I was stretching my legs. Instead, I found myself telling him about the stories.

"Inventing people," I said. I pointed down at two girls walking together down one of the sidewalks. "See them? They're off to rescue their brother from a wicked prince who kidnapped him. Without him, their kingdom isn't safe. It takes three to hold the magical wards."

"Naturally."

Glancing over at him, I was relieved to see a smile. He didn't think I was silly. Or crazy.

He leaned closer to me so I could follow the point of his finger as he chose a boy and girl walking down a different path. "Forbidden lovers," he said softly in my ear. "From warring kingdoms. They keep their love a secret, because no one understands. That just makes it all the more real."

I turned my head slightly to face him and for one wild moment I thought he was going to kiss me in the middle of the library. Sure there weren't people around right now but someone could walk up at any second. I could hardly breathe for wondering what he was going to do next. My body was so tense I thought I might explode.

And then he said, "Until next time," and walked away, ghosting his fingertips along my lower back as he went. Even though he didn't make contact with my skin, I felt the heat of his touch warm my whole body. It made me want to follow him.

Drawing myself away from the glass and out of the memory, I start re-shelving the last of the books. That was the other thing about Eric. Not only did I feel a real attraction to him, but he knew so much more about how to flirt than the boys in high school. I'd never flirted with someone who knew how to make every cell in my body watch him with just a small, innocent touch. When those boys touched me, their hands were too rough or too light, too unsure of themselves. Eric was different.

He knew what he was doing.

I sigh as I shelve the last book and head for the elevator. I wish I could be like that. So sure of myself. If the tables were turned, if I'd been the one to break up with Eric, he would know how to get me back. It wouldn't be difficult for him to figure out what to do, what to say. I push the button for the first floor and as the elevator takes me down, I wonder what he would say, if he were the one who needed to say it.

One true sentence.

"It's just us."

One true sentence.

"No one else matters."

One true sentence.

"Come back to me."

One true sentence.

"It's all going to be okay."

He would know how to say it so it made sense. So it was right. If I said it, it wouldn't have the same effect. He would smile down at me and explain all the reasons none of it was true.

But that doesn't mean I can't try. I have to try. And this is all I have.

When I get back to the front desk, the person taking over my shift is already there. I look at my phone. Excitement and nerves swell and tumble together in my chest.

Finally.

Finally finally finally.

It's time to go see Eric.

EIGHT

When I reach the stairs that lead up to the front door of the Letters and Arts Building, I take them slowly, counting each step in my head so I won't race up them. It's hard to go slow when all I want is to run back into his arms.

One.

It's just us.

Two.

No one else matters.

Three.

Come back to me.

Four.

It's all going to be okay.

Five. Six. Seven.

It's all going to be okay. It's all going to be okay. It's all going to be okay.

Inside, I head for the classroom at the end of the hall. There isn't a class being held in the room this period so I can walk right in.

It's a small classroom, with tables set up in a big U along the walls and sprouting from the middle like ribs. I hover in the doorway, surveying the empty desks, debating. No one else is here yet, so I have my choice of where to sit. Eric always sat in the front so I usually sat there too, as close to him as possible. This time I'm not sure where I should set up camp. Before I would have said Eric wanted me at the front, but I'm not sure how to navigate these waters now.

We can't do this anymore.

It's a small classroom so he'll see me the second he walks in the door. If I sit up front I might look too eager, like I think everything is the same between us when it clearly isn't. On the other hand, sitting at the front could remind him of how it used to be. How we used to sneak glances at one another during class, sharing entire stories without ever saying a word. If I sit in the front, maybe he'll look at me that way again.

If I sit in the back, that might tell him I don't want to be near him anymore, which is the opposite of what I want. But if I play it right, it could also be some version of hard to get. That's what girls are supposed to do. Play hard to get. Some internalized way of putting a challenge in the guy's path so he has to work to reach you, prove he really wants to be the one knocking on your tower door. If you don't require effort, surely you aren't worth it. Everyone knows being called easy is an insult.

Maybe that's what Eric wants. I never played hard to get with him before. Maybe that's what I did wrong. I didn't make him search through the village, slipping a glass high heel on every woman until he finally found me. Maybe I should have made him answer a riddle, defeat a champion, slay a dragon. But it hadn't crossed my mind. I was too busy thanking whatever gods do or don't exist that he had any type of interest in me at all. But maybe that had been a mistake. Maybe if I didn't make him fight for me then he wouldn't think I was *worth* fighting for.

Which means, obviously, I should sit at the back.

I chew on my lip, shifting from one foot to the next, still

standing in the doorway. It's all so much harder now, when I can't ask Eric what to do, when I can't read his cues and act accordingly. Choosing wrong could mean I don't ever get Eric back. And I can't let that happen.

The day he finally gave me a clue he liked me too, all I wanted was to turn the pages faster, to see how our story would go. Still, I let him take the lead. I let him turn the pages. I didn't push for knowledge. I didn't scream down from the heights of my tower and beg him to tell me how I ended up there, beg him to show me how to escape. Instead I waited. I soaked up all the knowledge he had to offer—about fairy tales, about the world, about life, about me—trying to decipher what it was he was saying, what it was he was trying to tell me. And I thought I was starting to understand, starting to see the pieces. My story. Our fairy tale. The prince and the princess. Happily ever after.

You're magic.

I want that feeling back. I want to feel like someone wants to know me. I want to feel like I'm a coveted book, a story so captivating that whoever is reading me would ignore everyone and everything else around them. Eric made me feel like that right from the start. Like he could spend his whole life reading me and still not be bored. Until now.

We can't do this anymore.

It's getting hard to breathe.

No. I'm fine. I'll *be* fine. *We'll* be fine. I just have to remind him what he saw in me. I can do that. I can be the girl he saw before. The princess in the window. I can be that girl. I am that girl. I'm whatever he wants me to be.

"I'm telling you," a female voice says from behind me. "It's true."

I glance over my shoulder and then walk into the classroom ahead of two students coming in after me. I know them from some of my other literature classes. Zoey and Emilio.

"Hey Kara," says Emilio as he takes a seat at the front of the room. I offer a small wave and smile in return.

"Hi," says Zoey, pulling out a chair next to Emilio and turning back to him. "Callie told me where to look Emilio. I saw it. Right there on the wall."

"It's just a stupid rumor Zoey. Don't believe everything you hear."

I'm going to look awkward if I don't sit down now. I choose a seat in the middle of the room, facing forward. Far enough back that I won't seem too eager but close enough that I won't seem like I'm trying to keep distance between us.

"Come on, you don't believe a professor would sleep with a student?" Zoey asks.

"That's not it. I just don't like gossip."

Carefully, I take what I'll need for class out of my bag. Pen. Notebook.

"All you're doing is spreading a rumor," Emilio says. "You don't have any facts. You're just making it worse. Fake news."

Zoey makes a scoffing sound and I glance up. She looks like she's about to pull me into their conversation but my phone dings its text alert noise and I avoid her gaze by pulling it out of my coat pocket. Another student walks in and Zoey turns to her to continue the conversation.

A text from my mom.

Hey honey. Just wanted to see how you're doing.

I don't have the brain space for this. Not with the possibility of Eric walking in any second. I don't want to be texting when he comes in. I want to glance up and meet his gaze, see myself reflected in his black eyes, which have become my favorite mirror. But I can't not answer my mom.

She'd work herself up into a worried-mother-panic-frenzy and then she'd probably do something crazy like call the school or the national guard. Or Shush.

> Hi mom. I'm doing good.
> Just waiting for class to start.

Someone else walks into the classroom and I look up hopefully, but it isn't Eric. My phone buzzes again.

Ok. Just wanted to tell you I love you.
I'm here if you need anything.

I stare at her message, wondering what would happen if I told the truth. But that would require so much explanation, so much back story. She doesn't know about Eric. Slowly, I type back.

> Love you too mom.

That seems to satisfy her because she stops texting me. For now at least. I set my phone down on the table and stop. The fake wooden surface is etched with markings—doodles, initials, words—left from who knows how many years' worth of students. Most of the writers stuck to the edges, but a few dared the middle of the table. And that's where I see it, the word etched deepest of all.

FUCK

Someone carved it into the wood with the harsh tip of a pen, forcing ink deep into the depressions. I reach out and trace it with my finger, trying to discern all of its rises and dips as if it's braille I can read. I'm so focused on it, I don't see Eric walk into the room. But I feel him. It's the same inexplicable pull I felt last year when he walked through a classroom door and into my life.

Slowly, I lift my gaze.

He's looking back at me. His ink-black eyes lock with mine and my body tenses. I feel his name surge up my throat and into my mouth, the taste familiar and intoxicating. Forcefully, I swallow it back down. I'm sure it only lasts a second, maybe two, but in that small expanse of time, I feel his arms around me, his mouth on mine. I feel all the words he's ever said to me.

You're magic.

It's all going to be okay.

We can't do this anymore.

I try, in that second of eternity, to get a read on his feelings. I'd been so good at reading his feelings. Once upon a time. I could sense his emotions and adjust myself accordingly. If he seemed happy, I would be flirtatious, the girl who read a book over his shoulder just for the chance to press her body up against his. If he seemed sad, I would be comforting, the girl who wrapped her arms around him in the dark. If he seemed angry, I would be apologetic, the girl who looked up at him meekly from beneath dark eyelashes and slipped her hand into his like a question.

But this time there's nothing. Just a black wall.

When he looks away without any hint of emotion, it's like he's yanked the world out from under me. I feel a bit unsteady, gripping the table for balance. He starts talking to Zoey and Emilio and it's all I can do to stay in my seat. I want to go to him, take him by the hand and lead him out into the hallway so we can have a private minute to talk. I want to fold myself into his arms, here in front of everyone, press my face into his strong chest, and tell him how hard it's been this past week without him.

But I can't do any of that.

He hasn't given me any signs it would be okay. And I can't be that girl. I'm not the ugly stepsister, demanding you look at my blood-covered foot and see that your glass slipper fits me. But the need is overwhelming. If not to get up and physically demand his attention, then to shout at him.

Eric.

Eric look at me.

Look at me.

I dig my fingernail hard into the surface of the desk.

FUCK

Look. At. Me.

But he doesn't.

My skin feels wrong. It's too tight. Too loose. Not mine. Not me. I want to get up, run to him, throw myself into his arms to see if he'll still catch me. I want to sink into this chair like quicksand and disappear. I want a dragon to turn me to stone. I want to prick my finger on the point of my pen and fall asleep until he comes back to wake me. To return me to my body, to skin I want to live in.

You're magic.

But he won't look at me. He hasn't angled his body away from me but he hasn't angled it towards me either. Now what do I do?

Anything else you want to ask me?

Why? I want to ask him why he had to end it. Why now? But more than that I want to ask him why he *started* it. Why me? Why did he want *me*? What made me special? I'm magic, but what kind? Do I need to know specific incantations or does it follow my will? What language are the spells in? Do I need a wand? Is it the kind of magic where I need to know what phase the moon is in or is it the kind of magic where I need to sacrifice a small animal? Is it blood magic? Will I find it beneath my skin if I keep searching?

In all the time we'd been together, I'd never really gotten an answer from him. I'd only gotten clues, clues I'm not sure I can piece together on my own. A touch of his hand on my hair, a kiss on my skin, a few words whispered into the dark. Without him it's all gone.

Look at me.

I try to send the desperate demand out into the air. Like a spell. A tendril of an incantation to hook around his heart and turn his gaze towards me. But nothing happens. I send it out again and again.

Look at me. Look at me. Look at me.

What do I do now?

I could get up and join their conversation, just casually put myself back into his proximity and see how he reacts. I'm still trying to decide when class starts. And I'm left with no recourse but to go back to my old ways.

Before we got together, I used to pretend he was sending me secret signals. I looked for hidden meanings in the way he held his pen, in the way he spoke, in the words he said. The exact tilt of his head when he was reading from one of the books, the angle of his smile, how many times he blinked. When he said something funny, the whole class laughed, but he would glance at me and I pretended he told the joke just for me. We had entire conversations without saying a word. Another student would say something and Eric would turn the page of his book in a way that said *Well that's obvious* and I would tap my pen on my notebook twice, saying *Everyone knows that.*

Now, I watch his mouth move and I can remember the way it looked when he said each of the things that don't reconcile.

You're magic.

It's all going to be okay.

We can't do this anymore.

I want to ask him how he can say them all and mean them. He wouldn't lie to me but I don't see how all of it can be true at once. I take my pen and trace over the graffiti in my desk, making it darker.

FUCK

I shift in my seat and my jeans rub over the cuts I'd made last night, causing the slightest amount of pain as denim meets open flesh. Biting the inside of my cheek, I shift again, focusing on the pain as it cries out from the skin on my thigh.

What do I do now?

Class goes on around me, the lecture and the discussion and the questions and answers. It all seems to be happening at a distance, like it's on the edge of a bubble, blurry and muffled. I can't quite connect to it. Eric hovers on the edge of it, bright and distinct, and if he would only look at me, I know I could pull him fully into the bubble with me. We could have our own conversation with just a look. That's all I need.

Look at me.

I need him to show me he knows what I'm feeling. That he has some inkling of our story and how it's all crumbling at the edges without him to hold it up. Just a look. Something to show he still sees me. But he won't. It's like nothing has happened. Like none of it ever happened. Like I never belonged in his fairytale world.

Look at me. Look at me. Look. At. Me.

I have to do something. Force his hand, make him look at me so I feel real again, not like everything that happened between us was a dream, a figment of my overactive imagination. I need to know I didn't make everything up.

At the end of class, he starts putting his books back in his bag along with everyone else, and I make my move. Standing, I sling my bag over my shoulder.

It's just us.

The words I planned to say to him feel hollow now. He still hasn't looked at me. As if he doesn't want to spark a flame and burn everything down around him. He doesn't need to worry about me making a scene in front of everyone. He knows I wouldn't do that. I just need to get him on his own.

No one else matters.

I start walking towards him, holding onto the strap of my bag with a tight grip, digging my nails into the palms of my hands for stability, for courage.

Come back to me.

I stop in front of where he's sitting, but he says nothing, doesn't even look up. As if I'm going to walk right past, head out of the classroom. As if I'm going to act like nothing ever happened between us. Making the first move like this feels wrong, like I'm going against everything I've been taught, but I have to try.

It's all going to be okay.

"Hi," I say.

Look at me.

He looks up as if he just noticed me there. His gaze connects with mine and somehow it's both easier and more difficult to breathe all at the same time. He looks at me expectantly, waiting for me to say something else. His

hands are resting on top of the desk, folded together. I want
to slip my hand between them, feel the warmth of his skin,
the strength of his fingers. The reassurance that always
came when he took my hand in his. A silent way of saying
*Follow me. The world is full of dragons but I will protect you.
You're safe with me.*

"Can we…" I glance around but no one seems to be listening to us. I lower my voice anyway. "Do you have a minute?"

*It's just us. No one else matters. Come back to me. It's all going
to be okay.*

There it is. In the corner of his mouth. Sadness.

"Sorry Kara. I've got to get going. I'm going to be late to
my next class."

Anything else you want to ask me?

I try to smile but my mouth doesn't move the way I tell it to.

Can you tell me what I say?

"Oh okay."

It's hard to breathe.

What do I do now?

I force a smile onto my face. Casual. I need to be casual.
To pass whatever test this is. Because that's what it must be.
A test. After all the time we shared, he wouldn't be blowing
me off like this. That isn't him. "I'll umm… I'll see you later."

"See you next time."

He stands up, taking obvious care not to touch me as
he passes me and leaves the classroom. I can't move. My
whole body strains to follow his out the door. It's a cruel
parody of the way it used to be. How he used to take advantage of chances like that to brush up against me, a casual
contact that no one else would think twice about, but a
brushing warmth of his body against mine telling me he
wanted me. It was always the small things. He didn't need
to shout his affection for me for the world to hear. He just

needed to casually make contact with me in plain view of everyone. Subtle but enough. Enough for me to know he cared enough to take the time to reassure me of his feelings. Enough for me to feel like I mattered.

I'm here.

I stare at the doorway even after his familiar form has disappeared down the hall.

The air leaves with him.

Kara we can't do this anymore.

Other students move past me and I know I need to get out of their way but I can't move.

It's over.

The tidal wave crashes.

It's over.

It really happened. It happened to me. He broke up with me.

It's over.

The air is gone. I can't breathe. A vast expanse of blank pages stretches out in front of me, so terrifying with its absence of story that I can't take a single step.

Fuck

I need to move, leave the classroom, before people realize I'm standing here like an idiot.

Anything else you want to ask me?

Breathe. Just breathe.

That's it.

I start walking, leaving the classroom, the building, heading back to my dorm room. I'm inside my room before I realize I never put my coat on. I drop it and my bag on the floor.

What do I do now?

It's all going to be okay.

I need to say my prayers.

NINE

I'm good at disappearing.

I'm good at being the inconsequential character in the story. The fourth victim of the serial killer. I'm not important like the first victim or the survivor who gets saved at the end. I'm just part of the pattern. A picture in the middle of a row of dead girls, taped to a police whiteboard. A nameless tragedy.

I came by this persona naturally but I've cultivated it over the years. Keeping my hair long, hiding behind it and my books. Staying quiet, only speaking when necessary. I become different people in different situations, doing everything I can to blend in. That's what a nameless victim does. You're not supposed to notice her until she's dead.

But Eric noticed me.

Maybe that's why I'm having such a hard time letting him go. He saw me. He spent time analyzing the details, measuring the distances between my freckles, learning my facial expressions. He asked me questions and he listened to the answers. With him I became someone new. Not the nameless body a local hiker finds in the woods. A princess.

I like that person. I like that skin, soft and smooth to the touch.

You're magic.

I want it back.

Look at me.

I need it back.

If Eric doesn't see me anymore, then I'm not his princess. Which means I go back to being the nameless tragedy. But I don't fit inside my old character anymore. Like I'm too big for that skin after living a fairy tale for so long. It doesn't fit properly. It makes it hard to breathe.

It makes the need to pray hum a little louder under my skin.

The first time Eric kissed me, we were leaving the library. We'd met a few times at the library and leaving was always the worst part. I never wanted to say goodbye and Eric always seemed to linger for a few minutes, stretching whatever we were talking about just a bit farther. We would walk slowly, meandering, heading nowhere. I followed his lead, letting him choose the direction. We were talking about fairy tales.

He wandered around the side of the library, into the shadows, away from the more brightly lit sidewalks. And when he stopped, turning to face me, it was hard to make out his expression but I knew something was different. I could feel it. Like the air had gotten thicker.

"Do you know the fairy tale behind the invention of the kiss?" he asked me, his voice soft.

I was rooted to the spot. "No."

"Would you like to hear it?"

I nodded and then, wondering if he could see me in the darkness, said in a voice that was a little breathless, "Yes."

"Once upon a time at the beginning of time, there was a man and a woman." He moved even closer to me. "He was in love with her and she with him, but they didn't know how to tell each other. Language was still being created. There weren't words for love, for the feelings taking over everything inside them."

Reaching out, he brushed the hair back from my face, his fingers lingering on my cheek, warming my skin despite the cold night air. I couldn't breathe.

"One day they met, and when they tried to tell each other how they felt, neither could understand the other. They opened their mouths and shouted out sound but it didn't match what they felt inside. It wasn't enough."

He was so close to me I could feel the heat of his breath on my face.

"Overwhelmed, they reached for each other, and then…"

When his mouth met mine, it was soft and warm and wonderful.

It was like waking up. Like I'd been asleep all this time and this was the thing I'd been missing. He held my face between his hands like I was made of glass, like he might break me. I curled my fingers into the lapels of his coat, holding on, pressing into him.

I don't know how long the kiss went on, but when he pulled back, I found myself breathing in deeply, my lungs aching for air. But I didn't care. He was still holding me, looking down at me like I was everything he'd ever imagined me to be. Like he'd started reading and he was happy with the story he found. Like he'd gotten through the first chapter and all he wanted was more.

"I've been wanting to do that since the first moment I saw you," he said softly, and waves of delight rose inside me. He'd noticed me. He'd *seen* me. He'd seen *me*.

"You're magic," he whispered. And in that moment, as he kissed me again, I knew it was true.

That, *that*, was what I had to get back. That feeling. That knowledge. My fairy tale.

You're magic.

If he knows I'm a princess worthy of admiration,

worthy of love, then that's what I am. But if he doesn't think that—

Yesterday plays over and over in my head, in disjointed pieces that refused to let me sleep all night. I watch Eric walk into the room, watch him pretend I don't exist. I watch myself, pathetic and unsure, walk up to his desk, watch him dismiss me.

I can't make it stop. But that isn't the worst part.

The worst part is me, screaming at myself. Interrogating myself, trying to get me to see what I could have done differently, berating me for doing the wrong wrong wrong *always* the *wrong* thing.

The same argument again and again.

Until the sun creeps up, letting light into my room. Until Ella starts texting me, letting me know she's headed my way.

I'm supposed to meet her to work on math homework and ambush Jake in the common room. But after what happened yesterday, I really don't want to face her chipper self. But I can't fail Calc. If I lose my scholarship, I can't stay here, and if I'm not here, there's zero chance I'll get Eric back. Not to mention disappointing my parents and ruining my whole future and all that. Rather than spur me to get out of bed, the weight of everything presses me into my mattress.

Come on Kara. Get up. You can do this.

At least I don't have class today. All I have to do is get through homework with Ella and her plan to get Jake to notice her. Then I can curl up in bed again.

Get up.

Just one step at a time.

Get. Up.

I can do this.

I throw off the covers. Swing my legs over the side of the bed. Get to my feet. And reach for my tabernacle.

On days like this, my ritual is all that gets me out of bed. Under the water, with the blade in my hand, I already feel a little better.

Pressure. Pain. Blood.

Breathe.

After, I get dressed slowly, carefully pulling up my underwear and jeans over my new cuts—shallow enough that they've already stopped bleeding. Ella texts me, letting me know she's at the door downstairs.

I sigh, gathering up my books and notebooks and laptop, and head down to let her in. It's not that I don't like Ella. It's just that she's *exhausting*. She's one of those people who wear all their emotions on the outside and all of her emotions seem so… *bright*. And it's not that I want Ella to be sad. It's that I don't have the energy to handle her.

I reach the front door and push it open for Ella.

"Hey," she says brightly—always brightly. I am not going to survive this.

"Hi." My smile feels okay on my face, like a real smile and not a fake grimace-looking thing.

Her gaze moves past me to the rest of the room. "You haven't seen him yet have you?"

"No," I say, not mentioning I've been curled up under the covers all morning. This had been the plan she'd finally landed on. Doing homework in the common room all day until Jake inevitably walked by. Then I could introduce them. She thought it would look casual.

We start on the math homework and it's not too bad. It's only the start of the semester so the work isn't that hard yet. I only have to ask Ella for help a couple times. And to my surprise and relief, she's really good at the whole tutoring thing. Maybe I won't fail Calc this time around.

Ella sits up straighter in her chair, scanning the other

people in my building's common room, searching for Jake with a slight hint of desperation. The common room is littered with tables and chairs, armchairs and couches.

"When do you think he'll come down?" Ella asks.

"I don't know."

She starts tapping her pen on the table so fast and loud that some of the other people are starting to look at her. "Ella," I say, "take a breath."

She glances down at her pen and sets it on the table, running her fingers through her hair. "Sorry. I just… I just want him to show up."

Her bubbly fairytale princess exterior is cracking a little, exposing an interior that's a little desperate. It's coming out in the way she keeps looking at the door, keeps running her hands through her hair. In the edges of her eyes, a little too wide, and in the tone of her voice, a little too high pitched.

She sighs, picking up her textbook and then putting it back down, glancing at both entrances to the common room. When she sees I'm still watching her, she groans and slumps over, putting her forehead on the table.

Her voice is a bit muffled as she asks, "You think I'm crazy don't you?"

"No." How can I call her crazy for arranging this thing with Jake when all I've been doing for the past week is planning how to get Eric back? This is what we're supposed to be doing anyway. Princesses planning to get their princes. When she looks back up at me, she looks like she's debating telling me secrets.

"I just want everything to be perfect," she says.

I nod. "I know."

She props an elbow on the table and turns her body to face me, resting her chin on her hand. "I never had that before."

I wait for her to explain.

"I'm not... well I'm not what you'd call beautiful, you know." She rushes on from this statement, not giving me the opening to say what I know I should—some variation of a rebuttal. "And what I look like now is nothing compared to what I was in high school. I used to be... well I used to be heavier and I had really bad acne and I didn't know how to use makeup or like, conditioner. So I never had a boyfriend. I've never..." Her face gets red. "I've never been kissed. Before college, I went on this crazy diet and I did all these makeup tutorials and I swore college was going to be different. I just... No one knows me here. I thought it would be a fresh start."

It's all starting to make sense. The way she's so desperate to get Jake's attention. She's gone through a transformation and now that she looks more like a fairytale princess, she wants a fairytale prince to complete the picture. That's how it's supposed to work. That's how it goes in all the stories.

"God," Ella sighs. "I'm such a crazy loser."

I think back to all the time I spent stressing about the writing I showed to Eric because I wanted to impress him. I agonized over every choice of topic, every word I put down on the page. I was sure each way I phrased a sentence was part of the magic spell I needed to get his attention, to keep him looking at me.

"No," I say. "You're not. You're really not."

There's a moment of silence as she gives me a small smile. And then she straightens, going back to her homework, the time of secrets passed. It all makes sense now. The way she's so hung up on Jake. She just wants him to give her what she's always thought was out of her reach.

You're magic.

Something sharp digs at my lungs and I take a deep breath, trying to loosen the sudden tightness in my chest.

Anything else you want to ask me?

I stop in mid-turn on a page of my biology book.

That's it.

So much of the time Eric and I spent together was about stories. Telling stories, analyzing stories, reading and listening and disappearing inside stories. That's what I have to do. I have to show Eric I understand. That I know what our story is. That I've been listening to him.

You're magic.

I flip to a new page in my notebook. All I have to do is figure out the right words to say it.

One true sentence.

The beginning is easy. I start it the way all fairy tales start.

Once upon a time…

This is it. This will get him back. I'll show him I've been paying attention. That I understand. I'll show him how we can make this work, how we can have our love story, no matter what.

"Kara," Ella hisses, kicking my leg under the table. I look up from my notebook and see Ella's would-be prince walking across the common room. Jake's nearly to us now. When he reaches our table, he does what he always does, and gives me a small nod of greeting.

"Hey Jake, how are you?" I say. There's a slight look of surprise on his face as he stops. Rarely do we ever exchange words in our passing hellos.

"I'm alright. You?"

Ella pushes her knee against mine, as if I need the reminder that this whole thing is a setup to introduce her to Jake.

"Good. I'm good. You know Ella right?" I tilt my head towards her and Jake shifts his gaze.

"Hey I'm Jake," he says.

Ella beams at him. "Hi."

"You're in Calc with Howards right?" Jake asks. Ella nods and I can sense the delight wafting off her at the fact that Jake had noticed her. "Have you done the homework?" He glances from Ella back to me and I'm about to say we both finished it half an hour ago when Ella jumps in.

"Just started," she says. I struggle to keep my expression straight. Ella flew through that homework. It took her about twenty minutes. Is she going to play the helpless math student, her plan from before, even though we'd decided that was a bad idea?

"Me too," Jake says. "I got stuck on problem seven. Math isn't really my forte."

"You should get Ella to help you," I say, seizing the opportunity. "She's a numbers genius." This plan is much better than Ella pretending she doesn't know what's going on.

"Yeah?" He shifts his weight towards her, his tone hopeful.

"I'm not a genius," Ella says sheepishly.

"She is. She's helping me." I sit up straighter and lean towards him. "Seriously, take the help. She's a great teacher."

He hesitates and I think maybe I've pushed it too far and he's sensed there's some kind of plot unfolding around him. But then he smiles. "Yeah?"

"I'd love to help," Ella says, and I'm impressed she keeps her tone of voice in check. She sounds calm, not like the jumping-for-joy fairytale princess I know is celebrating on the inside.

Jake glances at the exit to the common room and then back to Ella and me.

"I'm heading to lunch to meet some friends. Will you guys still be here in a while?"

"Yup," Ella responds before I have a chance to say anything. "Still tons more homework to get through."

"Great," says Jake. "I'll umm... I'll see you in a bit?"

Ella smiles. "Cool."

He walks away and I press my lips together against a groan. I don't want to sit here for another two hours. But when Ella turns to look at me, sunshine pouring out of the smile on her face, I know I'm going to stay.

"Well that went well," I say mildly.

Ella does a few little bounces in her chair. "It's perfect!"

I can't help but laugh at her.

"This is excellent," she says. "Man, I hope he really sucks at math."

I laugh again and this time she joins me.

"Didn't you say you were hungry?" I ask. "Why didn't you ask if we could go to lunch with him and his friends?"

Ella makes a face. "That would be so… pushy. You know? I don't want to come off as desperate or, or crazy or something."

I know exactly what she means. It's the line I've been trying to walk ever since Eric broke up with me. How to show I'm interested without pushing too hard.

I shake my head and look back down at my notebook. At least I can spend the time we're waiting working on my story for Eric. It has to be perfect. If I can show him I was paying attention to our story while it was happening, maybe I can show him I'm worthy enough to be his princess.

I run a finger over the words I've already written.

Once upon a time a princess met a prince.

I glance back at Ella, reveling in the start of her own little fairy tale, happily pulling out her completed math homework and tearing it into little pieces so she can start over while she's helping Jake. I wonder if her story will turn out better than mine.

No. My story isn't over. I can get Eric back, get my fairy tale back. It's fine.

I'm fine.

Putting my pen to paper, I get to work.

∽

It's Sunday night when he texts me. I do a double take
at my phone, hardly believing that yes, it's his name on the
text message. Not Shush. Not my mom. Not Ella.
Eric.

Meet me in the library. 8 pm

I leap off my bed, nearly knocking my laptop to the
ground in the process. He wants to see me.
He. Wants. To see. Me.
Tonight. In less than an hour.
A smile—a real smile—stretches my mouth so wide it
hurts. I'm out of practice.
I type and erase half a dozen messages to him—*I can't
wait* at one end of the spectrum and *ok* at the other—before
finally settling on *see you then.*
It worked. My story worked.
I spent all day yesterday perfecting it, and then last night
I emailed it to him. Simple. Not pushy. Just a casual email.
Let me know what you think, I said. As if I was just sharing
a piece of writing I'd been working on. As if I wanted his
academic opinion. I didn't have to explain what it was or
that it was about us or why I was sending it to him. Eric
would understand. He always understood.
I realize I'm smiling. This is it. I'm going to get him back.
Tonight's the night.
I open my dorm room door to head out and nearly run
into someone in my rush.
"Oh sorry," I say, and then stop.

Eventually you'll forgive me.

No. No no no.

You can't avoid me forever.

My smile freezes, then melts into a determined grimace. She's not going to ruin this. I won't let her.

Shush stares back at me, holding her hands out in front of her like I'm a wild animal that might spook.

"Kara I have to talk to you."

TEN

I close my eyes. This can't be happening. It. Cannot. Be. Happening.

Of all the times for Shush to show up at my door, she's going to do it now? It has to be *now*, when Eric finally wants to talk to me. I open my eyes and turn back to lock my dorm room door. Then I head down the hallway, determined not to acknowledge her. I run down the stairs and she thunders after me, not giving up. She follows me outside into the dark and the cold, even though she isn't wearing a coat.

"Kara, stop. I'm your friend, you have to listen to me."

Ignoring her, I pick up my pace. I don't respond to any of her pleas for me to listen. I don't say anything to her. I don't even look at her.

But she's relentless. A predator in pursuit of prey.

"Kara please stop. Just look at me. I'm sorry for what happened, okay?"

She tags along at my elbow, lowering her voice only slightly when we pass other people. Before this we'd never really gotten into a fight. I know some friends do that, fight with each other and then make up because their friendship is more important than whatever happened between them. But our friendship was never like that. I never pushed back. She led and I followed. She talked and I listened.

But not anymore.

"I was just trying to help," she says. "Jesus, are you even going to look at me?"

I keep walking, keep ignoring her. The problem now is I can't have her follow me to the library. I have to get rid of her somehow. Maybe I could outrun her. Take off in a different direction until she loses sight of me and then double back to the library.

"I just want to warn you. I did something and I wanted to tell you before you found out from someone else."

I could shout at her. That has its appeal too. But I'm not sure what I'd say. *Leave me alone* seems like a good start but I don't know if it would work. I could tell her I don't care what explanations she has to offer. I'm not going to forgive her for betraying me like she did. I want her to go away and never come back.

"Kara please." She reaches out and grabs my arm.

I yank away, finally stopping to face her. Her expression is fractured, like she's breaking apart.

"I just—" she starts, then breaks off. She's shivering slightly, her breath puffing out into the cold night air. Not that long ago we would have walked down this sidewalk together, talking and laughing, so close together we bumped into each other as we walked. Now, we're only a couple feet apart but the distance might as well be a vast moat. I've pulled up my drawbridge. She can't get to me now.

"Kara I wanted to tell you… I just… I-I'm sorry… I…"

I narrow my eyes, turning my expression into a glare and crossing my arms over my chest. At the change in my posture, she stops whatever she was about to say. I harden my gaze further. She can breathe all the fire she wants. My castle walls will hold strong.

We stand there for a long minute, staring at one another.

Then, deliberately, I turn away from her and walk on into the darkness.

This time, she doesn't follow.

Heat hits my face as I push through the doors of the library building. I should be grateful for it after the frigid air outside. But my body already feels too hot. I unzip my coat as I walk through the lobby, looking behind me for the millionth time to make sure Shush isn't there.

Kara you have to tell someone.

My skin itches.

Why is it so hot in here?

I can't breathe.

Yanking at the sleeves of my coat, pulling it off, I walk quickly through the open archway into the main library. My gaze darts around, searching. Not for Eric. Not yet.

For the wooden edge of that table. The metal corner of that bookend. The scissors on the circulation desk.

Anything sharp.

I need to pray.

You can't avoid me forever.

Why did she have to show up now? I need to be calm and collected. I'm supposed to be put together when I see him. Not all off balance, ready to gnaw off my own leg if it gets me out of Shush's claws.

I keep walking, past the desk, the computers, and far too many people doing too much *talking.* I head for the stairwell. My boots pound on the stairs, echoing. I step harder, leaning into the noise, drowning out Shush in my head.

Every two steps—his name.

Eric.

Eric.

Eric.

Round the corner and then I'm on the second floor. He

might be here already. Hope swells in my chest at the thought, expanding my lungs, making it easier to breathe.

Once upon a time…

Exit the stairwell, turn the corner, move past one, two, three, four, five sets of bookshelves.

There.

Our place.

Our secluded table, our window, our chairs.

Empty.

He isn't here yet.

I deflate. Just a little.

We can't do this anymore.

The humming under my skin gets louder.

The edge of the windowsill. The corner of the bookshelf. Could I press against that hard enough?

I go to the window, rocking on the balls of my feet, my body thrumming with words that have nowhere to go.

I want to let them out.

Kara you have to tell someone.

I check my phone. 7:54 p.m.

Not enough time not enough time. I'm early and there's *still* not enough time. Not enough time to go back down-stairs and borrow the scissors from the circulation desk. Take them into a bathroom stall and release this pressure under my skin. Eric might show up, not find me, and leave again. I can't take that chance.

I'm pacing. I can't stand still.

Get it together Kara. Get it the fuck together.

Can you tell me what I say?

I can't breathe.

I fling my coat on one of the chairs, wrap my arms around myself, push my hands inside the sleeves of my sweater, dig my fingernails into the skin on my forearms.

Eric will be here soon. He'll calm me down. He'll drown out the hum coming from under my skin. He'll run his hands over me and tell me I am magic, and then it will be true.

It's all going to be okay.

He'll be here soon.

Soon soon soon.

I just have to make it a few more minutes. I can do that. I can. I can I can I can.

It's just us.

No one else matters.

Come back to me.

My reflection looks back at me from the window. I'm transparent. Like a ghost. Like I'm not all the way here.

And even though I feel like I am *shaking*, I look completely still. A statue.

Waiting.

Waiting for him to come kiss my frozen mouth and wake me up.

I slip one hand into the waistband of my jeans, find the ridges of my scars below my hip bone, find fresh cuts and push down—pressure—stretch the skin—pain—force them open.

Breathe.

I have the sudden urge to take off all my clothes. To see all my scars reflected in this window. To wait for Eric like that.

Honest. Open. Plain to read.

Once upon a time there was a girl with magic words written into her skin…

The first time Eric discovered my scars, we were here. In the stairwell I just climbed up. He was pressing me against the wall, kissing me.

My skin warms, as if I can feel him standing here now. His hand on my waist, his fingers slipping under the hem of my shirt.

I wrap my arms around myself, move back until I'm leaning against the bookshelf behind me, until I can feel the ridges of books cradling my head, bracketing my spine. I need something to help hold me up.

I thought about stopping him. When his fingers skimmed the skin above the waistband of my jeans, when they started to slip beneath it. I thought about keeping that part of me locked away, trying to keep myself magic for him. Just for a little while longer I could be what he thought I was instead of what I am.

But I did nothing.

I waited. Waited to see what he would do.

When his fingers dipped to my hip bone, I felt his hesitation. The small pause his body gave as his fingers found the smooth ridges of recent cuts, still scarred over. His mouth stopped moving on mine and he pulled back, confusion clear on his face.

I said nothing.

He pressed down slightly, with the tips of his fingers. Just hard enough that I flinched, giving him an answer to the question he hadn't asked out loud.

Still I made no sound.

When he moved, he moved slowly, like he was waiting for me to stop him. But I didn't. I wanted to see what he would do next. He knelt at my feet and gently lifted my shirt with one hand as, with the other, he tugged down the waistband of my jeans to reveal the scars he felt and countless more, healed into white lines criss crossing my skin.

I sucked in a breath, closed my eyes, and waited.

This was when it would happen.

Panic.

I hadn't even known Eric that long. He would be well within his rights to panic. I expected it. I braced for it. For him to take his hand away as if my prayers had burned his flesh. For him to stand abruptly, put space between our bodies as if my religion was contagious. Boys had reacted that way before. As if this part of me they didn't understand might hurt them.

Still, I waited, frozen in this moment of nonexistence, waiting for him to decide who I was. The princess. Or the girl they find in the woods.

This was when it would happen.

Anger.

Boys had done that too. They would demand answers, demand an explanation I had tried before to give. But they didn't understand the language my holy book was written in. I might have been speaking in tongues for all they understood. But their lack of understanding didn't stop them from demanding I give up my worship. They called it dangerous, harmful, mutilation. Evil. As if it was a curse they could lift, a demon they could exorcize from me.

Eric's body shifted, ever so slightly, and I clenched my teeth together.

This was when it would happen.

Ignorance.

He would go back to kissing me as if he hadn't seen anything. That had happened too. They just went back to what they were doing as if nothing had changed. As if they hadn't discovered this vast difference between us, a religion they couldn't comprehend. And if Eric ignored it I would play along like I always did. I wouldn't push him to ask me for answers because he wouldn't understand my explanations anyway. When his hands ran over my body and always managed to miss my scars, I would pretend he wasn't holding only part of me and ignoring the rest.

I braced myself, not just for his reaction now, but for his

reaction later. Like a ticking bomb with a clock I couldn't see. Because he wouldn't ignore it forever. They never did.

Then it would happen.

No matter what reaction they had, the end result was always the same.

They left.

I held my breath, slowly disappearing, waiting to see which reaction he would have, waiting to see which way he would try to erase my story.

And then, gently, his fingers traced over my scars. Tenderly, thoroughly, as if they were Braille he could read.

And there was no panic there. No anger. No decision to ignore them.

There was no fear.

Leaning in, he pressed the lightest of kisses against the story I had carved into my skin. Tears stung my eyes as they flew open, and I gasped as—all at once—he brought me back from the edge of vanishing. I shuddered as—all at once—he transformed the scars on my skin from a tragedy into a fairy tale.

I had no time to recover because then he was standing, taking my face between his hands, his handsome features creasing with a frown.

"Kara you look scared. What's wrong?"

I shook my head, words building up in my throat, tangling, choking me.

"Tell me," he said. It wasn't a question. He wasn't *asking* for an answer. But neither was he *demanding* one.

No.

He was giving me the *choice*.

The choice to turn another of my pages. To let him read more, let him learn more about me.

I hadn't known it until then. Until right that second when

he gave it to me. That *this* was what had been missing before.

The others who had discovered my religion had demanded answers, explanations. But they didn't want a story I couldn't read to them. They didn't want to understand. Not really. They wanted something else.

They wanted to skip this chapter. To move past these pages and pretend they never existed.

They wanted a way to take the blade to me themselves, a way to cut this part of my story out of me. As if it was a wholly separate plotline they could cast aside.

And when I failed to give them what they wanted, they left. But this was different.

Eric was different.

Their questions had risen out of fear, out of a desire to cut the thing that was me out of me. They didn't understand and they didn't want to understand. They just wanted to be rid of it. But Eric didn't seem scared. His gaze was unflinching as he looked at me. His hands were sure and true as he brushed his thumbs over my cheeks, tilting my head slightly up so he could look me full in the face.

So he could see all of me.

And he did. He saw me. He saw the tragedy I had written into my skin, the parts of me I hid from everyone, the parts of me that wouldn't fit so easily into a fairy tale. And he wasn't turning away. He didn't feel like he was waiting to let go, to reach for my book as soon as I read it to him, to rip out the pages he didn't like and throw them into a fire. He looked like he wanted to read more.

"Tell me," he said again, moving even closer.

"I..." I inhaled sharply, holding onto his wrists, his hands still holding my head in place so I couldn't escape his gaze.

He waited. He didn't push again. He just waited.

As if I had bared myself before him, opened my castle

gates and extended an invitation as well as a warning.

You might not like what you see.

And I was prepared for all the choices I thought he would make. I was prepared for him to turn and run. I was prepared for him to take me out of the castle and walk with me around the outside, ignoring the fact that I had ever invited him in the first place. I was prepared for him to storm the castle, sword drawn, trying to kill the thing he couldn't see was me.

I was not prepared for *this*.

For him to take me by the hand and say, *Show me. Give me all of you and I will be here, with you, just the same.*

"They left," I managed. "Everyone else, they... they didn't understand. They left."

He wrapped his arms around me, holding me so tightly that I couldn't collapse the way my body wanted to. He pressed his mouth to my hair as I cried in his arms.

"I'm here," he said. "I'm here."

Give me all of you and I will be here, with you, just the same.

"I can't breathe," I whispered. A tear ran down my cheek, hot on my skin. "I can't breathe."

He kissed me then, holding me tight so I would not fall.

I'm here.

You're safe with me.

It's all going to be okay.

Everything changed that day. From then on I knew for certain Eric was different from anyone else. I shared things with him I'd never shared with anyone. He looked at my scars and he didn't look away. He saw the story that everyone else had run from and he didn't leave. He stayed and told me I still mattered. Told me I could still be the princess from the fairy tale.

You're magic.

He stayed.

Until he didn't.

We can't do this anymore.

I press down harder onto my fresh cuts, digging into the sharpness of the pain, forcing myself not to devolve into a spiral of panic.

He texted me. He asked me to meet him. He read my story and now he wanted me back. That has to be it. It has to be.

It's all going to be okay.

I force myself not to watch the end of the bookshelves for him, force myself to look out the window and wait. It takes minutes, hours, days. A lifetime.

And then I see movement reflected in the glass.

I'm here.

I turn to face him, relief draining the adrenaline out of me so I feel a bit unsteady on my feet.

You're safe with me.

Eric's here now.

It's all going to be okay.

"Hi," I say.

Then I frown.

Something's wrong.

I see it as soon as I meet his gaze. A storm raging there, stirring up the inky black depths. I've done something wrong. I glance down. He's clutching pieces of paper in his hand, crushing them in his fist as if he can make them disappear through sheer force.

Oh no.

I shouldn't have pushed. I went too far. I should have waited. I should have been patient.

I failed his test. I failed him.

I sink back into the last time we were alone together, when he broke up with me. He'd done the same thing then, texted me and asked to meet. I'd been delighted, anxious to see him after a long three weeks apart. Three weeks that were agonizing after everything that happened with Shush. And I'd known the minute I walked into the room that something was wrong. I tried to pretend it wasn't, tried to pretend I couldn't sense the storm that was about to dash me upon the rocks.

But I'd been wrecked on them anyway.

I take another step towards him, searching for a hint he's reaching out to save me from drowning.

You're magic.

You're safe with me.

I'm here.

It's all going to be okay.

But there's nothing for me to hold onto. No warmth in his expression, no opening in his posture I can slip myself inside to curl up against him.

Even so, my body pulls towards his. I want to sink into him, to apologize with my arms around him, with his arms around me. I'd made a mistake. Somehow, writing the story hadn't been the right thing to do, but he would forgive me.

He had to.

"Eric…" I start, and then stop. My voice sounds small, tiny, like something to be crushed and then forgotten. He takes a slow, deliberate step towards me.

"Why'd you do it?" he asks. A thick red current of anger paints his voice, and I resist the urge to take a step back. I open my mouth but nothing comes out.

I don't understand.

"How could you?" Betrayal comes out at the edges of his words and stabs me. It's the wrong kind of sharpness. It makes the air too thick. I can't breathe.

I don't understand why he's reacting this way.

"I—"

"Don't you get what could happen? What this could do to me?" He comes closer, shaking his clenched fist at me, the papers clutched in it so tightly I think my words might be seeping from the paper into his skin.

"I…" I mean to say I don't understand but that's not what comes out. "I'm lost."

What do I do now?

Cautiously, I reach a hand out towards him, stretching it towards the papers. At first I think he isn't going to give them to me, but then he thrusts them out, angrily putting them in my hand.

I smooth out the papers, and as I skim the printed words, all the air leaves the room.

Oh my god.

Fuck

This could ruin everything.

People wouldn't understand.

I look up at him, helpless. He can't think this was me. He can't.

"I didn't write this," I tell him, desperation tinging my words. "This wasn't me."

"No?" he spits out, moving in on me. "You weren't angry that I ended it? Didn't decide to get a little revenge?"

It's like he punched me in the stomach. I can't breathe. How could he ever think I would do this? He knows me. He knows me better than anyone. He knows me better than I do. I would never do this.

Can you tell me what I say?

I shake my head. "No. N-no of course not."

He crosses his arms over his chest and looks at me, searching my face.

"It wasn't you?" he asks.

"No. No this wasn't me. I would never…" I would never tell lies about him like this. "Eric you… you know me…"

The end of my sentence tilts up like a question, a hook wanting to sink into something, anything. Just something to hold onto.

I'm lost.

He looks at me, hard, for another long minute, and then he gives a curt nod. "Okay. I believe you."

I take a step towards him, wanting to offer my help, my comfort, anything. "Is there—"

"I have to go," he says, interrupting me. "I have to figure out how to deal with this."

What do I do now?

"Did you get my email?" I ask before he can go, my voice too high. "Did you… did you read my story?"

Maybe, just maybe, I can salvage this. I imagine his expression softening, him taking me into his arms and apologizing. Of course he read my story. Of course he loved it.

You're magic.

"I don't have fucking time for this Kara."

I stagger back a step.

It's over.

He turns to leave and I reach out, grabbing his hand. "Eric wait."

When he turns back to me, his jaw is clenched tight. Deliberately, he pulls his hand away from me. He pulls something with it. Whatever it is that's holding me together. He rips it away and I don't know what's keeping me standing. He only says one thing before turning and walking away, leaving me again. Leaving me alone.

When he speaks his anger is like a book slamming closed, crushing me.

"I told you. Call me *Dr. Callahan.*"

ELEVEN

I heard Dr. Callahan's voice before I saw him.

Freshman year, first day of the second semester, I was in one of the large lecture halls, waiting for class to start. And then his voice, strong and sure of itself, came from the back of the room, cutting through all the noise.

"Once upon a time…"

A shiver ran down my spine. His words washed over me like warm breath on the back of my neck. The voice came from far away but I felt like he whispered it in my ear, like he said it just for me. I twisted in my seat, searching for who'd spoken. And then I saw him, slowly making his way down the steps to my left, the curves of a smile gracing his handsome face.

And he *was* handsome. That was immediately apparent. More than the thickness of his hair or the length of his torso, it was the sparkle of mischief in his gaze, the surety of his steps. The way he spoke with such confidence, like he knew everyone was hanging on his every word.

"I've got your attention now don't I?" he said.

Yes.

I almost said the word out loud. I'd nearly forgotten we weren't the only two people in the room.

"It's like a magic spell, isn't it? Once upon a time…" He

reached the front of the room and took his place behind the podium. "You don't know where I'm going with it—who starts a lecture by saying once upon a time?—but you can't help it."

He braced his weight on his elbows, leaning forward, and I found myself leaning towards him in return. "Your ears prick up, your spine straightens, you focus on my words. Because you know what happens next." His gaze locked with mine, and the smile returned to his lips. "I'm going to tell you a story."

Yes.

Again, I nearly said the word out loud.

I didn't care what he said next. I didn't care what kind of story he had to tell. I just wanted him to tell it to me. I wanted to know what happened next.

"Welcome to Introduction to Fairy Tales," he said. "I'm Dr. Callahan."

Dr. Callahan.

That was how I knew him for months. During lecture upon lecture where I tried to memorize every word he said. During all the time I spent agonizing over my assignments for him. During other classes when I couldn't focus on what the other professor was saying because I was analyzing a small interaction we'd had the day before. Through it all, he was Dr. Callahan. When I thought of him it was as Dr. Callahan, when I spoke to him I addressed him as Dr. Callahan. It wasn't until later, when he started helping me with my final paper, that he offered me his first name.

"Goodnight Dr. Callahan," I said one night as we were leaving the library.

He smiled down at me, reaching out to tuck my hair behind my ear, the gesture so natural and familiar we might have known each other our whole lives.

"Call me Eric," he said.

"Eric," I repeated, trying it out on my tongue and smiling at the feel of it.

I tucked his name into my back pocket like a note. *Eric.* I carried it around with me everywhere, taking it out to admire its edges. The curves and the straightaways. *Eric.* I took it out when I was bored in class, when I was lonely late at night, when I simply wanted to admire it, to remind myself he thought me worthy of such a gift. A small piece of magic all my own. The first page of our story. A story that made it easier to breathe. A fairy tale. Not a tragedy.

And of course Shush, being Shush, didn't take long to notice the difference.

"What are you smiling about?" she asked me one day while we were working on homework in her dorm room.

"What?" I pulled myself out of my head with a little bit of effort. I'd been remembering the day before, when I got to spend an entire hour with Eric in his office, just the two of us. Nothing had happened. Not really. But I swear at the end of it, he'd nearly kissed me goodbye.

"You're smiling," Shush said, pointing her pen at me.

"So?"

"So what are you smiling about?"

"Do I have to be smiling *about* something?"

Shush squinted at me, frowning, like she was trying to solve a mystery. "You look… happy," she said. "Like really happy."

"And that's unusual?"

"Well… yeah. You don't have resting bitch face like me, you have like, like—" She waved her fingers around in the air as she thought. "—resting slit-your-wrists face. That's it. And now you look *happy.* So out with it."

I didn't say anything, hoping she would drop it. But

she didn't. Because she's Shush and incapable of dropping anything.

"Ho-ly shit," she said after a moment of silence, a grin stretching across her face.

"What?"

"There's a *guy*."

"What?" I tried to keep panic from edging into my voice. "No there's not."

"A girl?" Shush asked.

I shook my head.

"Yeah I didn't think you went that way but you never know, maybe you're experimenting." She got up from her desk chair and came to join me on the bed. "So tell me about the guy."

"Shush there isn't—"

"You've been staring into space with a sappy love-struck grin on your face for like five minutes. Tell me about the guy."

I hesitated. It *would* be nice to tell someone about him. Even just a little. I didn't have to give her everything.

"Fine." I threw my hands up in protest, feeling my face turn red. "There's a guy."

"Oh my god I *knew* it." She bounced on the bed. "Tell me tell me tell me."

So I did. I told her I met him in class. I told her how he was so incredibly smart and he knew so many things. I told her that when he looked at me I felt like we were the only two people in the room.

Shush was desperate for details. "Have you asked him out? Have you guys swapped phone numbers? Have you kissed yet?" When I kept my silence, she groaned. "Come on girl, I'm going to die alone over here. Give me some romance."

I relented. It was kind of a relief to have someone to talk to about him. I didn't tell her a lot, but she was delighted with each small detail. She was happy to puzzle out his behavior with me—"Okay so after he looked at you, did he smile?"—to give me advice—"Don't wait on him to make the first move, just ask him on a date already"—to celebrate any steps forward— "Oh my god you *finally* kissed him, good for you."

But I didn't tell her his name. I didn't tell her who he was.

No matter how many times she asked me— "I might know him, I might be able to help. Why won't you tell me who he is?"—I kept his name folded into a small square, hidden in my pocket where no one could see, where no one else could take it away and wring the magic from it. I made excuses—"I don't want you to go up and push him to ask me out" or "I like keeping him all to myself." Then the semester ended. Shush went back to her hometown, and I stayed on campus with Eric.

We spent the summer wrapped up in our own little fairy-tale world, full of sunshine and castles and magic and no one there but us.

When classes started up again, I knew things would be different. We'd have to be more careful, there wouldn't be so much time to spend together. But I kept his name—*Eric*—the first secret we ever had, like a talisman. To remind me of the magic. To make it easier to breathe.

Call me Eric.

Now, that's all been broken.

Call me Dr. Callahan.

I'd never stopped to think about the distance his title created between us. *Dr. Callahan.* So small I hardly noticed it. A door we could see through but couldn't open, defining our relationship as professor and student. With those three small words—*Call me Eric*—he'd held out his hand, a key in his palm, inviting me to unlock it. And I'd done so without hesitation.

Now, he's ripped it all away from me.
Call me Dr. Callahan.
The castle.
Call me Dr. Callahan.
The magic.
Call me Dr. Callahan.
How am I supposed to breathe now?

TWELVE

I take Monday off.

When my alarm breaks the morning stillness, I'm already staring at the ceiling, watching the shadows change as the sun comes up. The small amount of sleep I managed to get last night was sporadic and plagued by dreams of dragons.

The alarm feels far away. I let it go, waiting for its shrill beeping to pierce the hazy cloud around me making me feel like I'm not really here. Someone else is curled up under these sheets. I'm just watching her, waiting for her to move, waiting for her to become real.

Eventually, I shut off the alarm, but I don't get up.

I don't even *tell* myself to get up. Not this time. Not today.

I'll just rest, take a mental health day. Rest is supposed to be a good thing. This is normal. A college kid skipping class to catch up on sleep. It's fine. I'm fine. I need it. I need to rest. I'm exhausted. Like I've been running the whole night. Even now, just laying in bed, I feel my energy seeping out into the mattress. As if I've been running where the air is too thin and I can't get enough in my lungs, can't get enough oxygen in my blood to keep myself going, to get myself back down to where I can actually breathe.

I don't have the energy to face the world today. I can't face what I know will be happening all over campus. I can't face Shush in Biology with her dragon fire. I can't face Creative Writing with Dr. Leery asking us to come up with true sentences. I can't face any of it. Not while everyone will be talking about nothing but lies.

So I stay in bed. I watch Netflix, read a book, try to sleep. I do anything and everything to avoid doing the one thing I end up doing anyway. Reading and rereading the stupid newspaper story Eric had handed me over and over again, as if I'll be able to make the lies disappear by reading them enough, by absorbing the ink into my skin.

TRIGGER WARNING

The following section contains graphic depictions of sexual assault. If you are not in a place where you feel up to reading that, please skip to the next section.

Remember, you're not alone. Mental health resources can be found at the back of this book. Take care of yourself.

My freshman year, I was sexually assaulted by my professor.

The night started out normal. It was a little late, past regular office hours, but I knew he was busy. I appreciated that he was taking the time to help me with my paper. I didn't think anything was wrong.

When he closed the door of his office, I thought it was because of the vacuum someone was running in the hall. When he brushed up against me, I thought it was an accident. When he touched my shoulder, I thought he was being friendly.

I should have left then, should have listened to the prickle of warning running up my spine.

But I didn't.

I told myself I was imagining things. I'd been watching too much television, reading too many books, reading too many news stories about other people.

I'd known him for months. Everyone loved him. I loved him. He was a well-liked and respected professor. He wouldn't do anything to hurt me.

I told myself over and over I was just imagining things.

When he leaned over my shoulder to look at my paper, I told myself I was imagining his hand on my back was anything other than an innocent touch.

When he took hold of my hand, tracing patterns in my palm, I told myself I was imagining he was crossing a line.

When he asked for a hug goodbye, I told myself I was imagining this could be anything inappropriate.

When he pressed himself against me, I told myself I was imagining the way he pushed his hips against mine.

When he kissed me, I told myself I was imagining it all. It wasn't really happening. It couldn't really be happening.

When he shoved his tongue into my mouth, I knew I wasn't imagining anything.

I tried to get away, but he just held me tighter. He rubbed himself against me. His hands were everywhere all at once. Groping me over my clothes. Under my clothes. He kept kissing me, telling me I was beautiful, wonderful. Showering me with compliments as he assaulted me.

I stopped struggling. I stopped doing anything. I just stood there, a statue, trying to pretend none of it was happening, praying it would be over soon, praying he wouldn't go farther than this.

Then he let me go. And I ran.

I ran back to my dorm room and I locked the door behind me and I cried myself to sleep. I didn't tell anyone. I knew I should. But I couldn't. I still couldn't believe it had happened. Couldn't believe it happened to me.

The next day in class he didn't acknowledge anything had happened and again I told myself I imagined it. Surely this professor, a professor I admired and respected, wouldn't have done something like that. It must have been a misunderstanding. A mistake. It took me weeks, months, to admit to myself that he'd assaulted me. I'd been sexually assaulted by my professor.

And I never told. Not until now.

I can't keep this in any longer.

I won't be silent now.

I've read the thing so many times I know it by heart. I close my eyes and its lies traipse across the insides of my eyelids.

I was sexually assaulted by my professor.

I can't believe her.

I can't believe Shush did this.

Because of course it's her. It was published anonymously but I know she's the one who wrote this horror of a fiction. I realized it last night, somewhere around midnight when the rest of my world disappeared inside this terrible nightmare of a story.

I've read everything Shush ever wrote in the student newspaper. I know this is her. I know from the familiar way the sentences are strung together, from the sound of the words in my head as I read them.

I won't be silent now.

It's her voice.

Kara you have to tell someone.

I know from the look on her face last night when she tried to talk to me on my way to meet Eric. This, *this* was what she'd been trying to warn me about.

As if a warning would be a strong enough shield to protect me from this monstrous lie. The paper burns my skin as I hold it, a lie too terrible even for a dragon.

I can't believe she did this.

When he took hold of my hand, tracing patterns in my palm, I told myself I was imagining he was crossing a line.

She used what I told her against me, against him.

This is why Eric thinks it's me.

She's managed to take a single line of truth and anchor her lie around it.

I remember the first time Eric did that with me. We were in the library, talking about Hansel and Gretel. When he reached out and took my hand, I lost all focus on what he

109

was saying, but he kept talking as he traced the lines on my palm with his thumb, almost absentmindedly, like it was habit. And all of me warmed at his touch.

I remember telling Shush about it. How we'd giggled and how she'd been so happy for me, saying he finally took a step towards showing he was attracted to me.

And now she's ruined it. She's ruined all of it.

She's taken it and twisted it, turned it into something horrible.

And she's only guessing. Guessing that when I told her about a guy, I was talking about Eric.

She didn't *know* I was dating *him*. I never told her his name. I never let any hint slip that the guy I told her stories about was anyone other than another student. Over the summer, when my relationship with Eric became more serious, I stopped telling her any stories at all. The longer I kept his name from her, the more she wanted to know it. So I told her he'd left for the summer, that he'd stopped talking to me, that whatever it was we had was over and I was okay with it.

But Shush couldn't help herself. She had to sniff out a story everywhere she went. Any hint of something that smelled of drama and she had her claws into it faster than I could blink.

She caught me looking at Eric one morning in the library.

He was walking with another professor and nodded his hello to both of us as they walked past. I'd felt gleeful, because I knew I was meeting him later in his office, and it was our little secret. No one here knew he'd given me his name, that I could taste it in my mouth as he disappeared around the corner.

Eric.

I wanted to linger over it, search out hints of the popcorn we had the first time we went out to the movies. I wanted to roll it around in my mouth until I tasted the wine we had the first night he invited me to his house. I wanted to hold it on my tongue until I tasted the salt on his skin.

But I should have known better than to lose myself around Shush.

"Who are you looking at?" she asked me, and I knew I'd been smiling at him. She followed my gaze, still trailing after Eric, and when she looked back at me, she was frowning. "Dr. Callahan?"

"No," I said, but I knew I was blushing. She was still staring at me, hard, and I knew she wasn't going to accept that answer. So I relented. Just a little. "Okay fine. Fine. He's just… really hot don't you think?"

At the time, it was almost a relief. To actually admit some small portion of my feelings for him. Sometimes all I wanted to do was scream my happiness from the rooftops. But I knew I couldn't.

"I think this should be our secret," Eric had said after he kissed me for the first time, his arms still wrapped around me. He didn't have to say it was because I was a student and he was a professor. I knew that. It was obvious. I hadn't been thinking about telling anyone. Not even Shush. Especially Shush.

I liked that we existed in our own world.

"Our secret," I agreed, and tilted my face up so he would kiss me again.

But surely this would be okay. Admitting to Shush I thought he was good-looking. Students have crushes on professors all the time. There's nothing wrong with that. She wouldn't know there was something deeper going on. Except she didn't take it like I thought she would.

"No," she said. "I think he's old."

I hadn't read anything into it then, just brushed it off as

Shush being Shush. She was always pretty abrupt. Didn't believe in sugarcoating anything. But over time she got more and more suspicious. Any time we were anywhere together—the cafeteria, the library, the café—and he walked in, she'd start up her investigation again.

"You're not actually into him are you?"

I managed to hold her at bay with shrugs and short answers for a little while. Then finally, one night, she ambushed me outside the library after I'd said goodnight to Eric. We'd spent the whole evening together in the library, going over my latest paper. We were planning to meet up later, at his house, and all I could think was that it had been ages since I spent the night in his bed. Since I fell asleep in his arms and woke up the same way.

"I saw you," she said, stepping out of the shadows. "I saw you with Dr. Callahan."

I blanched, thinking back. But we hadn't done anything. It was dark out but there had been a lot of students around so we hadn't kissed goodnight. We hadn't even touched. We were saving that for later. Looking from the outside at our exchange, no one would have thought us anything more than professor and student.

"So?" I asked. "We were talking about class."

There was an edge to her voice. "Kara he's not what you think."

"Shush, really, you're looking for a story where there isn't one."

After that night, she wouldn't stop pushing me to tell her more. Tell her how much I liked him, why I liked him, what exactly he'd said to me. I maintained that she was imagining things. It strained our relationship, and when everything finally blew up right before winter break, I'd already been pulling out of our friendship. What she did then was just the final straw.

Eventually you'll forgive me.

And now this.

I thought she couldn't get any worse, thought she couldn't claw her way any deeper into my life than she already had. But I was wrong.

She's given up on talking to me and now she's telling her lies about Eric to everyone.

I don't understand why she would do it. Why she would try to tear his whole life apart like this. For attention maybe. This type of story would get her that, even though she published it anonymously. It's entirely plausible someone will figure out Shush is the writer—hell she might even leak it herself—and once that happens they could figure out what classes she took her freshman year. Then it would only be a matter of time before a handful of male professors were under scrutiny.

That wasn't the worst that could happen though. At least then there'd still be some doubt about who she was talking about.

The worst thing would be if she leaked Eric's name.

If everyone who loved and respected him believed these lies about him, even for one second, it would ruin him.

And what if the administration decided to investigate? I know that's one of the reasons we kept our relationship a secret. Our relationship was legal—I was eighteen when we started dating—but I highly doubted our rather religious administration would look favorably on a professor dating a student. Eric could lose his job.

I read Shush's story so many times I can see the words on the insides of my eyelids whenever exhaustion pulls my eyes closed. I can feel them running just under my skin, running through my bloodstream. I can feel them sinking into my bones.

I was sexually assaulted by my professor.

Lies.

Groping me over my clothes. Under my clothes. Showering me with compliments as he assaulted me.

Lies, lies, lies.

I remember the first time Eric kissed me. How gentle he'd been. How he'd gone so slowly, giving me time to stop him if I wanted to. He didn't do these things. He couldn't do these things. He would never take advantage of someone like that. There's just no way. Shush is lying.

She always thinks she's right. He's my professor, so he must be taking advantage of me. She looks at everything so black and white, right and wrong and she's the one who knows the difference. She doesn't understand it isn't like that at all. He isn't taking advantage. We're in a relationship.

We *were* in a relationship.

It's over.

I clench my jaw against the tears threatening to fall.

I can't believe her.

She keeps making decisions like this, deciding what I should and shouldn't do, deciding how I should live my life. She doesn't know what's best for me. She doesn't know anything about me, anything about what I want or about what's good for me.

Kara you have to tell someone.

I realize I've crumpled the story into a ball in my fists. Lies. They're all *lies*.

I won't listen to her.

I tear the story into pieces. I tear it into pieces and then I tear those pieces into pieces and then I tear those, until nothing is left but confetti, scattered over my bed. Getting up for the first time today, I scoop them up by the handful, sentences torn to shreds, words without their meaning. I throw them in the trash.

I'll ignore it. That's all. It'll be a big story for a few days or a few weeks and then it will blow over. I'll just wait. I'll weather the storm and then, when everyone's forgotten about it, when everyone's talking about the latest thing the president said again, I'll try to talk to Eric.

He's under attack. *We're* under attack. But it's okay. *It's all going to be okay.* We just have to bunker down, wait out the siege. We'll outlast them. What we had, what we *have*, is stronger than them. Stronger than Shush.

I just have to wait. Keep my head down, act normal, go to work and my classes and it'll be fine. Sure, everyone will be talking about it. But I don't have to. I can talk about other things. I can think about other things.

Like how it felt when Eric gave me his name.

Call me Eric.

And how it will feel when he gives it back to me.

Call me Eric.

Like I can breathe again.

THIRTEEN

I decide to avoid it as much as I can. The Lie. I don't talk to a lot of people anyway, so it shouldn't be very difficult. Just put in some headphones to avoid catching any hint of it from other people's conversations and I'll be fine. I figure I'll manage at least part of Tuesday without having to slog through it all again.

But I'm wrong. Right from the start, I'm thrown back into it. A text from Shush wakes me before my alarm.

You ok? Skipping class again?

I stare at my phone, not quite believing I'm actually reading those words from her.

I know she'd have noticed I missed Bio yesterday but the fact that she's checking on me pisses me off. I'm still dealing with all the ways she's ripped my life apart, and now she's trying to dig her claws into my business *again*.

It's almost casual. As if she expects me to text her back. As if she has a right to check in on me. Well she can just forget it. No way I'm going to text her. If she wants me to start speaking to her again, trying to ruin Eric's life—and mine—isn't going to do it.

I put my phone facedown on the bed and close my eyes.

Skipping class again?
Maybe.

I'll go to class with Eric this afternoon but do I really need to go to Calc this morning? Ella will be there. All happy and bubbly and wanting me to help her flirt with Jake. I'll have to make conversation. I'll have to pretend I can breathe like everybody else.

Just thinking about it makes me pull the covers up over my head. Class with Eric is going to be hard enough. Being so close to him without being able to offer him my support is going to be torture. Eric—

No.

Dr. Callahan.

He's Dr. Callahan now.

My bed feels like quicksand, slowly pulling me under until I can't breathe.

I don't make any effort to get up.

I don't care. I really just don't care. Caring requires energy. I want to go back to sleep.

My phone buzzes again.

What now? I don't want to look at it. It's going to be Shush, raking her claws through my life again, trying to sink them into me. But still some sad, desperate bit of hope flares in my chest. It could be Eric. I have to check.

I'm wrong on both counts. My mom is checking on me. Again.

Morning sweetheart.
Just wanted to see how you're doing.

Anger eclipses hope.

Had Shush texted her? Told her I missed class? Told her I needed someone to check in on me? Make sure I'm okay?

Why won't everyone leave me alone and let me handle my own life?

Then, of course, comes a crushing sense of guilt.

She's my mom. She loves me. She wants what's best for me and—unlike Shush—she does have some kind of right to check in on me since she gave birth to me and raised me and was always a good mom.

Just wanted to see how you're doing.

I can't skip class again. I especially can't skip Calc. I can't fail. I can't do that to my parents. They're worried enough already. I have to convince them everything is fine. Failing Calc isn't going to help me make my case.

I type a quick, placating reply to my mom.

> **Just getting ready for class.**
> **Everything's going great! Love you.**

I check the time and sigh. If I want to get to class, I have to get up now.

Get up. You can do it. Covers off. Feet on floor. Stand up. One thing at a time.

Get up.

I want to pray. I need it to help me get through today. But it's taken me too long to get out of bed; I don't have time. I'd be late to class.

You can do this, I tell myself as I strip off the clothes I was sleeping in and put on a pair of jeans and a sweater I find on the floor. You can do this. You just have to be patient. Hold your resolve. Stay strong. Do it for Eric. If he can survive this, you can too.

And after it all dies down maybe we can try to be together again. I'll try harder this time to keep things secret. I won't let Shush pull down our castle. We aren't friends anymore, eventually she'll stop trying to run my life. Eventually she'll leave me and Eric alone. And then we can be happy.

But—I zip up my coat and take a deep breath, staring at the door—for now he has to be Dr. Callahan.

I put in my headphones before I make it downstairs to the lobby of my building. They usually help me tune out the world. I keep my head down and my music up loud and I manage to make it all the way to Calc without hearing The Lie.

That's as far as I get.

Ella's already sitting down, the paper spread out on the table in front of her. How will I get out of this? Can I keep my headphones in? Plead a migraine? A bad day? Something. Anything to make her not talk to me about that paper.

My professor sexually assaulted me.

I walk as slowly as I can—without looking like an idiot—over to the table. Ella looks up, smiling in greeting, and then her smile widens, her gaze going behind me. I turn and see Jake walking through the door.

Maybe I'm saved. Maybe she'll talk to Jake and forget about The Lie.

And maybe she won't.

As soon as I pull my headphones out of my ears, she starts in on it.

"Did you hear?" There's a hint of glee in her tone, her gaze moving back and forth between Jake and me.

I feel sick.

Jake shakes his head. At least The Lie hasn't gotten to everyone.

"This." She picks up the newspaper off the table and passes it to Jake, who takes it and starts reading.

I'm watching The Lie infect someone new in real time. I

want to sink into my chair and pass through it into another dimension of space, a fairytale world where it's just me and Eric and no one else can come and judge us.

Jake's expression gradually forms into a frown as he reads the story. "That's terrible," he says finally, handing the paper back to Ella.

"I know, who would've thought that could happen here?"

Jake raises his eyebrows and gives a slight roll of his eyes in a well-the-world-is-pretty-awful kind of expression. "That kind of thing happens everywhere. All the time."

"I know, I know," Ella rushes to say. "I just... but can you imagine one of *our* professors doing that?"

I shake my head but say nothing, pretending to be interested in something on my phone. I don't want to participate in this conversation. I want to sit here and pretend it isn't happening. I want to pretend it isn't happening even more than I want to jump to Eric's defense, to say that no, of course not, the whole thing is probably made up.

"No," Jake says. "I can't."

I like him more and more every day.

"Who do you think it's about?" Ella asks. She's just a bit *too* into the gossip. I know she's using it as an excuse to start a conversation with Jake, but still. There's too much excitement in her tone.

Jake shrugs. "I don't know."

Don't say anything, I tell myself. Stop paying attention.

"Maybe if we figure out who wrote it? Do you think it's someone who works for the paper or like a randomer? It doesn't really say."

"They obviously wanted to remain anonymous," Jake says.

I'm not here.

I'm walking down a beach with Eric, my hand held securely in his. I can feel the sunshine on my skin and the strength of his fingers wrapped around mine.

Or is it that I'm gripping my phone so tightly the edges of my case are making indentations in my flesh?

Ella leans forward eagerly. "Yeah, why do you think they didn't put their name down?"

You can't avoid me forever.

"Well, then everyone would ask them about it," Jake says. "It's a pretty private thing to have total strangers coming up to you about."

Unable to help myself, I look up from my phone. "Or they don't want to have to prove it."

"What?" Ella frowns.

Shit.

I shouldn't have said anything. Shit. But I can't stop now. Everyone's taking Shush's stupid anti-fairytale Lie as the truth. No one's questioning it.

"Think about it," I say. "If she—"

"Or he," says Jake. "It could be a guy."

"If she or he or they put their name down, then the administration would want them to actually name the professor. They'd want some kind of proof. If they don't put their name down, they don't have to face any hard questions."

"You don't believe it?" Jake asks.

I hesitate, unsure how to proceed here.

What should I say?

Of course I don't believe it. But that's only because I know who wrote it and who they were talking about and why they wrote it. I can't tell Jake and Ella any of that.

So I just shrug.

Ella picks up from there. "That's interesting. What if it's a lie?"

Jake shakes his head. "Yeah. People don't really lie about that."

"No one?" I ask.

"Fine, a small percentage."

"A small percentage lie about that *to the police*," I say. I know the statistics he's talking about. The percentage is in single digits. I couldn't be friends with Shush for a year and a half without picking up some of this. "But they aren't reporting this to the police are they?"

Jake has a stubborn expression on his face. "Maybe they did."

"Then why tell the story this way?" asks Ella.

"You guys are treating this like it's some big mystery you have to solve," Jake says.

"Isn't it?" Ella leans forward. "I mean, don't you want to know who the professor is?"

I shake my head. "You can't go around thinking all your professors are rapists."

Jake takes a breath and starts to push back. "But what if—"

And then Dr. Howards walks in, rushing up to the front of the room.

"Sorry I'm late everyone," she says. "We'll jump right in. Open your books to Chapter Six."

I'm grateful for the reason to stop the conversation. I was pushing too hard. I could see it on Jake's face and even a little on Ella's. They were starting to get suspicious. But I couldn't just let them talk about Eric like that, even if they didn't know it was him they were talking about.

Class goes smoothly after that. There isn't a chance to continue the conversation and Ella's meeting another friend after class, which means I don't have to deal with her following me to my shift at the library.

It isn't too difficult to avoid The Lie at work. At first I think I'll be safe at the circulation desk, especially since Tom doesn't seem to want to talk about it. But so many people walking past are talking about it that I retreat to the safety of shelf-reading. I take my headphones and lose myself in simple counting.

I need to prepare myself. Because soon I have class with Eric.

No. That's not right.

I have class with Dr. Callahan.

TRIGGER WARNING

The following section contains graphic depictions of self-harm. If you are not in a place where you feel up to reading that, please skip to the next section.

Remember, you're not alone. Mental health resources can be found at the back of this book. Take care of yourself.

FOURTEEN

This is how you write a note you will always remember:

First, you need to know that where you write the note is crucial.

People write notes in a variety of places. Planners, sticky notes, apps on their phone. An addition to the grocery list or a phone number for work. They use a pen or a marker, write it down on the palm of their hand.

None of these are right. This is not that kind of note.

This isn't a casual reminder, something that can be forgotten without consequence. This is important.

This is how you write a note you will always remember:

Go to your bathroom and lock the door. This is a note to be written in a place of worship, within the walls of a place familiar with this type of language. Take off your clothes and get in the shower. This is how you open the book. You must write your note at the start of your shower, you will need time to let it set before getting out.

Prepare yourself. This is not a reminder to pay your bills or pick up your child from soccer practice. This is not that kind of note.

Take up your pink-handled razor, with its three silver blades, meant for making your skin clean to the eye and smooth to the touch. Choose the skin on your hip, for this is where notes will make the best impression, where your hip bone protrudes the farthest. This is the closest you will get to putting your note on your bones.

Write your words in a manner not quite precision but not quite desperation. Notes are not as precise as a prayer but they are still deliberate.

This is how you write a note you will always remember:

Hold the handle of the razor firmly in your grip, press the head of it, the blades, to your skin atop the bone. Press down. Hard. You will need to crush the skin against the bone, create enough pressure that the blades, designed to merely glide over your skin, will dip into the cache of red ink below.

Don't be alarmed when your teeth clench against the biting intrusion of the blades, when your breath catches as you break into your own body.

This is how you write a note you will always remember:

Sacrifice.

Pain.

After you have made a cut, lift the pen from your skin.

And then there will be the sweet, beautiful red.

Admire it as it glides down the skin of your leg. Don't wash away the excess ink until you have completed the note. You may need to write your note more than once. Don't worry. You will know how long each particular note needs to be, how often it needs to be repeated to sink in.

When you are finished, turn into the water, and let the stinging spray wash you clean. Wash your hair, then your body. Get out of the shower, and if the note has stopped weeping excess ink, continue getting dressed. You may have to hold pressure with a towel, or folded toilet paper, to stop more red words from coming out.

If you look in the mirror and feel guilt that you need

a note like this, don't worry. Each letter, each word, will appear angry at having been created. At having been etched into the surface rather than allowed to roam with freedom through your blood. Notes don't always want to be written, but they often must be. Writing them is necessary. Otherwise you would not have done it.

When the note doesn't make sense immediately, don't worry, there will be many readings. You will read the words after your shower is over, in your room while you are getting dressed. You will read them in the mirror, bright on your pale skin. You will read them with your fingertips, instinctively seeking out the opening in your skin.

When you can't quite make out the words you had intended to write, don't worry. When they scar over you'll be able to read them more easily.

Over the next several days, when you walk or shift your position, there will be a stinging pain at your hip, caused by the waistband of your pants. This is why you must put the message there, at the hinge of things, so there will be no chance of forgetting.

You will read them again the next morning when you wake and roll over, wincing at the pain, the reminder you were hoping for. The message will be rewritten for days afterward, reopened by your every movement.

And when it fades, when it seals itself, the red ink retreating back below the surface, you'll still have the reminder. It will be less apparent, not quite so easy to feel, but still there. You can always carve the words again if needed.

Sacrifice.

Pain.

This is how you write a note you will always remember.

FIFTEEN

I manage to make it into the classroom without overhearing any conversations. Headphones are marvelous things. I don't even have to worry about where to sit anymore because everyone has claimed seats for the semester now. I just sit where I did before, greeting the familiar graffiti on my table like a favorite book.

FUCK

It's welcoming. A sharp-edged stone I can clutch in my palm.

When other students start to trickle in, I resolutely look at my phone, thumbing through Facebook with music blaring in my ears. When the voices start to get too loud, I turn up the volume.

I won't do this here, sit here and listen to others believe the Lie. Not now while I wait for him.

He'll be here soon.

It's all going to be okay.

When he finally walks in, I look up, taking out my headphones, hoping for some type of reassurance. The ghost of a smile, a hint of affection in his gaze. Something to keep me going. I need to know he isn't mad at me. I need to tell him I know what to do. Stay away from him until the storm passes. I need to tell him I'm waiting for him, waiting with him. I need to tell him we're in this together. But before I can do that I need to know he isn't mad at me.

But there's nothing.

He almost looks as if this were any other day. The only sign there's anything wrong is a tightening in the left corner of his mouth, so his smile doesn't quite reach its usual height when he greets the class.

"How're we all doing today?"

Even his tone sounds normal. No one would know that under the surface there's a storm waiting to rip him apart. No one would know he's facing down the dragon with Shush's face.

For the first time, watching him, catching small hints he's struggling, I wonder if I should tell him. What would happen if I told him I knew who wrote The Lie? If I told him it was Shush, would that fix this? Would he be able to get her thrown off the paper? Maybe even print a retraction?

I hope for just a moment, and then admit to myself that probably isn't what would happen.

And as I watch Eric start class, willing him to look at me, to see I'm still here for him, I realize there's another problem with that plan. It might not solve anything and it might make matters even worse. If I tell Eric Shush wrote the story, he's going to want to know why, and I'm going to have to tell him. I'll have to tell him she's trying to burn down our castle because she doesn't think we should be living in it together.

And then he'll blame me.

He'll think I told her about us even though I didn't. Not really. He'll be angry about the things I did tell her. He'll blame me for being careless and letting her find out I was attracted to him at all.

And he'll be right.

It *is* my fault. I didn't tell her about us. I did everything in my power to keep her from thinking we were together, but she still found out. I wasn't careful enough.

She was *my* friend.

I ruined this.

I ruined our fairy tale.

It's all my fault.

I want to go up and tell him I'm sorry. I want to throw myself at his feet and beg forgiveness. I want to ask him how I can fix this. He starts the lecture and I want to stand to my feet and scream it out.

What do I do now?

I'll do whatever he says, whatever he wants. I just need him to tell me what I should do next.

I shift forward in my seat, and a slight stinging pain at my hip brings me back to myself. My note, reminding me to keep it together.

There isn't anything to be done. If there was, Eric would have done it. If he needed me right now, he would have asked, he would have told me. If there was any solution other than what he was currently doing, he would have thought of it, of course he would have.

I have to stick with it, stick with him. I have to wait.

I try to focus on what he's saying. I used to be so enraptured by his lectures, trying to soak up every word he said, pick up as much of his knowledge and pieces of him as I could. But today I can't. Every word he says makes me want to go to him. Every time he scans the classroom and doesn't meet my gaze the way he used to, I want to run into his arms, force him to acknowledge my existence, force him to acknowledge our story.

I try to distract myself. I try to take notes, write down

what he says. But I can't focus.

Kara you have to tell someone.

Zoey and Emilio are sitting in front of me, writing notes back and forth to each other, and I know what they're talking about.

You can't avoid me forever.

They have it right there between them. The newspaper. The Lie.

I was sexually assaulted by my professor.

I'm so angry at Shush I can hardly breathe, much less think straight.

I dig my nail into the tabletop.

FUCK

I want to run. I want to scream. I have to do *something*.

I could raise my hand. Ask a question. Something about the lecture.

Anything so he'll look at me.

I shift in my seat and feel the ache at my hip from the note I wrote before class. I know that soon the message will be scarred over.

Patience, it says. *Wait.*

A reminder not to speak to Eric. A reminder to act as though nothing ever happened between us. A reminder that I won't have a chance at getting him back if I don't wait until Shush's sensational fabrication blows over.

Eric—Dr. Callahan—smiles, laughing at something Zoey said, and I deliberately cross one leg over the other, again causing a slight stinging pain at my hip.

Wait.

I trace over the graffiti on my table top.

FUCK

Then Eric—
No.
No.
No.
Dr. Callahan. Dr. Callahan. Dr. Callahan.
I need to take the note out of my back pocket. Set it on fire.
Eric.
But I can't let it go now. It's all I have left.

FUCK

The most versatile word in the English language. A noun, a verb, an adjective, an adverb. An insult or a compliment. Agony or delight. How many students had sat here as I am, feeling this word, tracing it, making it deeper? How many different meanings did it have to them?

Anger, frustration, sadness, pain.

FUCK

Did it have movement for the first person to begin the carving? A river that swept them away in its current. Or had it been solid? A rock to hold them in place.

I glance up at Dr. Callahan, the taste of his title bitter on my tongue, and wonder which I want it to be for me.

SIXTEEN

Come on brain, focus.

I stare at the Calc test, trying to force numbers into equations that make sense. Next to me, Ella's writing so fast I'm surprised the paper isn't on fire. But I'm stuck on the first problem.

I read it. Then I read it again.

And still I can't make my brain put pencil to paper.

All I can think about is Shush.

It's been a couple weeks since she told The Lie and for the most part I've been successfully keeping my head above water. I'm not sure if things have actually gotten better or if I've just gotten used to the exhaustion that comes with constantly treading water. But I've been going to all my classes, doing all my homework, eating regular meals, going to work, even spending time with Ella. I'm handling everything.

I'm fine.

Be patient, I keep telling myself. Keep it together. Just wait. Wait until it all blows over.

It's all going to be okay.

Nearly every morning I wake up to a new text message from someone other than Eric, the one person I actually *want* to text me. My phone vibrates and I pick it up, hoping to see his name on the screen. But it's never him. It's Ella. Or my mom. Or Shush.

And I'm handling it.

When Ella confides in me that she's worried Jake isn't interested in her, I listen. They've been spending more time together, sometimes even without me there, but he still hasn't given her any sort of indication he's interested in her as anything but a friend.

I have plenty of worries rolling around in my head, I don't need any from Ella to join them. But she's my friend. And she's stressed about it. I know how to be a supportive friend. I'm handling it. I texted her one night:

Why don't you just ask him on a date?

The problem, Ella explained to me in half a dozen text messages, is that if she asks Jake out and he isn't interested in her that way right now, then it would end their friendship and he'll never have a chance to see her in a romantic light. What she really needs to do is get him to see her as more than a friend, as girlfriend material, as a possible princess to his prince. The trick is how to do that. A pretty outfit, a situation where he needs to save her somehow, something. The plan is still a work in progress, but I'm being her friend, figuring it out with her.

I'm handling text messages from my mom too. I know how to play the happy daughter. It's easy to lie via text. *I'm fine Mom* over and over again. *I love you,* which is true, but in most of these cases it's just a digital long-distance reassurance I won't do anything to make her worry.

Phone calls are harder. It's difficult some days to make my voice sound real, to force words that don't ring hollow.

I tell her stories about Ella and Jake, trying to make her

laugh, trying to show her I have friends. Whenever she asks about Shush, I say we're doing fine. I make up stories about us working on homework, attending basketball games, going to the movies. White lies, I tell myself. Not a big deal. It's all to comfort her. And it works. I'm handling it.

Shush's text messages are the worst ones. She's stopped texting me a million times a day and settled for once or twice, just a little reminder about the knife she stabbed in my back. Just a little wiggling it around to remind me of all the pain I'm in. To remind me she's the reason I'm feeling it. Her texts vary slightly, but they basically stick to the same theme.

Please talk to me

I'm sorry.

Talk to you in class?

You can't ignore me forever.

I read the text messages, and for some reason I can't fathom, I don't delete them. Just let them build up as a string of unanswered blocks forming a wall on one side of my phone screen. A wall she won't ever get through.

Everything else seems like it's evened out. I'm exhausted, but it's an even level of exhaustion. I can handle it. I can deal with Ella. I can deal with my mom. The only thing that hasn't died down is how angry I am at Shush.

It's all her fault.

She's the reason I have to tell myself not to be angry with Ella for chasing down her prince when I can't chase down mine. She's the reason I'm walking on eggshells with my parents. She's the reason Eric and I aren't together. She's the

135

reason I have to go around reminding myself all the time to think of him as Dr. Callahan and not Eric so I won't go up to him in random places like the café and the library and try to strike up a conversation the way I used to.

I thought the more time went on, the easier it would get to be around him and not be *with* him. But it's getting worse, it's getting harder. The longer I go without him looking at me, the more I feel like I'm disappearing.

I grip my pencil a bit harder, moving forward in my chair and bending my head down towards my Calc test.

I write something down for the first problem. It's probably right. Maybe.

But when I try to move on to the second, I hear Shush.

I know there are women at this school…

Get out.

Get out get out *get out of my head.*

This past weekend was our college Women's March. Back when Shush and I were friends, I helped her start organizing the whole thing, and I knew she was still one of the people in charge of it. Which meant there was no way I wanted to be there.

I've managed to avoid another in-person confrontation with her so far. She's tried to ambush me a few times, but I'm not going with her old-fashioned face-to-face fighting style.

No.

When a dragon calls you out and says *Face me, you coward,* you don't fall for it. Ignore the insult, it doesn't matter. Hide. Because your only weapon when fighting a dragon like Shush is to survive for as long as possible. To wait until they lose interest.

So I've started going in and out of my dorm room as little as possible, spending entire days with Ella in her building or not leaving my dorm room at all, anything to avoid Shush. Several times I've spotted her walking into the library and left my post at the desk, going back to the staff-only break room under the pretense of getting another cup of coffee. I've varied my class arrival times, sometimes arriving really early and sometimes late, so she can't get me on my own in class. A few times she's managed to catch me in Biology. Come up to me when I was sitting in class. But I kept my headphones in and ignored her.

I wondered if she could feel the anger radiating off me. If she could feel she shouldn't push me any farther.

I've been doing so well avoiding her and going—on purpose—to a place I knew she was going to be went against all my self-protection instincts. But when Ella asked me if I wanted to go to the Women's March, I couldn't think of an excuse to get out of it. She's already starting to suspect something's up with me.

"You've been awful quiet lately. Even more than usual," she said to me at lunch the day before.

I don't need *another* person worried about me.

Except, of course, Eric. I wish *he* would ask me how I'm doing.

But I'm fine. I'm fine.

I *would be* fine if everyone would just stop asking me how I am.

So I had to go. And at first I thought it would be fine. It started out okay. All the typical protest things. Ella carried a sign, chanted, the whole bit. I walked with her, carrying a sign she made for me, but I couldn't summon the energy for chanting. I told Ella I had a sore throat.

We marched in the middle of the crowd and I kept my head on a swivel, looking for Shush. In the end, I didn't see her until the actual march was over, until it ended at the steps of the administration building where speeches were set to take place.

And there was Shush, up on a platform, in all her fiery glory. "Hey all you *nasty* women!" she shouted into the mic, and a cheer went up around me. I stared at her, a cold knot of fury tightening in my chest. A couple months ago, I would have been cheering along with everyone else, but now I just wanted everyone to stop celebrating her.

Everyone thinks she's so amazing. No one else sees what a terrible dragon she really is, how she ruins lives and claims it's all in the name of doing "the right thing."

"It's great to hear your *voices*! That's why we're all here. To speak out. To speak up. To let our voices be heard. Because I know there are women at this school who've been silent. Who are still silent."

I tensed up. I was expecting her to talk about the election, the new president. I wasn't expecting her to talk about The Lie. I wasn't prepared. Treading water suddenly got a whole lot more difficult. I wanted to leave. But Ella was next to me, just as wrapped up in Shush's speech as everyone else.

"I know there are women at this school who've been assaulted by people in positions of power. I know there are women at this school who've felt helpless to speak out. I know there are some of you here, right now, in this crowd."

She searched the audience and I moved behind my sign. I knew she was talking about me. But she was wrong. I'm not one of those women. She's got our story all wrong.

"*This* is why we're here. For all the people who need to tell someone their story but feel like they can't. To let them know they're not alone. To speak for them. To tell their stories. To be a voice for the voiceless."

She let this sink in for a minute, let a hush settle over the crowd. And then she raised a fist in the air.

"So get loud!" she shouted, and again a cheer went up.

I wanted to scream at her.

I wanted to rip the microphone out of her hand, shove her down off the steps.

I wanted to run away, get the hell out of there, but I couldn't. Because if I did, Ella would want to know what was wrong. And I couldn't tell her anything. So I had to stand there and listen to Shush, stand there and listen to everyone else cheer her on. As if she was a knight in shining armor come to rescue us all. Instead of the dragon constantly trying to eat me alive.

It pulled my head right under the surface.

I skipped Biology yesterday. No way I could handle being in the same room with her. I'd gone to Creative Writing but for all I paid attention I might as well have skipped that too.

Somehow, until now, I've been managing to handle all my schoolwork pretty well. I always get good grades in Eric's classes because I pay attention to the lectures and understand the material. In Biology I can hold on with my ability to read quickly and retain information. In Creative Writing I get by as long as I write something for each class and make at least one comment on what everyone else reads. And Ella's been holding my head above water in Calc.

I studied with her and Jake last night. This test isn't even supposed to be that difficult. It's just covering what we've done so far, all stuff I should be able to do, all stuff I've done with Ella on the homework—all stuff I'd done last year even.

But I'm just sitting here, staring at the numbers on the page as Ella writes down answers so fast she's probably nearly done with the test. I can't remember a single thing we reviewed last night during our study session. It's like the numbers are melting on the page. All I can see are letters.

Once upon a time…
We can't do this anymore.
Kara you have to tell someone.

139

It's all going to be okay.
So get loud!
You're magic.
I'm lost.

Focus. Focus. If I fail this test, I won't get a good enough grade to keep my GPA up. I'll lose my scholarship and I'll have to leave and I won't be able to see Eric anymore. And on top of that my parents will both be panicked that I failed out of college. Plus the actual fact that I will have *failed out of college.*

I have to pass it. My mom and dad's disappointed faces swim through my head, clouding the numbers on the page.

And then Shush.

And then Eric.

Do you know the fairy tale behind the invention of the kiss?

Focus.

You can't avoid me forever.

Focus.

You're safe with me.

Focus.

Kara he's not what you think.

Focus.

Can you tell me what I say?

Dammit. Focus. Focus focus focus.

I press my hand against my thigh, where I made my prayers this morning.

Focus.

Pain blossoms sharply where the cuts are still fresh, pulling me back to the present. Come on Kara, focus. I press harder, not letting up until Eric and Shush are forced to the back of my mind, until the numbers on the page form themselves into problems I recognize, problems I can solve.

I start writing.

I think I do fine. Not great maybe, but not terrible.

Which is why, on Friday, when Dr. Howards hands the tests back, I don't expect to see the large, red letter F on the top of mine.

But there it is anyway.

It looks like Dr. Howards took a katana to a living thing, slicing it to absolute ribbons. There isn't a single problem that doesn't have some sort of correction on it.

"Jesus, your test is bleeding," Jake says, looking over my shoulder. I stare at my grade, forcing myself to keep a normal expression on my face.

I don't fail tests. I'm not the type of person who fails tests.

Except now I am. Plus, I remind myself, I did fail this entire class last semester.

Ella looks over at my test and winces. I glance at hers. Not a single red mark.

"If Ella didn't have a score on top of hers I'd say Dr. Howards skipped grading it," I say, if only to get the focus off my own test.

Ella blushes. "How'd you do, Jake?"

"Solid B minus. Not too bad."

Ella turns to me with a sympathetic expression and I suppress the urge to either cover my face with my hands or run away. I can't handle her being sorry for me right now. If she feels sorry for me then there's something to feel sorry for. Which turns this into a big deal, something I won't be able to handle.

"Don't worry Kara," she says. "I'll work with you on it."

I don't tell her I failed this class before, that I'm probably just not cut out for math and should give up and drop out of the class and the whole entire school while I'm at it. Why keep pretending I can do this when I so obviously can't?

I take a breath.

Come on Kara, keep it together. It's just a failed test.

"I have to get to work," I tell her. I get up, throwing my things in my bag and getting out of there without giving her a chance to follow.

Thankfully, she doesn't try.

SEVENTEEN

I spend work putting books back on shelves and shelf-reading, anything to keep me from sitting at my desk sinking into despair. Tom obviously senses something is wrong. I can tell from the looks he gives me out of the corner of his eye, but he doesn't say anything, just lets me disappear into the upper floors of books without comment.

Surely my day will get better, I tell myself after work, heading to class with Eric. At least I'll get to see Eric. Maybe I can come up with a good class-related question to ask him at the end of class, give us a chance to talk. Maybe it won't be talking to him *alone* but at least it will be talking to him. He hasn't said more than a sentence directly to me in weeks now, and that sentence was: "Kara can you please pass out these papers?"

He hasn't even written me any messages on my assignments.

Every class period we have some type of assignment to hand in, a few short answer questions about the required reading or a longer response to a discussion question. When we were together—even at the beginning when our relationship wasn't romantic—he always left me little notes on my assignments. At first they were in the margins, questions or comments on what I'd written. Nothing that he wouldn't write on any other student's paper. Later, he'd written them on sticky notes attached to the front, and they'd gradually become more and more personal, going from *Really excellent thinking here Kara* to *You look really pretty today* to *Library, 7pm.*

Now he doesn't even write his professor comments. The only thing he writes on any of my papers is a score. Ten out of ten. Always.

I've been working hard to write really thoughtful responses to the questions because I want to impress him. I want to remind him he enjoyed talking with me about stories, about the things we both loved. But since the Women's March I haven't been able to pull my thoughts together for long enough to form a coherent paragraph, much less a whole page. The response to a discussion question I handed in on Tuesday wasn't even a whole page, meaning he should have automatically deducted points.

But there, at the top near my name, is the score. Ten out of ten.

Instead of this filling me with relief—at least I'm doing well in this class, even if I'm failing Calc—it fills me with worry.

I look down at the paper in my hand and wonder, for the first time, if he's giving me special treatment. Never, in all the time we spent together, have I thought he was treating me differently than any other student as far as my school work went. Sure, I get good grades in his classes, but I thought that was because I work hard and I actually enjoy the subjects he teaches. Books, stories. These are things I love. It only makes sense I would be good at studying them.

Now, staring down at the circled ten out of ten mark he made at the top of the page—which is only a third of the way full of writing—I start to question that.

You're magic.

144

Have his feelings for me been affecting the way he grades my work? Am I not really as good at this as I think I am?

Is this why he broke up with me? Because he realized I'm not really that smart, I'm not really that perceptive, I'm not really *that* anything.

I'm not anything he thought I was.

Had his judgment been clouded by his feelings? Maybe he'd finally seen the truth after we spent three weeks apart during the holidays. It was the longest amount of time we'd been apart since we started dating. Maybe he'd gone to grade my final paper and realized I'm actually so much dumber than he thought.

Maybe he finally finished translating the book of me and realized I'm not what he thought. I'm not beautiful or interesting or magic. I'm not a princess. I don't belong in a fairy tale. I'm not a book he wants to keep reading. I'm hollow, plain, a tale told so many times it's lost its sting. I'm just a sad story.

And now? Now that he's realized it? He's taking pity on me.

I glance up from my paper and try to see it in his eyes.

Pity.

Sickly sweet so it sticks in my throat, gagging me.

Maybe he's seen the dark circles under my eyes the way I've noticed the ones under his. You wouldn't see the signs of the stress these last few weeks have caused him, not unless you were looking.

I've noticed.

His handsome face is marred by signs of the struggle. Dark depressions have grown under his eyes, his cheekbones seem more pronounced, the warm parchment tone of his skin has paled. The signs of gray in his thick black hair seem more obvious, less like wisdom and more like old age.

I set my paper on the table in front of me, beside the word FULK carved into its surface, and fold my hands in my lap to keep myself from ripping it in two.

Does he pity me now? Now that he's left me alone? Now that he's discovered I'm not magic? Maybe I should have tried harder to warn him. I look up at him, lecturing at the front of the room, and remember the way his eyes had shone with understanding the first night he discovered my scars.

Tell me.

I remember the feel of his arms around me, holding me up. The feel of his lips pressed to my hair, reassuring me he didn't think I was broken and worthless now that he knew the worst of me.

I'm here.

Except now he's not.

It's over.

Suddenly I have to bite my lip to keep the tears gathering in my eyes from falling down my cheeks.

Don't cry. Not here in class like a stupid, soft little girl who can't handle her own emotions. That isn't the way to get Eric back.

I am not a person who cries in public. I just don't. I've got a better handle on my emotions than that.

I dig my fingernails into my palms, glancing up at the clock at the front of the room. Class is nearly over. Just a few more minutes and then I can get out of here, then I can get to my room, get to my church.

When Eric dismisses class, I give up on going up to him, trying to ask him a question. He'll see it on my face. The tears I'm barely holding back. And the understanding in his expression will rip me apart.

Can you tell me what I say?

I leave as quickly as I can.

The tears start falling down my cheeks as soon as I get outside. I pull the hood of my coat up, using that and my hair as a shield, keeping my head angled down so no one will be able to tell I'm crying as I hurry across campus. I have to get back to my dorm room.

Inside, I shed my clothes and turn on the hot water, feeling myself starting to calm down. But it isn't until the thin razor blade slices into my skin, releasing the pressure my tears were trying to but couldn't, that I feel like I can breathe again. Three more prayers, three little red lines in the company of the ones I made this morning and the ones I made two days earlier, and then I'm no longer crying.

Calmly, I stand in the hot water, letting it wash my cuts clean, wash out as much blood as it can. There's too much of it, too full of words. It just needs to be released sometimes.

So I can get a handle on everything. So I can get some control.

Maybe Eric's right, I think as I get out and dry myself off. Maybe I'm not the girl he thought I was. Maybe he was wrong before. Maybe I'm not magic. Maybe I'm just… something else.

I thought at least I was smart. I'm not the prettiest girl around and I'm not the most outgoing, but I thought I at least had some kind of something going on in my head. But if I'm failing math tests and Eric thinks he has to take pity on me in order for me to pass his class, then I'm obviously not a good student. I'm… what? A failure? Stupid? Too unintelligent to even pass my classes, much less keep Eric around?

I'm still, casually, circling around this drain as I go to dinner with Ella and Jake. I don't want to go but I know I have to act normal, have to act like my math test isn't a weight wrapped around my neck with all the others, adding to everything trying to pull me under.

I'm not losing it. I'm not. I'm just… searching.

Can you tell me what I say?

If I'm not the person Eric thought I was, and I'm not even the person I thought I was, then who am I?

What do I do now?

Jake and Ella studiously avoid bringing up the math test, talking about anything and everything else instead. But I don't care.

I'm not really here.

It's like I'm watching myself sitting at this table with them, watching myself cut up a chicken breast smothered in pasta sauce, stab a piece with my fork and bring it to my mouth. Watching myself respond as Jake asks if I've watched anything good on Netflix lately. Watching myself laugh at Ella tell a story about something that happened in one of her classes.

I'm not sure what the show would be called. Kara Fakes Normal maybe. Or Kara Tries Being Human. Or Kara is Well-Adjusted and Definitely Not Falling Apart. I'd be okay with watching it rather than living it.

Watching what I say and the way I say it, watching my posture as I sit in my chair, watching the expressions I use. None of the expressions really connect with my face. They're all just masks. I've painted them well. Jake and Ella don't seem to notice they're not real.

I study myself. Like I'm a stranger. Like I've just met myself and I'm trying to pick up context clues to figure out who I am. Why does she sit that way? What's she thinking now? Why does she say that? Why does that make her laugh?

What do I do now?

Maybe the better question is *Who am I now?*

Everyone keeps giving me different clues to figure out the puzzle. Ella thinks I'm her friend. Eric used to think I was his lover and now… now I'm not sure what he thinks. And Shush? Her expression comes into view, pity in her dark eyes, and a hint of rage flashes through me. Shush thinks she knows me better than anyone. *Victim* her eyes say. She has no idea what she's talking about.

I force my mind back to the table, back to Kara Eats Food and Has Friends. I'm just in time for something interesting to happen.

"Hey my friend Greg's throwing this party tonight," Jake says. "You guys want to come?"

"Definitely," Ella says so quickly Jake's hardly finished his sentence. Then they look at me.

I watch myself carefully, trying to figure out how I feel about this.

Instead of the prospect of spending a night surrounded by drunk and horny college kids—and a possibly drunk and definitely horny Ella—making me search for any excuse to get out of it and then reluctantly being guilted into going by Ella's puppy freshman eyes, I feel a slight hint of excitement.

I make my expression into some version of what Ella's is, push my voice up a pitch as I say, "Sounds like fun."

If I'm not a good student, maybe I'm a party girl. It's a skin I've never tried on before, but who knows, maybe it will feel just right covering my bones. Maybe this will be the character that finally fits.

EIGHTEEN

"Oh my god what are you supposed to wear to a party?"

Ella rifles through her closet, shoving aside hangers one by one, a slight panic to her movements. I watch from my perch on her bed, wondering why she thinks I would know the answer to that.

"Umm... something cute."

She shoots me a glare. "Not helpful. Do I wear a dress? Something revealing? Or will that be really obvious? I mean it's only, like, twenty degrees out." She pulls out a black sleeveless dress that looks more suited to a formal occasion than a college party. "If I show too much skin will I seem sexy and confident or slutty and desperate?"

I am entirely the wrong person to be answering these questions. This is the kind of thing I would have asked Shush if we were still speaking. My wardrobe consists largely of plaid flannel, loose sweaters, and jeans with holes in them.

I take a swig from the water bottle Ella filled with vodka and Coke. She bought the vodka off her roommate, who I've never met because she basically lives with her girlfriend, and who—from what Ella had told me—would probably have been helpful in this situation. Unfortunately, she went home for the weekend. The Coke has a slight bite to it from the vodka, but it doesn't taste very strong.

"I don't want to get like really drunk," Ella had said as she mixed the drink when I first came over. "I just want to be... I don't know. Relaxed. You know? So I don't freak out. Besides this is what you do in college right?"

I dutifully agreed. "Definitely. You're supposed to pregame."

It isn't the alcohol—I don't think I've had that much—but I can feel myself starting to gain a little confidence. A little arrogance. A little devil-may-care-ence.

A party girl would feel that right? This version of Kara, the one who drinks vodka and goes to parties and doesn't care if she fails Calculus, this version of Kara might not know exactly what she's doing, but she doesn't care. None of it matters anyway, right?

She's a tragedy. Might as well have fun on the way down.

"Not that dress," I say. "It's not a funeral." I get up and go to Ella's closet, going through the hangers until I find something suitable. I throw the clothes at her. "This is perfect. Sexy but not desperate."

I keep going through the clothes until I find a top I can pair with my jeans and black boots. We get dressed, taking turns drinking from the vodka and coke, and I can tell the vodka is already starting to loosen Ella up. She's so excited she can hardly stand it.

"Tonight's the night!" she says as we do our makeup. I don't usually wear a lot of makeup, but tonight I rim my eyes with a thick black liner. It makes them stand out, bright and shining, a little bit with the alcohol and a little bit with my new-found attitude.

When we're done, I look in the mirror and see an entirely different girl staring back at me. Regular Kara dresses like a background character. Just enough makeup not to be pointed out as someone who doesn't wear makeup. Loose, casual tops. Jeans. Boots that make her look put together but aren't enough to make her stand out. See her in a crowd and your gaze slides right over her. It's part of the reason I was so surprised when Eric noticed me.

I wonder what he would think of my new look.

My jeans and boots he would recognize, but my top is definitely not my usual style. It's a black, long-sleeve v-neck, slightly translucent and cut low enough that I should probably wear a tank top under it. On Ella it would produce significant cleavage; on me, it just shows the hint of my bra at the edges.

But it's my face that looks the most different. A heavy amount of black eyeliner and eyeshadow makes my eyes pop from my pale face, surrounded by a mess of light blonde hair. I look older. I look sophisticated. Like I have mysterious meaningful tattoos and go to bars for poetry readings. I look like a book you'd want to read. I look like a book that might smack your hand away and refuse to let you.

I look like I don't care if Eric broke up with me or not. I look like the kind of person who could laugh and say, "Your loss."

I sure as hell don't look like someone who cares about a damn Calc test.

Ella comes up next to me in the mirror, her brown freshman eyes shimmering with alcohol and excitement. "Ready?"

She's wearing a blue button-up dress over leggings and a large black belt that hits her in just the right place. At my urging she's left the top few buttons undone, letting her cleavage out for a show Jake will definitely want to buy a ticket for.

I grin and even that seems different. It feels different on

my face. Like I'm a different person. I pick up the drink and down the rest of it, like I'm the girl from the movie who doesn't care at all.

"Ready."

~

"Oh my god it's freezing," Ella says. I glance over at her. She has her arms crossed tightly in front of her chest, and her lips are turning blue. She isn't wrong.

We decided not to wear our coats, a debate that had been ongoing the whole time we were getting ready. Do you wear a coat to a party? Is there a place to put it once you get there? Or do you have to carry it around with you? In the end, Ella looked up the address of the house, and when Google maps told us it was only a ten-minute walk away, we'd decided to forgo coats.

"It's not that bad," I say. "Just think about something else."

"Like what?" Ella asks.

I nudge her with my shoulder. "Like Jake."

For my part, I'm embracing the cold. I'm embracing it the same way I'm embracing this new skin I'm trying on tonight. Party Kara doesn't care about the cold. Party Kara has vodka flowing through her blood and a confidence to her walk that cuts through the frigid air. Party Kara isn't worried about failing out of college. Party Kara isn't heartbroken over Eric. Party Kara is single because she wants to be. Party Kara is going to have fun and nothing is going to stop her.

"Maybe he'll kiss me tonight?" Ella asks, and even the fragile hope in her voice isn't enough to pierce my I-don't-care shield. Party Kara doesn't feel a stab of pain every time Ella shows exactly how breakable she is.

"Maybe *you'll* kiss *him* tonight," I say.

I hear Shush saying it even as the words come out of my own mouth. She's always doing that, flipping the script around to push people to act outside the story we've been given all our lives. She'll tell girls they should ask boys out instead of waiting to be asked out themselves. Fighting the patriarchy. Or whatever the fuck she's doing.

No.

I'm not going to be angry tonight. I'm not going to let her ruin something else. I push thoughts of Shush away. Somehow it's easier now, with alcohol buzzing under my skin. Party Kara doesn't care about Shush. Shush can't hurt her, can't hurt me. Not now.

Because I don't care.

We step off a curb and my jeans rub up against the cuts on my thighs. Somehow that small blossoming pain only pushes me deeper into my new skin.

I don't care.

I don't care at all.

"What do you think the party will be like?" Ella asks, huddling closer to me as we walk, as if she can steal my warmth even though I have none to offer. I'm not warm. I'm numb. I am a shield of armor, and nothing can get to me, not even the cold.

"I don't know." I look both ways and then cross the street, leaving campus. "Did Jake say how many people were coming?"

Ella shakes her head.

I've been to exactly two parties in my life.

The first had been in high school. The guy I was dating at the time was a football player, and the captain of the team was throwing the party. The parties I'd seen on TV were always packed full of beautiful people, with loud music and red cups of alcohol everywhere. Everyone always seemed to be having the time of their life. The party I went to with him was a sad imitation.

Most of the football team was there, as were some of the other jocks, and all of the cheerleaders. The ratio of girls to guys was off though, and there weren't enough girls to keep the guys occupied. But they didn't seem to mind. They spent their time doing keg stands and getting so drunk they could hardly stand. The guy I was dating followed suit, and when he fell down the stairs trying to get me up into a bedroom, I left and walked home. Our relationship ended that night.

The second party I'd been to was with Shush. I hesitate to even call it a party. Shush did, but to me it felt more like a get together. Everyone there seemed to know each other and there were only about twenty people. There was drinking and some people smoking pot, but altogether it was a much more sober affair than the football fiasco.

I spent all of it glued to Shush's side, letting her introduce me to people and listening to the conversations she had with her other friends about the presidential primaries and the state of U.S. politics. There was music but it was at a low enough level that everyone could easily have a conversation without worrying about shouting.

Walking to this party with Ella, I start to picture some kind of hybrid of both of the parties I'd been to. With more people and more drinking than Shush's get together, and less sloppiness than the football party. But whatever images my head conjures up are wrong.

We hear the music before we reach the house, the characteristic bass *thump* pushing through the cold air to reach us. If we thought we were going to have trouble finding the place, we were dead wrong. It sounds like the whole college is here. There are groups of people outside, smoking and drinking and laughing. Some are wearing coats and some aren't. Some are finding different ways to keep warm.

Ella glances at me, her steps faltering as we near the people. If Shush were here, I would follow her, do what she did. But she isn't. And I don't want her to be.

I don't need her.

Party Kara doesn't need anyone.

"Come on," I say to Ella. "Let's go find Jake."

I push on, moving through and around people, taking the lead as if I know where I'm going. As if I know what I'm doing. I can do this. Nothing to it really. Party Kara belongs here. She leads Ella through the crowd outside and when people turn to look at her, it isn't because she looks like she shouldn't be here. It's because she looks like she should. Like she knows why she's here. Like she knows what she wants and exactly how to get it.

I can do this.

I lift my chin and push through the front door without knocking.

Inside, there are just more people. I'm instantly glad we didn't bring coats, because it's warm and clammy, a fine haze of beer and sweat in the air that instantly sticks to your skin. I keep my eyes peeled for Jake, knowing Ella is doing the same. We walk through the entrance hall and into the dining room where people are playing beer pong. Beyond that is the living room, where I can see people playing some kind of card game. Still no sign of Jake. Maybe he isn't here yet.

"Do you see Jake?" Ella asks. "Do you think he's here?"

I falter slightly. What would Party Kara do now? Without Jake here? I feel Unsure Kara lifting her head through the barrier of alcohol-induced-confidence. I look around for a familiar face and see only Ella, who looks as uncertain as I feel. I want a drink. Everyone else has one in their hand, and we look out of place without one. Is there communal alcohol at parties like this? Or should we have brought our own?

"I don't see him. Why don't we—"

"Hey!" The voice comes from behind us and I turn around to see Jake, holding a red plastic cup and grinning widely at us. "You made it!"

He has great timing. Also, he's drunk.

I can tell right away, from the too-wide grin and the happiness in his eyes. From the way he slings his arm around Ella's shoulders and gives her something between a squeeze and a hug. Ella, for her part, turns bright red and I'm surprised she doesn't faint from happiness at the physical contact.

He doesn't seem too sloppy though, as he leads us through a door into the kitchen. He's at least walking a straight line.

"Let's get some drinks in your hands ladies," he says brightly. There's a keg and a variety of beer scattered over the kitchen counter. Gallantly, Jake fills up two red plastic cups from the keg and hands them to us. We thank him and obediently knock our cups together as he offers up a toast. "To a great night."

The beer is warm and tastes sour. I prefer the bitter stinging bite of the vodka. But whatever. It's alcohol. Party Kara drinks it, finishing half the cup in a few large gulps.

Ella shoots me a panicked glance and I know she's trying to come up with something to say to Jake, something to keep him around, as he's already eying the room beyond us like he's looking for someone.

"Another toast," I say, holding up my glass. Jake grins at me, holding up his own cup and clearly on board for whatever this is. "To free booze."

"To free booze," Jake echoes agreeably. Ella follows suit and everyone drinks. I take another two large swallows of my beer.

"Your turn," I say to Ella, nudging her.

"What?"

"Toast to something."

She holds up her red cup and gives her bottom lip a nervous nibble. "Umm… to the best years of our lives?"

"Here here," shouts Jake a little too loudly, even with the state of the music. This time, I finish my beer.

"Damn Kara, thirsty?" Jake asks, laughing. I say nothing, just offer him a smile. Party Kara doesn't feel nervous. Party Kara doesn't care what he thinks, what Ella thinks—what Eric or Shush thinks—she doesn't care what anyone thinks.

Dutifully, Jake takes my cup and gets me another, filling his back up as well.

"Ella you're behind," I say, taking another sip of my fresh-but-really-still-stale-tasting beer.

"Oh god. I can't keep up with you two. I'd, like, die."

"Sounds like a plan to me," I say under my breath, taking another long drink. I should be drunker than I feel. I had more of the vodka than Ella. It's like my brain is fighting back against the alcohol, trying to surface even as I try to drown it. It's not going to win. Not tonight.

I want to stop thinking.

I don't want to think about what anyone else thinks. I don't even want to think about what I think. Not right now. Maybe not ever again.

"Jake!" The shout comes from behind us and I turn to see a guy smiling widely, making his way over to us.

"Guys this is Greg. It's his party," Jake says. "Greg, this is Ella and Kara."

Party Kara doesn't worry about whether or not it's

appropriate to shake hands in this situation or if that would make her look out of place. Party Kara holds out her hand and takes Greg's, hanging on just a second too long, enjoying the strength in his fingers.

"Nice party," I say, and am surprised to hear the tone of my voice. Filled with innuendo and flirtation.

"Thanks," says Greg. "Glad you guys could come." He looks around at us. "So what are we doing?"

"Toasting," says Jake jubilantly, holding his cup in the air.

Greg grins, and I like the slight crooked edge to it. I shift my weight, move a bit closer to him, and not just because I'm intellectually calculating that doing so will make it clear there are pairs here—Ella and Jake, and me and Greg—but because I want to.

"I've got something better for that," Greg says. "Follow me."

We go upstairs to Greg's bedroom, where he takes a bottle of whiskey out of the closet. "I keep the good stuff for my friends," he says.

Unscrewing the cap, he lifts the bottle into the air. "To tonight," he says. "Fuck the morning." He takes a healthy swallow before passing the bottle to Jake.

"Fuck assholes," Jake says. Greg laughs so hard at this while Jake is drinking that I think it must be a private joke.

Ella's next. She hesitates, as if she can't think of anything. Then her face hardens, and I know she's thinking of something or someone very specific. "Fuck high school."

Jake gives a hoot of agreement. "Fuck fucking high school, damn right."

When it's my turn, I look down at the bottle of whiskey like I might dive into it and drown. I think I want to.

Can you tell me what I say?
Kara you have to tell someone.
What do I do now?

"Fuck," I say, and the edges of the word cut at my cheeks, my tongue. It feels good. "Fuck *everything*." I turn the bottle upside down.

NINETEEN

After that, the boys teach us how to play beer pong, which neither of us have played before and which Ella is surprisingly good at.

"Woo, yeah, go Ella!" I cheer from my spot leaning against the wall as Ella sinks another shot against Jake and whoops in victory. She's already beaten me.

"What do you think Greg?" Ella says, hands on hips, grinning.

"Oh get the fuck outta my way Jake." Greg pushes off the wall where he was standing next to me and goes to the other side of the table. "I'm taking her down."

Jake throws his hands up in a gesture of defeat, laughing. Ella looks so happy she could burst.

"Hey you need a refill?" Jake asks me.

I look down at my red cup, still a third of the way full. "Yeah," I say, and down the rest of it.

Jake shakes his head, laughing.

"What?" I ask, following him as he heads back to the kitchen and the keg.

"Nothing just…" He turns to me as we wait behind a group of boys filling their cups, eying me shrewdly despite the booze shining in his gaze. "You're in some kind of mood tonight aren't you? Doesn't seem like you."

A flash of fear runs through me like ice water down my spine, shaking Party Kara loose. He sees the mask. He's going to ask me what's wrong and bring all the bad back into my night of fun. I force myself to shrug.

"I don't know what you're talking about."

He opens his mouth to respond but then a guy nearly tackles him from behind. "Jake! Holy shit man! Been a minute."

Jake starts talking to him and I use the excuse to get away, heading outside. I need some cold air. Need to breathe. Get the mask back in place.

Fine Kara. Party Kara. I Don't Care Kara.

The Kara who could shrug off Jake's comment instead of feeling like I'm about to shatter.

It's freezing out on the porch. Good. I lean against the house and take a deep breath, letting the cold air wake me up. I'm not crying. I'm not falling apart. I'm fine. I'm fine I'm fine I'm fine.

"Hey babe you alright?" The voice comes from my right, and a tall good-looking guy with brown hair steps closer to me, smiling. "It's cold out here."

"Yeah," I say, "it is."

"You uh, want something to warm you up?"

"What'd you have in mind?" I know that's the line to say here. The way to get him to smile wider, the way he's doing now. I know the way to tilt my hips first towards and then away from his, the way to lift my chin just slightly, as if I'm thinking about kissing him. And it's easy. Playing this character. This is Party Kara. Party Kara is fine. Party Kara has fun. She flirts with strange guys and doesn't ask their name. She wants to see where it goes. She doesn't really care, she just wants to push. Just a little farther. Just to see if the edge of this blade will be sharp enough to cut through skin.

The guy leans into me, bracing himself with one hand

against the wall next to my head. He eyes me up and down. "Damn. I'm thinking all sorts of things babe. But we can start with this." He reaches into his coat pocket and pulls out a flask, extending it out to me.

And I want to take it. Even though I shouldn't. Because you don't accept drinks from people you don't know. It's one of those rules. From all the stories. Don't take gifts from strangers.

And suddenly I'm laughing, because fairy tales have gotten all mixed up with don't-get-raped lessons, and maybe they're all the same anyway and I'm laughing so hard I can't breathe.

The guy looks a little confused but he's still smiling. "What's—"

"Kara?" Jake's voice cuts over my laughter and the din of the conversation and the music. I look over and he's walking towards us with a purpose. "Hey Kara, come on."

He grabs hold of my wrist and pulls me away, back inside, upstairs and into Greg's room. "Fuck Kara, what are you trying to do?"

I don't answer him, going to rummage in Greg's closet instead, coming away with a heavy glass bottle as my prize. I twist off the cap and take a swig of Greg's whiskey. I hold it out to Jake.

"Damn." He takes it, upending it and swallowing with a wince. "Look, hey, pick someone else to fuck. Not that guy. He's—look he likes to get girls drunk okay? Don't go off with him."

And then I'm laughing again. I'm laughing and Jake's looking at me like I'm crazy but I don't care. "It's all fucking little red riding hood isn't it? It's all fucked. The whole thing. God why doesn't anyone see it?"

Jake's frown deepens. "See what?"

"We're just paper dolls Jake. I'm not me and you're not

you. Fucking paper dolls—just characters doing whatever society told us to do or doing exactly the opposite just so we can say we're doing the opposite. Don't take the drink because you might end up eaten by the wolf *slut* but you should take the drink because you're not supposed to see wolves everywhere *bitch* and by the way shouldn't you have just stayed tucked up at home living a life that isn't a life so you can be safe. And no one no one no one's talking about the fucking wolf."

I look at Jake, waiting for him to agree, to understand. But he just looks lost. "Kara. What are you *talking* about?"

"God Jake I—fuck I want the fairy tale. I want the prince and the castle and I want all of it and why? Because *they told me to*. They told me to want it, over and over they told me to want it until I can't tell if I actually do or if it's just them putting things inside me that aren't me. But there's no way to tell so why does it matter?"

I take the bottle back from him and take another drink.

"That, see that." He yanks the bottle away from me. "I know what you're doing. Tell me what's wrong. Because you're talking crazy and you're drinking like you want to disappear and—"

"That's the whole point!" I throw my hands up in the air. "The whole fucking point Jake. I'm supposed to disappear. It's what I'm for. It's my fucking purpose. I'm a tragedy. I'm not the princess, I don't get the fairy tale. I'm the girl they find in the woods."

"Kara what—"

I grab him by the shoulders, shaking him, determined to get him to understand. "They lied Jake. They lied they lied they *lied*. They told us to want the fairy tale but they didn't tell us there weren't enough to go around. Some people have to be side characters, which means some people have to be the tragedies. Some people have to show up dead in the first act and then fade out by the end. Some people don't get happy endings. Some people have to have sad stories or else who would motivate the heroes and the heroines? You can't have the good without the bad. So what the fuck else am I supposed to do besides drink with that guy down there? The guy that everyone seems to know is a bad guy but no one is really willing to do anything about it. It's fucked. The whole thing is fucked. It's—"

"Kara you're losing it."

I push him away from me. "And why shouldn't I be? Everyone should be losing it. Losing it is the only thing that makes sense. God-fuck-Jake. Fuck. Everyone's just walking around like it isn't all fucked. You can't have the princess without the girl in the woods and everyone's just walking around like it doesn't matter. So fuck it Jake. Just fuck it."

I'm breathing hard when I finally run out of words. Jake looks at me like I might explode again at any second. Gingerly, he hands me the whiskey bottle.

"Thank you," I say, and take another drink. And I shouldn't have said it. I shouldn't have said any of it. But somehow, right now, I don't regret that I did.

"So—" he starts to say, but I don't let him finish.

"Look," I say, running a hand through my hair, "can we just forget this ever happened?"

"Kara—"

"I just want to have fun tonight? Okay? I had a bad week, that's it. I just need a night to have fun."

He hesitates. But then nods. "Alright. Whatever you want. I know exactly what to do."

And he does.

We head back to Ella and Greg and Jake grabs Ella's hand. "Come on," he announces, pulling her towards the basement stairs. "I want to dance."

Ella turns back to look at me and mouths "Oh my god" with a slightly tilted look of glee on her face. She grabs my hand and pulls me after her, and I grab Greg's, pulling him after me.

"Wow," I say to him as we reach the basement. Greg had turned it into a little club of sorts, pushing all the furniture to the sides of the room and setting up speakers all around the place.

I've never really been the dancing type of person. Too worried I would do it wrong, that people would look at me, laugh at me. Dancing always seems to happen only in front of a bunch of other people. You're always the center of attention when you do it. I studiously avoided dancing in high school.

But here? In Greg's basement with alcohol burning in my gut and swimming in my head, surrounded by people who don't seem to care they might not be dancing exactly like they're supposed to, who don't seem to care about anything at all other than the drink in their hand and the person they're with. Here? I dance. Party Kara knows exactly what to do, and when she doesn't, she does whatever she wants. Because she doesn't care.

I don't care.

I let the beat, loud enough that I think it's syncing with my heart, move my body. I laugh more than I can remember laughing in months. I sing loudly, surprised at myself for knowing all the lyrics. I dance next to Greg, close enough for our bodies to brush up against one another. I take Ella by the hands and spin the pair of us in a circle while the boys watch. I have *fun*.

And I don't care about anything other than that. I don't care about anything other than the beat of the music, the smile on Ella's face, the warmth of Greg's body when he moves against me.

I don't care.

I'm not sure how long we dance for, only that suddenly Ella is gripping my shoulder, pulling me closer.

"I've got to pee," she yells into my ear. "Be right back."

I look around, at all the drunk college boys surrounding us, some of whom are eying the dance floor like it's a buffet table. I look at Ella, who's swaying slightly on her feet, and not just because she's dancing to the music. I'm probably not any better off than she is, but two is better than one when you're facing a pack of hungry wolves.

"I'll come with you."

We turn to Jake and Greg. "Be right back," Ella shouts and Jake gives us the thumbs up.

"I'm getting another beer," he says, and Greg moves to join him.

We wind our way through the party to the bathroom, where Jake and Greg leave us to go to the kitchen for beer, and I wait outside the door while Ella goes in to pee. It's after she's inside, while I wait against the wall, looking out at the party, when I see him.

Jake, with his arms around someone else. Jake, whispering in someone else's ear. Jake, with his mouth on someone else's lips.

Oh my god.

I'm not sure if I say the words out loud or not.

Suddenly I understand. I understand all the times it felt like there was a friendly distance between him and Ella. Why it always seemed like he treated her like a friend and not a potential girlfriend. Why no matter how many buttons Ella undid on her shirt, she would never get Jake's attention.

Because Jake is wrapped around Greg.

I go back over all the time Ella and I had spent with Jake, and wonder how I didn't realize. I never thought to ask. No one in my small high school had been gay—or at least they hadn't been out—and although I've met plenty of gay people since I've been at college, I still default to thinking people are straight. And, apparently, so does Ella.

This isn't good. This is not good at all. She's going to be crushed.

I watch him make out with Greg and hope he's bisexual. But somehow, I don't think fate is going to be that nice.

I try to think of ways I could make it better, ways I could spin it so this doesn't seem like such a disaster. At least this means the fact that he isn't interested in her has nothing to do with *her*. Maybe she'll take some kind of comfort in that. Probably not.

Greg takes Jake by the hand and pulls him away through the crowd, heading in the direction of the stairs, and I know they're going back up to Greg's bedroom. This time, I doubt we'll be invited.

At least Ella's not going to walk out of the bathroom and see Jake wrapped up in another man's arms. She can be spared that slap across the face.

Fuck

How am I going to tell her? Should I tell her here? Maybe get her another drink to help blunt the pain? Or should I wait until tomorrow, when we're both sober? What state of mind would I want to be in when I found out the man I wanted wasn't what I thought?

Kara he's not what you think.

Shush's voice pushes back into my head and I press both hands to my temples. Get out. Get out get out *get out.*

Ella comes out of the bathroom behind me. "Jake still getting drinks?" Eagerly, she looks towards the kitchen.

168

"Ella…" I hesitate, still not sure what to do. "Wait for me?" I ask her, and then disappear into the bathroom she just vacated. This will give me a few extra minutes to figure out what to say at least. Except when I look into the mirror and see myself—my hair a mess, my eyeliner starting to smear—I'm not thinking about Ella. I'm thinking about Eric.

I wipe my fingers under my eyes, trying to straighten out the eyeliner. I look exactly how I wanted to look. Like a girl who doesn't care. Like a girl who's seen it all before. Like a girl who's lived some part of her life, instead of hiding away in her books. I look older, like I know more. Like I've embraced my tragedy, run towards it, instead of digging in my heels and looking the other way.

If I looked like this, would Eric still be interested? Would he want to invite me in if I went to his house now, smelling of alcohol and sweat? Would he be jealous if I went downstairs and grabbed some drunk guy to dance with? To disappear into a bedroom with? Would that make him feel like he had to fight for me? Like I have other options, like I'm not just waiting around, pining for him. Would that make him want me back?

Or would he take one look at me, in my low-cut sweater with my black eyes and my drunken smile, and see it's all pretend? That I'm just playing dress up in someone else's skin?

Fuck

His face flashes through my mind, the expressions different each time. Excitement. Arousal. Interest. Disappointment. Sadness. Disgust.

I feel like I'm going to be sick.

And then I straighten, running my hand over my jeans, pushing against the cuts there.

I don't care, I remind myself. Party Kara doesn't care. Party Kara just wants another drink.

Leaving the bathroom, I open my mouth to tell Ella as much, but the words die on my lips. Because there, talking to Ella, the girl who has *become* my best friend, is the dragon who *used to be* my best friend.
And she's looking right at me.
Fuck

TWENTY

I want to scream.

I want to punch something.

Or someone.

What the hell is she doing here? Why can't she just leave me alone for one night? Let me enjoy one damn thing.

"Hey," says Shush. As if a simple greeting is going to make me forget everything she's done to me.

That one word pierces my comfortable haze of alcohol. Everything comes back into focus.

And it hurts.

My failed math test. My worried parents. Eric. Shush. It hurts so much I can't breathe.

I have to get out of here.

What can I say to make her go away? Make her vanish in a spark of flame, a puff of smoke. What can I say to flip our story back to the beginning so I can stop myself from ever meeting her? So none of this will have ever happened. How do I burn our whole book to ash?

"Hey Kara, Shush says you guys are friends?" Ella is smiling, but there's a slight falter to it as she looks back and forth between me and Shush.

A wave of panic pushes bile up into my throat. What did Shush tell her? About Eric? About me? What lies has she been telling? Or—and I can't decide if this would be better or worse—what truths did she tell her?

Shush is going to poison Ella against me. I have to get her out of here. She's already taken Eric from me. I can't let her have Ella too.

When I don't say anything, Ella pushes on. "Did you know she knows Jake and Greg too?"

I meet Shush's gaze and I can tell she knows. She knows about Jake and Greg. She's going to ruin everything. Again.

I want to grab Ella and get her behind me, to shield her from Shush. Because Ella doesn't know. She doesn't know how Shush can take the truth and twist it, so even though it's technically true, it's all completely wrong. She doesn't know how Shush can make you question your own truths in favor of hers.

"Kara, we need to talk," Shush says, taking a step towards me. I move back, away from her, fear lancing through me.

What's she going to say?

What's she going to do?

I have to get out of here.

I have to get Ella out of here.

I know there's a party going on around me but all I can see is Shush, staring back at me. I'm tense, unmoving, prey caught in a predator's gaze. I'm waiting for her to make a move. For her to reach for me with her right hand so I know to move left.

And then a girl crashes into us, laughing and wrapping her arms around Ella, nearly pulling her off her feet. "Ella, oh my god Ella you're here."

"Heather," says Ella, smiling back. "Oh my god hi, how are you?"

"We're dancing, come on, come dance with us." Heather looks at a few other girls gathered nearby, obviously waiting for her. They must be individual people but I can't tell them apart.

All I see is escape.

Ella looks from this new girl back to me. I take her by the hand and pull her away, joining the group of girls heading down the stairs to the dance floor. I won't let Shush ruin this, not now. Ella's supposed to be having fun. I'm supposed to be having fun.

"Kara what's going on? What was that?" Ella asks as we go down the stairs.

I shake my head. "I don't want to talk about it."

She looks like she's about to argue but when we reach the basement, she's distracted. Her head twists around, searching the crowd. "Where's Jake?"

"I don't know," I lie. "Don't worry, he'll find us."

"Ella," Heather says, shoving a fifth of vodka into Ella's hands. "Want some?"

Ella looks around nervously, obviously still searching for Jake.

"Hey," I tell her, taking her face between my hands. "Let's have fun."

I say the words to *her*, but I hear them echo inside *my* head. They bounce off the inside of my skull. I try to make them bigger, make them take up more space inside my brain. I try to make them big enough to overshadow Shush.

Let's have fun.

I want Party Kara back.

Ella hesitates, just for a second, but then she nods. I let her go and she unscrews the cap, drinking before passing it to me.

Let's have fun.

I take a large swallow. Heather grins at me, and somehow we're instant friends. Bonded by alcohol and the rush of bodies pressing in around us. She takes Ella by the hand and pulls her to the middle of the dance floor.

I follow, wanting nothing but to lose myself in a crowd. Safety in numbers or something like that. I move as close to the speaker as possible. I want the music louder, I want it to drown out all the screaming in my head.

Kara you have to tell someone.

You can't avoid me forever.

Eventually you'll forgive me.

I've never been the type of person who had close friends. I mean, I've had friends. People I went to movies with and sat with at lunch in high school. People I laughed with in classes and did homework with. But never someone who really *knew* me.

Shush was the first.

We never should have been friends. I'm quiet, more likely to be found sitting alone with a book than interacting with other human beings. Shush is exactly the opposite. Nine times out of ten if you go looking for her she'll be with at least one other person.

I never expected us to become friends, and I can't pinpoint the moment where our story changed. Where we went from outgoing RA trying to help her shy resident make friends to being friends ourselves. I'm not sure when her inviting me to lunch and study groups stopped being her just being nice and turned into a habit. I'm not sure when her being nice and me being too quiet to say no when she invited me places turned into us being friends. But it did.

Stop it.

I force myself back to the present. Back to the party, the music, the dancing.

Move, body.

Hands. Hips. Feet.

Move.

It's fine. This is all fine. Forget about her. She doesn't matter. I don't care.

Party Kara doesn't care.

The warmth of the vodka moves from my throat and my belly into my head, making everything a little hazy, giving all the moving bodies a slight shimmer. It's good. It's exactly what I want. I let the music wash through me, force myself to laugh with Ella and all these girls I don't know.

Party Kara is fine. Party Kara fits here. Party Kara is having fun.

A hand curls around my hip, tugging me backward into a warm, solid body. "Dance with me," says a male voice in my ear.

From the look on Ella's face, she has no idea who the guy is. Neither do I. For all I know it's the guy from before, the one Jake told me to stay away from. But I don't care. His hands are strong and sure on my hips, his body a wall behind mine.

I don't even turn around.

I reach up and wrap my arms around his neck. I move with him, closing my eyes. All I want is to dance. All I want is to have fun.

I listen to Party Kara. I forget about Shush. I just dance. I just dance with him.

With Eric.

God his arms feel good. It's been so long. So long since I've been able to let go, so long since I've let another body hold mine up. I lean into him, giving him control. I just want him to take me away.

Eric Eric Eric.

His name pulses through me with every beat of the music. The world is spinning under my feet, spinning inside my head. But I don't care. Eric's holding me steady. He always holds me steady. He knows what to do.

His arms around me, his mouth on my neck, his hands slipping under the hem of my shirt.

It's all going to be okay.

"Don't you have a girlfriend Adam?" Shush's voice screeches over the music.

And Eric is gone.

I open my eyes and find her standing in front of us, arms crossed over her chest, a parental eyebrow raised.

"Calm down," the guy says. "We were just dancing."

I turn and see him for the first time. He's about my height. Good-looking. Not the worst dance partner. Not the guy Jake told me to stay away from.

But he's not Eric.

Shush rolls her eyes. "Whatever. I'll be sure to tell Danielle that."

"Fuck you Shush," he says. But then he leaves.

I stare at her, remembering a time when she would have joined me on this dance floor. When she would have run off that guy but then pushed her way into our group, dancing so wildly you couldn't help but look at her. The center of attention. Like the sun, pulling everything into orbit around her, shining so brightly some of her light warmed you up too.

She turns on me. "Kara I need to talk to you."

"No."

The word comes out with force, sharp, biting through the party atmosphere. Shush has the decency to flinch. At least now I know *something* can get through her thick dragon scales. It's the first word I've said to her since she ruined my life. And it feels so *good* I say it again. "No. No, no, no. *Fuck* no."

She hardens her expression but doesn't move. "God Kara, after everything that happened and now you're—"

I cut her off, turning to Ella, who's stopped dancing to watch us. "I'll be back Ella." I turn to Shush, sinking into the fact that I can't put this off any longer. I shove a little steel into my spine and say, "Let's go then."

I can't let her go on and on about everything with Ella here. Ella's already going to have questions about Shush, about why I'm acting the way I am. I don't want her to know anything more. I don't want Shush to run her off too.

I lead Shush upstairs to the kitchen, because if I'm going to be listening to her talk, I need a drink in my hand. I need some kind of shield between us.

I pour myself another beer even though what I really want is Heather's vodka. Or maybe the whiskey Greg has upstairs. Something that burns its way down my throat instead of sitting like sour water on my tongue.

Shush comes up beside me, eying the drink I'm pouring. "Kara," she says, her tone dripping with reproach.

"You want one?"

She narrows her eyes at me. "What the hell is wrong with you?"

"I don't know but I'm sure you're about to tell me."

Her mouth falls open in surprise and I want to laugh. She doesn't know Party Kara. Party Kara isn't quiet. Party Kara is sarcastic and outspoken and comfortable in her own skin. I lift my chin and meet her gaze. Maybe Party Kara will be too much for her to handle. Maybe Party Kara is the suit of armor I need to finally withstand the dragon.

Someone pushes past us to get at the alcohol and I move off to the side, leaning against a counter and taking a large gulp of beer. Shush comes after me, moving in close. I'm grateful that at least she isn't shouting, making a spectacle. I settle in for the long haul, thinking maybe if I let her go on, she'll blow herself out. Her fire has to die eventually. Maybe then she'll leave me alone.

I sip at my beer, torn between wanting to make it last as long as possible and wanting to down the whole thing now in one gulp. It gives me something to do, something to focus on, an anchor to hold onto inside the storm of Shush's beating wings.

"Okay," she says finally, "I know you're mad at me."

I snort and take another drink. Mad at her? She says it like she borrowed my favorite book and never gave it back, not like she spent the last two months ripping my life apart.

She presses on. "I did it to help you Kara. I did it because you're my best friend."

I take another drink. I want to drown in this stale alcohol. I want to drink so much I'm not me anymore. I want to drink so much I stay Party Kara forever. Because Shush is right.

She was my best friend.

She's so entwined into my life it's hard to separate one from the other. I keep finding things of hers mixed in with mine. A pen. A sock. A sweatshirt she once lent me. The *I Voted* sticker on my laptop. All my memories since I've been at college are twisted up with her.

She was there for me while I was figuring out this whole college thing, helping me every step of the way. And I was there for her all through election night, when she couldn't stop crying, and the days after, when she couldn't get out of bed.

When Eric broke up with me, even though I wasn't speaking to her, she was the only person I wanted to tell. Even as I desperately avoided her, I wanted so badly to run to her instead, to tell her everything. She would have known how to make me feel better.

Even now, when just seeing her face causes me pain, there's a part of me that wants to talk to her about this fight. As if I'm fighting with someone else. And Shush could help me get through it.

It's all so twisted in my head that I can't sort it out. I can't separate my best friend from the dragon she's become.

I don't say anything to her, just make a noncommittal noise of acknowledgment that yes, we used to be friends. And then I take another drink.

My silence just seems to make her angrier.

"And now you're what? Stonewalling me? Ghosting me? I don't deserve that Kara."

Another drink.

I could be good at this game, the way Ella is good at beer pong. Every time Shush opens her mouth and says some ridiculous statement, I drink. If I'm still standing at the end of it—and let's face it, Shush likes to talk, so I might not be— then I win.

"You ignore my text messages, you ignore me in class. I deserve the chance to explain."

She really doesn't. I drink. She's just going to twist everything to make it look like it's all my fault, like she was just trying to help.

But she betrayed me. This isn't my fault.

"I was just trying to help," she says.

Drink.

"And now you're treating me like shit."

Drink.

"I was your best friend."

Drink.

Shit. Cup's empty.

"Hold that thought," I say, moving past her to top up. If I'm going to make it through tonight alive, Party Kara has to stick around. She's strong. Confident. Carefree. *She* can handle this.

I'm not sure *I* can.

I bump into someone on my way to the keg, stumbling a little. "Sorry," I say, snorting out a laugh as I reach for the keg to refill my cup.

Shush comes with me, frowning. "Since when do you drink beer?"

"Since tonight."

"Since tonight? Kara." She has that tone again. That lecturing I-know-better-than-you tone she gets when she's about to get up on her soap box. So fucking certain she's right about everything.

He's not what you think.

A knot tightens in my chest and I focus on the beer pouring into my cup.

"Do you really need that right now?"

I don't answer her. The knot pulls tighter. I have to focus on not clenching my fingers around my plastic cup.

"How much have you had to drink?"

"Not enough." I shut off the tap and go to take a drink. That's when she stops me, trying to take the cup out of my hand.

"I think you've had plenty."

The knot inside my chest rips open. That does it. "Still fucking trying to decide what's best for me?"

Her expression hardens. "I'm going to ignore that. Because you're drunk. You—"

"What does me being drunk have to do with it? You've been ignoring me since we met."

She glances around. I realize my voice has gotten louder, realize people are starting to look at us. I don't care. Party Kara doesn't care. She says what she wants.

"Look—" starts Shush, but I don't let her finish.

"Shut up!" I scream it so loud it echoes clearly above the beat of the music. "God Shush don't you ever stop talking?

Are you really so in love with the sound of your own voice?"

She stares back at me as if I've slapped her, obviously affronted I would do anything besides run away, anything besides just listen to her. As if she thinks I'm incapable of standing up to her.

And suddenly, I can't take it. Maybe it's the alcohol, or the fact that I'm not me right now, I'm someone else, someone a bit more like Shush, a bit more capable of making noise. But the newspaper article and Eric ignoring me and everyone cheering for Shush at the Women's March despite all her lies—all of it rushes through me at once. I can hear it like my blood whooshing through my ears. It's like I've been standing on the edge of a cliff, my toes hanging over the edge, and she's just pushed me off it.

"What the fuck do you want? Why can't you stop trying to ruin my life?" I stalk towards her and she backs away from me until she's pressed against the kitchen counter. I know the other people around are staring at us. But I don't care. Not right now. Not tonight.

"Kara I know—"

"You don't know *anything*!" I throw my cup at her feet and she jumps back as beer splashes everywhere. "You think you do, but you don't. You go around preaching at everyone, like you know what's best, like you know what's right and what's wrong. Like you're the one who gets to decide what's a fairy tale and what's a tragedy."

She opens her mouth but it's like something inside me has broken, a tap that won't shut off, and I can't stop the vitriol pouring out.

"But you're wrong Shush. You're just wrong. You were wrong about my parents and you're wrong about that—that *lie* you told—I can't believe you would do something like that. Lie about something so important. Aren't you always going on and on about how we should believe women and now you're lying like this? God. I never knew you at all."

I start to walk away and she reaches out for me again.

"Kara—"

"Don't fucking touch me!" I scream at her.

"What is *wrong* with you?" She's looking at me like she doesn't recognize my face. She's looking at me like I'm the dragon.

"You," I say. "You're what's wrong with me. I trusted you. I *trusted* you. And now you've ruined *everything*."

The words come out before I realize what I'm saying. That this, *this* is what hurts most of all. She betrayed me. It makes every single second we spent together feel like a lie. All the times we laughed and the times we were there for each other. All that time I didn't know she was capable of something like this. It makes our whole friendship a lie. Something that cracks the ground under my feet instead of holding me up.

I take a breath and realize it's shaky. I'm shaky. Because everything is coming back into focus. The party. The people watching me like I'm a drama on TV.

Fuck

Shush is staring at me like I've stabbed her in the chest. What did I say? What did *I* say?

Because it wasn't Party Kara who said that. It was me.

My eyes sting with tears.

No. I won't cry in front of her. I won't.

I have to get out of here.

I turn and push my way through the crowd, heading for the door. There's too many people in here. Shush is taking up too much space. Crushing me. I feel sick. I need air. I can't breathe.

I push through the front door, jump down the porch

steps, nearly falling. I walk down the sidewalk, leaving the party behind.

Fuck. Oh fuck oh fuck oh fuck.

What did I just do?

The worst part is Shush is the only person I think would understand what just happened.

I read something somewhere about how you know who your best friend is when you figure out which of your friends you'd call if you murdered someone. That's a bit extreme. But maybe someone you would tell about your worst thoughts, tell about all the terrible things you want to do, all the awful things you want to say. I never had anyone like that. Shush was the first.

I've never been a person who yells at other people. I can't remember the last time I did it. I'm just not that kind of person. But Shush would have understood. Not only would she have understood, she would have cheered me on. She would have nodded, clapped me on the back, said, "Good for you standing up for yourself."

Except all of that's wrong. Because she's on the wrong side now. None of it makes any sense.

I push my hair out of my face, taking a deep breath of cold air. Where am I? How do I get back to my dorm? I stop to look around and that's when she catches me.

She followed me. Of course she fucking followed me.

"Kara what the hell—"

When I turn around, my hands are balled into fists. "Leave me the fuck alone. I *never* want to speak to you again."

She looks back at me, her mouth open, as if I stabbed her. As if I'm the one in the wrong here. "I just wanted to help."

"Stop saying that! You didn't. You didn't want to help Shush. You wanted to *get your way*. You wanted to make it about *you*. Just like you always do."

"Is that what you think?" Her voice is so low and broken I almost can't understand her. I've never heard her sound like this before. In the dim light of the street lamp, I think I see her eyes shining with tears.

"I thought we were friends," I say, spitting the words at her. "I never thought you'd ruin my life just to get a little attention. Because that's all you care about isn't it?"

The hurt in her eyes is like a knife I can cut myself on. I push down into the blade.

"Well congratulations. You got what you wanted. Enjoy the spotlight."

And then I leave her standing there, finally silent.

TRIGGER WARNING

The following section contains graphic depictions of self-harm. If you are not in a place where you feel up to reading that, please skip to the next section.

Remember, you're not alone. Mental health resources can be found at the back of this book. Take care of yourself.

TWENTY-ONE

Some days I feel like an alien in my skin.

On those days, I cut to ask questions.

I am not a devout worshiper, standing in a cathedral with stained glass windows, wearing holy robes. I am a scientist, standing in a laboratory, wearing a white coat and gloves. I am not praying, I am investigating. I am clinical. Detached. I am studying a subject. I am studying me. I am at once holding the scalpel and also spread-eagled on the stainless-steel table, waiting patiently for my skin to be peeled away.

On those days, I cut to find answers.

Every cut is a hunt for something living, something sentient, something determined to hide from me. I can feel it, running beneath my skin, burrowing into my bones. Something that doesn't belong. Something eating me from the inside out. I just don't know what it is. A foreign body, something extra-terrestrial, a new species.

I hunt to catch it, to trap it so I can peer through the wire mesh of its cage and discover its shape. To take it back to my laboratory and dissect its body piece by piece. To weigh each organ and discover its circulatory system. To trace the outline of each bone and find the framework of its skeleton so I can rearticulate it and hang it from my ceiling, a dead model of the thing I found inside me. A warning to not let it in again.

On those days, I cut to find more blood.

I need as much as possible to run more tests. To discover how this thing has poisoned me, how it's making me into someone I don't recognize. I take my blood between my fingers and examine it. Its consistency, its color, its feel. I touch my finger to my tongue, to make sure it tastes like blood and not like ink.

On those days, I cut to understand.

When I fail to trap the monster, when the testing reveals nothing extraordinary, I keep going. I try to find something I might call it. I write my name in blood on the white wall of the shower and search for the shadow of a new name beneath mine. I search until I don't recognize my own name anymore. It becomes unfamiliar. Like a word from a different language. Like each letter is a symbol from a language no longer spoken and I know they all mean something. I just don't know what.

On those days, I cut to make sure my body cries out at the intrusion.

To make sure some part of me is mine. That my body resists my blood being taken from me. That I can't simply peel off my skin and put on another one without effort, without sacrifice. To make sure not all skins feel the same on my bones. That there is one that fits better than all the others. One that belongs to me. One that is mine.

On those days, I cut to test myself.

I cut to make sure my body responds. To make sure that when the blade slices into my skin, I feel a sharp gasp of pain. To make sure my blood comes out red. To make sure it hasn't turned black inside my veins.

On those days, I cut to make sure I'm human.

TWENTY-TWO

When I wake up, it takes me one groggy, throbbing minute to remember what happened the night before. It comes back in disjointed flashes.

The taste of the whiskey.

The press of flesh against me on the dance floor.

The feel of a smile on my face.

The music of my laughter.

The sound of me ranting at Jake.

The way Jake kissed Greg.

The hot stickiness of a strange guy's tongue on the side of my neck.

The hurt in Shush's eyes before I walked away.

But nothing really stays in focus too long. Not the feeling of fun the night started out with, and not the feeling of sick, guilty satisfaction it ended with.

I watch my memories like a show, wondering who that is drinking whiskey from the bottle, spilling her guts to Jake, dancing with that guy, screaming at Shush. She doesn't look like me. I don't recognize her.

I don't understand how she shares my name.

Why did Party Kara seem like such a good idea last night? How could I do those things? I know I'd been drinking, something I'm not used to doing, but alcohol doesn't make you an entirely different person. It just lowers your inhibitions.

Am I actually Party Kara? Somewhere inside me, do I want to do those things? Shots with strangers? Screaming at Shush? Dancing with strange guys? Do I want to lose control that way?

Am I actually that person?

I can feel a sense of panic somewhere in my chest, but it's dim. It can't fully break through the hangover fog. I'm trapped in limbo. Like I'm staring down the dragon but I can't summon the energy to care, can't summon the energy to run. Because it doesn't matter. Nothing matters.

All I can do is lay here, curled up under my covers, too exhausted and on this edge of nausea to fall back asleep, even if that's all I want to do. Because even though I'm not feeling the onslaught of my emotions right now, I know I will. I know eventually this haze protecting me will fade, and then I'll have to feel it.

I'll have to feel it *all*.

The pain for Ella. The embarrassment at all the fairytale nonsense I told Jake. The disgust for the way I acted with not just one but two guys. The guilt for how I screamed at Shush.

I don't want to be here. I'll even take the hangover, as long as I don't have to be in my bed alone, watching all my emotions grow larger until I suffocate beneath them.

I want to be in Eric's bed. In Eric's arms. Wrapped up in the strength and the warmth of him, where I know everything will be okay. He'll protect me. He's my prince. He'll pull me up from underneath the surface, keep me from drowning. He'll save me.

Except he's not here.

I'm all alone.

I close my eyes. I just want to fall back asleep. To wake up tomorrow. Or next week. But I don't. My phone buzzes and I hope, dimly, it's Eric. Something warm to wrap myself in so I can fall back asleep, safe and protected. Or maybe even Shush. Something sharp to cut myself on so I can wake up, so I can run.

But it's neither.

You make it home okay?

I stare at Ella's message, wondering if it's worth the effort of answering it. Because it won't just be a simple answer. This is the start to a conversation. And I can't do a conversation right now. Not with another person.

I can barely keep up with the conversations happening in my head.

The conversation I had with Shush last night. The conversation I'm having with myself now. The conversation I want to be having with Eric.

But I have to respond to Ella. Because above the text message she just sent me is a long string of unanswered ones she sent me last night, all asking where I was and if I was okay. I never responded. I must have been home already, passed out, when she sent them.

I can't just not reply now. Then she might do something crazy to make sure I'm safe. Like call me. Or come over. I text her something obvious, easy.

I'm never drinking again.

My head is killing me.

I wonder if I should tell her about Jake now. When I'm all fuzzy and can't feel things properly. Maybe the hangover will blunt the difficulty, the pain. For both of us.

190

But it's probably something I should tell her in person.
So I can comfort her, or whatever it is I'm supposed to
do. Bring chocolate and offer hugs. Something like that. It
all feels a little like it doesn't matter. Like I'm looking at a
mountain I need to climb but it's still so far in the distance I
can't bring myself to care yet.
Ella texts me again.

Did you see Jake before you left?

No, I say, because that's easier and it's true. I didn't see
Jake before I left because he was upstairs with Greg.
This is where I should tell her. Phrase it in some way to
let her down easy. If I'm not going to tell her in person then I
have to at least try to ease her into it.
But I don't know how.
I don't know how to do anything anymore.
Then a hopeful thought makes its way through my hangover fog. Maybe she already knows. Maybe she saw Jake
before she left. Maybe that's why she's asking me. To see if I
know about him and Greg. Only one way to find out. I text Jake.

Hey does Ella know about you and Greg?

A little blunt for a good morning text probably. But after
everything I said to him last night it hardly matters what I
say to him now. It takes him a few minutes to reply.

No. I didn't know you knew about me and Greg.

So much for that little spark of hope. I close my eyes, setting
my phone down and pulling the blankets tighter around me.
I want Eric.

191

I want to fall asleep and wake up a year from now, when all this mess has sorted itself out. I want to fall asleep and wake up a year ago, before this whole mess started.

I want to fall asleep and not wake up at all.

My phone buzzes again. Jake.

Hey so can you not tell anyone?
About me and Greg? I'm not exactly in
the closet but I'm not really out either.

Dimly, I feel a stabbing pain of empathy in my chest at how he still feels the need to keep who he loves a secret. But it feels far away. Like everything else. I should reassure him. But I don't have the energy.

Ok.

I put the phone down and tell myself to go back to sleep, but then my phone goes off again. It isn't Jake like I expect. Or Eric like I hope. It isn't Ella or even Shush. It's my mom.

Good morning honey, how are you?

Hungover.

Ella texts me then.

Come be miserable and Netflix with me?

Hungover and that's the least of my problems.

I can't do this. I really can't do this right now. I can't juggle multiple conversations and the question of should I keep Jake's secret or should I tell Ella. I just want to go back to sleep. I text my mom.

> I'm good, Just heading to the
> library to get some homework done.

That's what I should be doing. I should be getting up and going to do homework. Or I should be getting up and going over to Ella's so we can commiserate about our hangovers. So I can tell her about Jake. Or not tell her. I don't know anymore.

Besides just keeping Jake's secret, part of me wants to give her another day of believing last night had gone well for her. Of feeling light and happy. Because Jake invited her to a party. Because he smiled at her and laughed with her. Because he danced with her. I want to give her a little longer of living the memory of that fairytale ball, perfect except for its ending, where she didn't get her kiss.

But the longer you believe something, the harder it hits you when you find out it isn't true.

I trusted you.

You're magic.

It's all going to be okay.

The longer Ella basks in memories of how she thought last night had gone, the more devastated she's going to be when she finds out it was all a facade. A fairy tale but not *her* fairy tale.

And besides, the longer I leave it, the bigger the chances Shush will find her first. Shush will tell her and break her and not stick around to hold her together. It's just like Shush to say things at the worst possible times. To hide behind the fact that she's telling the truth and ignore the way the truth can hurt worse than a lie, worse than just keeping your silence.

I need to tell Ella before Shush tells her. Before she finds out some other way. Before she texts Jake and digs herself deeper into the fairy tale. The farther in she goes, the more it's going to hurt when I have to drag her up out of it.

I know the lines I'm supposed to say. I can watch it all take place in my head. Me going over to Ella's and bonding over our hangovers, over our shared misery. Me telling her about Jake. I know my lines. *You'll be okay. There are other princes out there.*

Even in my head they ring hollow. They're true. Of course they're true. *Ella* will find someone else.

The problem is, *I* won't.

I just want Eric.

I don't want to have to take care of Ella. I want to be with Eric. I want to let him take care of me. I want to let his strength hold me together because I'm too tired to do it myself right now.

He's the only one who ever understood me, who saw all of me and accepted all of me. I can't handle Ella right now, can't handle her questions as I tear her fairy tale down. Can't handle the question of if I should tell Ella or if I should keep Jake's secret like I said I would. Because all I can think about are all the questions I have for Eric.

I want to ask him why I lost control last night. Why Party Kara was so appealing to me. I want to ask him how I could be like that—so ready to be someone else.

Maybe that wasn't someone else. Maybe Party Kara is me and I hadn't figured that out until now.

How do you figure that out? How do you know if you're the kind of person who parties every weekend? Who does shots with strangers and chugs down stale beer. Who dances in the middle of a house party and doesn't care who sees. Who wakes up hungover, groggily trying to remember what happened the night before. How do you know if that's who you want to be? Or if you'd rather have curled up with a book and gone to bed at nine p.m.

Anything else you want to ask me?

The questions rise up to my lips and I stare at my phone, wanting to text Eric, wanting to call him. He's the only one I want to ask. He's the only one I think will understand not only the question but also how to tell me the answer in a way that makes it all make sense.

I'm lost, I would tell him, wandering into his arms, covered in dirt and scars from my time in the woods.

I'll find you, he would say, and take me by the hand and lead me into the castle to clean me up. To make me shiny and new and beautiful. To make me into someone who belongs in a castle. Who belongs in a castle with him.

He would take me as a student to his teacher and show me the secret languages I'd never understood.

How do you know who you are? How do you know if you're doing the things you're supposed to be doing? How do you know if the choices you're making are the right ones? How do you know if you're living the life you're supposed to be?

Anything else you want to ask me?

I want to go up to him and kneel at the foot of his desk, surrounded by his books, and beg him to take me back, beg him to show me.

You're magic.

How did he know who I was?

I pull up his messages on my phone, reading the last few, where he asked me to meet him at the library. My fingers hover over the screen, wanting to type something. Would he come if I said I needed him?

I feel perched at the edge of a precipice, the way in front of me so thick with fog I can't see my next step. I might step forward and find a bridge, sturdy and waiting to carry me across to Eric's castle. Or I might step forward and find nothing. I might step forward and fall.

Before I can decide, my mom sends me another text message.

What's your schedule like this week?

Oh no.

Dread makes me sink even deeper into my bed. That sounds like she's planning something. Like she wants me to come home. Or she wants to come visit.

I know what she wants me to say. That I'm not busy. Then she'll spring her plan on me. And I won't be able to say no. Because if I say I'm busy and try to avoid it, that will make her worry anyway. She needs to see me, I know she does. She needs to reassure herself I'm okay. She needs to run her hands over my arms and make sure I'm not cracking apart at my edges.

I'll have to go and put on one of my masks and pretend like everything is fine when all I want is to crawl back into bed and not lift my head above the covers.

And I can do it. Pretend. I can.

Because I'm fine. I am.

Just not today. Today I'm too tired. I can't put on Fine Kara's mask today.

I just need some time.

I'm not sure about my schedule. What's up?

Your father and I are going to be in town.
We thought we could take you out to dinner.

I close my eyes.

I know what to do. What I'm supposed to do. I'm supposed

to say yes to them both. Yes to Ella and yes to my mom.
Ella texts me:

Kara? You want to come over?

And another text from my mom:

What do you think? Do you have time for dinner?

I can't do this. I want to shut off my phone and roll over,
bury my head beneath my covers and not get up for a week.
Maybe not even then.
Why can't they just leave me alone?
I take a deep breath. Just push through it. Wrap up the
conversations and then you can go back to sleep. Or at least
back to staring at the wall in silence.
I text my mom.

What day are you coming?

Then I text Ella.

I don't think I can make it.

That bad?

Yeah.

And it is. I'm not lying about that. It just isn't all the hangover.
Another text comes in from my mom

Tuesday work for you?

I'm in the middle of texting my mom back when Ella texts me again.

I think I'm going to text Jake.

Shit.

Don't do it.

Why not?

I don't respond right away this time, not sure what to say. I go back to my mom's message and tell her Tuesday will work. Then I go back to Ella's and stare at the blinking cursor. I can't put it off anymore. I know I shouldn't. I told Jake I wouldn't. But I don't have the energy to lie. Or even to coat this bitter pill with chocolate, to make it go down smoothly. Sometimes you just have to drink the poison and let what happens happen.

Because he's with Greg

So?

I can't handle this right now. I can't spend time pulling Ella together when I only have until Tuesday to pull myself together for my parents.

No, Ella, he was with Greg last night.

Yeah we were too.

I groan. She's just not getting it.

They went to bed together Ella.

What?

He's gay. I should just say it. I should just tell her
outright. But I can't.

I know what it's like to bury your head in the sand, to
spend so much time believing one thing that you can't let
yourself believe its opposite. And maybe on a different day,
I could have been more understanding. I could have tried to
break through her fairytale bubble gently instead of smash-
ing it all to pieces.

But then my mom texts me again.

Why don't you see if Shush wants to come too?

And I nearly shut off my phone. I nearly shut off my
phone and determine to not ever turn it back on, to not ever
get out of this bed. Because *of course* it comes back to Shush.
It always comes back to Shush.

I need to end these conversations. I can't do this right now.
I text Ella.

I saw them making out, He's gay.
Jake's gay. He isn't into you. He never was.

Then I text my mom.

I'll see if she has time. Got to go study. Love you.

And then I turn the phone off.

Goddamn Shush for making my parents worry about me
like this. I want to scream. I want to hate her. But the desires

are half-hearted. They lack bite, lack energy.

It's like I've been drained.

I shouted all the words I had at Shush last night and now I don't have any left to give. The memories of what I said raise their monstrous heads above the surface one by one, a relentless torrent of my worst faces.

Are you really so in love with the sound of your own voice?

You're what's wrong with me.

I trusted you. And now you've ruined everything.

Leave me the fuck alone. I never want to speak to you again.

You didn't want to help Shush. You wanted to get your way.

You wanted to make it about you.

I never thought you'd ruin my life just to get a little attention.

Enjoy the spotlight.

I don't recognize the person who said all those things. I don't recognize the person who kept pushing until she drove Shush to tears.

But it isn't my fault.

It's Shush. If she'd just accepted it when I stopped talking to her, none of this would have happened. She refused to let things go, to let our friendship fade away quietly the way it should have. She just had to make things difficult.

I'm not the dragon here. I didn't tear apart her life. She tore apart mine.

She's the one who hurt *me*.

So why is it that all I can see is her face, staring back at me as if I'd run her through with a blade?

Why is it that my guilt is slowly starting to push through the hangover?

Why do I feel like I've done something terrible?

Why do I feel like someone I don't know at all?

I look back at my phone, now silent. Which is what I wanted. Except I never meant to tell Ella about Jake like that.

Not only to break his confidence but to tell her and then leave her all alone.

And I can't even make myself text her to apologize. I can't make myself go over to her dorm room and comfort her the way I know I should.

None of it makes any sense.

I feel, not just that I don't understand myself, but that I don't understand *anything*. I don't understand what it means to be human. I don't understand how we get up and live our lives. I don't understand the fairy tales and the tragedies and how they're all somehow twisted up together. I don't understand why we need the things we need. I don't understand why we want the things we want. I don't understand how we hurt each other. I don't understand how we break and keep breaking. I don't understand why we keep getting up in the morning.

I don't understand how I can know so little about myself. How I can be a person Eric loves and a person who makes her friends cry. How I can be a person who never knows what to say and still knows exactly what words to use to cut Shush down, to sever Ella from her fairy tale in the harshest way possible.

I don't understand how I can remember doing something and not recognize the girl wearing my face.

I don't understand anything.

My questions are big and suffocating and I can't ask Eric for the answers. Not now. Not after what I've done.

I see myself flirting with a bad guy holding out a flask, fully prepared to let him take me wherever he wants. I feel Adam's mouth on the side of my neck, hot and pulling. My skin crawls, like something has found its way inside me that shouldn't be there.

Because then. In that moment.

Flirting with him.
Then. In that moment.
Dancing with him.
Then. In that moment.
Screaming at Shush.
I enjoyed it.
I enjoyed the danger in his eyes, the risk of the unknown. I enjoyed the want in his fingers, the desire in his mouth. I enjoyed the strength in my spine, the power in my voice.
I *loved* it.
And there's a part of me that still does. A part of me, somewhere down deep, that wants *more*.
I can't go to Eric like this. I can't let him see this terrible stranger wearing my face.
There's only one thing I can do now.
I get up, ignoring the way the world tilts around me, ignoring the throbbing behind my eyes, and head for the shower.
Some days I feel like an alien in my skin.
On those days, I cut to find something familiar.
I cut to make sure my body responds the way it always has before. To make sure that when the blade slices into my skin, I still feel that sharp gasp of pain. To make sure my blood comes out the same way it always has before. Beautiful and red. To make sure it hasn't turned black inside my veins.
On those days, I cut to feel like me.

TWENTY-THREE

Whenever I can't get out of bed, I cut everything into small pieces.

I don't have to go to class. I just have to take off the covers. I just have to sit up. I just have to put my feet on the floor. I'm not climbing a mountain, I'm just taking a step. Monday morning, I cut everything into pieces.

I don't have to survive two days of classes before dinner with my parents. I just have to make it through Biology. I just have to make it through Creative Writing. Another night of trying to sleep. Calculus. Work. Eric. Dinner.

It's not so huge, this list. Just small things. Nothing as big as the dinner at the end, and it starts with the biggest hurdle. Biology. Everything is downhill from Biology.

If I can make it through Biology, I can do the rest of it.

There's no way I can skip it. I'm already struggling in Calculus. If my grades slip in another class, I'm going to lose my scholarship for sure. But I don't want to go. I don't want to go for the same reason as always. Because Shush is there. Because I have no idea what she's going to do. And this time it's even worse. At the party, I might have put out the fire, ate up all her fuel with a blaze of my own, or I might have thrown gasoline onto the flames.

I don't know.

I know she's going to be angry with me. For nearly outing what she's done in front of all those people. For not accepting or believing she's trying to help me. For what I said. *You wanted to make it about you. Just like you always do.* For knocking high and mighty Shush off her pedestal. *Enjoy the spotlight.* But I'm not sure what form her anger will take. Breathing fire, like she usually does, would mean causing a scene. Calling me out in front of everyone, demanding I respond to her on her terms. Or she could completely ignore me. Which is what I'm hoping for as I slowly make my way to class.

I spent the whole weekend in bed but I still feel exhausted. Like each step takes nearly too much effort to complete.

My exhaustion might be a blessing in disguise though. Because I have so many things to worry about. Getting through all my classes. Keeping up with my schoolwork. Shush. What if she attacks me again? Eric. What if he sees what I've done on my face? Jake. What if he finds out I told Ella he's gay? Ella. What if she won't speak to me? My parents. What if I can't keep it together for dinner?

There's so much, but I don't have the energy to panic about all of it. I can't keep them all front and center in my head at once. I can only do one of them at a time.

Biology first. Shush.

Everything else feels somewhere in the distance. Right now, I only have the energy to worry about Shush. I only have the energy to worry about making it through Biology.

When I get to class, I scan the students already sitting down to make sure Shush is at her usual place in the front of the room and not sitting somewhere else to ambush me. When I see her, as if she can feel my gaze, she turns to look at me.

Oh.

I suck in a breath.

It hurts.

I know what Shush looks like when she's angry. The slight tightening at the corners of her eyes and mouth, the widening of her nostrils, the way the muscle in her jaw clenches. I know the fire that lights her gaze when she's furious about something. It happens easily, like her rage is always just under the surface, a geyser waiting to be tapped. But what I see on her face, in her eyes, isn't anger.

It's sadness.

A sadness so acute it feels like she's hooked a claw inside my rib cage and pierced my lungs. The corners of her mouth downturned, her eyes open slightly wider than usual. Exhaustion pulling all her features a little looser at the edges. She's looking at me as if I've wounded her. And more than that, she's looking at me as if she hadn't been expecting it. Like I snuck up and stabbed her in the back for no reason.

That isn't what happened. It's not. She attacked me first. I had to fight back. What else was I going to do? What happened this weekend wasn't my fault. It wasn't me. It was her. No matter how she looks at me, I'm not the dragon. I was defending myself.

I was defending myself.

I wrench my gaze away from Shush and take my seat, getting out my notebook and my pen, staring at the notes I took last class in a futile attempt to study, in an effort not to look at her.

And still, I feel guilt sinking into me, pain spreading from where she dug her claw into my chest.

I've never hurt anyone before, not like this, not intentionally. I've never even gotten into a shouting match with anyone, much less said things designed to hurt them. Before the party, I didn't know I was capable of it, didn't know *that* Kara existed inside me. Mean Kara. Cruel Kara. A Kara who would strike out on purpose and hurt someone she used to care about.

I think about how I betrayed Jake's secret. About the text message I sent to Ella.

A Kara who would hurt someone she *still* cares about.

I color in one of the lines of my notebook, pressing the pen hard into the paper. I want to fill the whole white page, cover all the words. Fill it all with black.

I want to talk to Eric.

Anything else you want to ask me?

There has to be a fairy tale to explain this. To explain how people can act so out of character they don't recognize themselves.

I glance up and eye the back of Shush's head, a mess of dark curls.

It's fine. I don't care if she feels like I've hurt her unjustly. I was just telling the truth. It's her who's been doing all the lying. And at least what I said seems to have had the desired effect. She doesn't seem like she's going to keep attacking me. My attack worked. I won't have to talk to her again. I won't have to avoid her because she'll be avoiding me.

It's fine.

I'm not the dragon.

I was defending myself.

And now I don't have to anymore.

As Dr. Nelson starts the lecture, I force myself to pay attention. Over and over I drag my mind back to what she's saying. I drag it away from memories of the party. I drag it away from dreams of Eric. I drag it away from wanting to write another note into my skin.

I am not the dragon.

By the end of class, I'm more exhausted than I was at the start.

"Don't leave yet people," Dr. Nelson says. "I've assigned your partners for the final project. I know it's still early in the semester but I want to give you plenty of opportunity to get started. I've assigned you randomly. No changes allowed so don't ask."

Great.

Now I have to work with a stranger on top of everything else. A new personality to figure out, to work around. Someone else who's going to try and make me talk.

I press the tips of my fingers hard above my left eyebrow, where a headache is starting to make its presence known.

It'll be fine. I don't have to start now.

I'll deal with this after tomorrow night. After I make it through dinner. *If* I make it through dinner.

But then the professor puts up the list of names.

It doesn't feel like a punch to the gut, like everyone always says surprises feel. It feels like someone slaps me on both sides of my head, over my ears, making my head ring.

This can't be happening. The universe can't be this cruel.

I squint at the name. I rub my eyes.

But no matter what I do, the name next to mine refuses to change.

Shush.

≈

I spend Creative Writing split in two. One half of me playing the character of good student and the other half arguing against dropping Biology to get out of working with Shush. Write down something Dr. Leery says. Tell myself I can't drop because I need the class to graduate. Comment on something somebody wrote. Ask myself what I would tell my parents.

Even when I decide on a solution—asking Dr. Nelson if she can make an exception and let me switch partners—I find it hard to focus.

"Today I want you all to dig a little deeper." Dr. Leery stands at the head of the class, leaning back against her desk. I'll go after class to ask Dr. Nelson about switching. I'll beg. Cry if I have to. Something. Anything. I glance at the clock. We just have our fifteen-minute free write left to get through.

"Today," Dr. Leery says, "I want you all to write something you might not be entirely comfortable sharing with the class."

Everyone else starts writing and I glance up at Dr. Leery. She meets my gaze and points down to the blank notebook page in front of me. Reluctantly, I pick up my pen.

One true sentence.

What did she say?

Write something we don't want to share?

If I don't want to share it, why would I write it?

So far, my writing pieces have all been abstract. They've dealt with concepts. Like the way grass grows in the spring. Inevitable. Persisting through late cold snaps and smothering frost. Insistent on existing even when it would be easier to stay beneath the surface, dormant. Or dead.

Or they've been about things that don't matter. Like the first time I went swimming. How, when I went beneath the water and all the sound—children laughing, Lake Michigan waves lapping at the shore, seagulls crying for food—disappeared, I panicked. I came up from under the surface terrified, screaming just to make sure I could still hear myself.

"Get going," Dr. Leery says. "I want to see pens moving. This is for participation points."

I stare at my notebook. What don't I want to talk about? What don't I want to tell people about?

Everything.
Ella.
My parents.
Eric.
Shush.
I latch onto something there. A feeling. An image.
One true sentence.
I set about putting it on paper.

∾

Monday night I don't sleep.
I stare at the ceiling and plan for tomorrow. For Calculus.
For class with Eric. For after that, when my Biology professor has office hours and I can go plead my case. She wasn't in her office after Creative Writing. I have to wait. I have to worry about this for another day.

When my eyes finally close, I still don't sleep. I dream. I chase myself around in the dark, running in circles until my lungs burn for air and my legs collapse beneath me. Sometimes I'm the princess, running from a dragon, breathing fire down my back. And sometimes I'm the dragon, burning the forest down, burning myself alive.

When the morning comes, I'm more exhausted than when I went to bed.

TWENTY-FOUR

I get to Calculus and stop outside the door, staring at a nearby bulletin board and sipping coffee from my travel mug without reading any of the flyers on the board. I don't want to go in yet.

I haven't spoken to Ella at all since I told her about Jake and Greg. Every time I pull out my phone to text her, I put it away again without sending anything. I can't figure out what to say. How to apologize. How to explain I was never supposed to tell her. How to explain I betrayed Jake and hurt her at the same time. How to ask for her help—please don't tell him you know he's gay—and her forgiveness at the same time.

I'm practically going to be sitting between them. If I'm still sitting in my usual place at all. Once I walk into the room, I'm going to have to decide whether or not I can still sit next to Ella.

I don't even know if she's in there yet. I don't know—

"Hey Kara." The familiar voice makes me turn my head.

"Hey Jake."

He comes up to me, carrying his own coffee mug. He pauses awkwardly a few feet away and takes a sip from it. Then he glances around at the other students in the hallway and moves closer. "So listen," he says, keeping his voice

210

quiet. "About… about the party."

I've never seen him look awkward like this, unsure, shifting from foot to foot. I don't know what to say to him. If I should pretend I never told Ella or if I should just tell him I'm sorry and get it out of the way. At least then if it's going to make him hate me, I'll know right away. I won't have to worry about the possibilities of the unknown.

"Ella knows," I say. He presses his lips together in a hard line and for a second I think he's going to be angry with me. But then he shrugs.

"Yeah I figured."

"I'm sorry."

He shrugs again. I take a sip of my coffee and look away from him. When I look back, he still looks uncomfortable.

"Listen, we don't… you could have told us."

"Yeah I just, I've had people ditch me before," he says. "Or preach at me. Sometimes I just don't want to deal with it."

I nod. "Makes sense."

"So, uh… friends?" He extends his coffee mug towards me, a half smile on his lips. And in spite of everything, I cough out a laugh, and clink my mug with his.

"Friends."

He nods, his smile widening, and starts to walk towards the classroom door. When I don't follow, he turns back, giving me a quizzical look.

"You coming?"

I sigh. "Yeah."

Not much choice.

I follow him in, and when I see Ella isn't even here yet, I roll my eyes at my own ridiculousness. After a split second of hesitation, I sit in my usual seat. I'll take that step first. Show Ella I still want to be here. That I'm here for her now. I wasn't before but I am now.

I shift in my chair, feeling the marks of my investigation crying out as my jeans rub against them, as my skin stretches with the movement, opening them again. My search went longer than it usually does. I've never had so many lines of questioning open at once, organized in neat rows down the inside of my left thigh.

But I've never had as many questions as I do right now. Questions about Eric. Questions about Shush. Questions about me.

Ella walks in, pulling me out of my head, and I tense. She pauses, glancing from me to Jake.

Oh no.

She isn't going to sit by me. She's going to find another seat. She's going to find another friend. I want to get up and pull her down next to me.

She has to talk to me.

She has to.

I figured it out last night, while I wasn't sleeping. I figured out how to pacify my mom since I definitely can't invite Shush to dinner. If I show up with another friend, maybe that will help set my parents' minds at ease. I can hold Ella up in front of me, bright and shiny, and say, See? I'm normal. I'm happy. I have friends. I have happy fairy-tale princess friends who are happy.

Ella has to come with me.

She has to talk to me.

Finally, she comes over and sits down in her usual spot.

I sag into my chair with relief.

"Morning Ella," says Jake.

"Morning," she says, and I notice it's missing its usual bubbliness.

"Hey." My voice is so soft I think she might not hear me at first. I don't want to push too hard. Don't want to scare her away.

She turns and meets my gaze. I search her face, trying to figure out what she's feeling. There's a bit of hardness to her gaze, something that isn't usually there. I'm not sure if it's anger though, or just a bit of a shield. Something she needs to get through the day.

I open my mouth and close it again. What should I say? I move my foot, just a little, under the table, until it's touching hers.

Sorry, I mouth, and feel a little lighter.

For a second there's nothing, and I start to panic.

What if she doesn't forgive me? What if I have to start avoiding another person who used to be my friend? What if I've ruined everything?

But then she presses her foot against mine, and the corner of her mouth crooks up in a smile.

She's forgiven me.

Jake turns to talk to someone else, and I lean in closer to Ella. "You okay?"

"I'm okay," she says. "I'll get over it." I'm not sure if she's talking about what I did or the fact that Jake's gay.

"You sure?"

"Yeah," she says, and even though her smile is forced, I think she will be. "It's fine. I'll... I'm glad he's happy. We can just be friends."

"He didn't know how we'd take it," I say.

She nods. "Yeah. I know."

I glance at the clock. Class is going to start any minute. I hurry to spit out my question. I don't want to spend all of class wondering about her answer.

"Hey, umm, do you have plans later?" I ask.

"What's up?"

"My parents are in town. They want to take me out to dinner. Want to come?"

Dr. Howards walks in. Ella turns to me and whispers, "Sure. I'll come."

I reach out and curl my fingers around her wrist.

"Thank you," I say. And I mean it.

"Good morning everyone," says Dr. Howards. "Let's get started."

∿

"You look stressed," Tom says.

I look away from my library computer screen and turn to him.

"Huh?"

"What's up?" His voice is pleasant, casual but caring. He's offering a hand but not pushing it on me.

Twisting in my chair, I look at him. We don't talk a lot, but we've always shared the easy comradery of coworkers. Tom is solid. Quiet and steady. Like one of the bookshelves.

I take a breath. I don't have anything to lose.

"You ever have Dr. Nelson?"

He nods. "Yup. Last year."

"Any chance she's going to let me swap project partners?"

He purses his lips, wincing and shaking his head. "Got a bad one huh?"

"You could say that."

"She's a stickler for that kind of thing. Thinks we all have to learn to work with people in the real world or something like that."

I feel a weight settling over my shoulders. She isn't going to let me switch. I'm going to have to work with Shush.

"Can't hurt to ask though," he says, offering me the tiniest amount of hope to hang onto.

"Yeah." I force a smile, because even though Tom seems

understanding, if I crumble into pieces at the thought of a Biology project, he's going to think I'm crazy. And I'm not. I'm fine.

"Figure out a logical reason to give her," he says. "Like it's going to hurt your learning experience."

This time, my smile is at least partially real. "Thanks."

A student comes up and I turn to help them check out their books, effectively ending the conversation. Tom doesn't try to strike it up again, and I'm grateful. Because all I can do is rehearse variations of my conversation with my professor in my head.

I have to get out of doing this project with Shush.

I have to.

~

I'm sitting at my usual table, alone in the classroom, waiting. Waiting for class to start. Waiting for Eric.

Everything is still.

I can feel the word pressing into my forehead.

FUCK

Students are coming in around me and I know I need to sit up, lift my head from the table. I need to not look like I'm about to fall apart.

But I can't gather the strength.

Because Dr. Nelson said no.

She isn't going to let me switch partners. I have to work with Shush.

FUCK

I wonder if I leave my head here long enough, will it leave an impression in my forehead?

Focus.

Sit up.

One thing at a time.

Just get through this class.

Worry about Shush later.

You can do it.

Sit. Up.

I manage to pull myself upright just as Eric walks into the room, and I must have a look on my face, because his gaze meets mine, and I see a flash of concern cross his features.

Oh.

It's like a calming, warm hand on my back, helping hold me up.

He still cares.

Then he looks away and starts the class, and I can't feel his hand anymore.

I feel Adam's mouth on my neck. I scratch at my skin, trying to rid myself of the feeling.

Guilt runs through me, thick and strong. I want to apologize. I grip the edges of my chair to keep myself in place. To keep myself from walking to the front of the room and kneeling at his feet.

I'm sorry, I try to say with my eyes. If only he would look at me again.

I should never have done it. I should never have betrayed him like that.

I don't understand, I want to tell him. I don't understand why I did it. It wasn't me. I'm not that person.

I'm not.

Shush's hurt gaze flashes in my head and I feel the guilt run stronger.

Keep it together.

It's not my fault. It's not.

And suddenly I can't look at Eric anymore. He's going to see it. He's going to see this other person on my face. Party Kara. Cruel Kara. And if he sees her, he's never going to want me back.

Come on Kara.

You're fine.

Be fine.

Do not fall apart now.

After this, I have to get ready for dinner with my parents. I have to figure out what to say so they don't get suspicious about Shush not being there. I have to put on my Fine Kara mask.

It's hard. It's hard because all I want to do is let Eric see how exhausted I am. He'll come for me then. A prince has to rescue a princess when she's in danger. It's in his nature.

I've been trying for weeks to hold it together in front of him, to show him I can handle everything that's going on. That I'm strong enough to deal with the fallout of our relationship, I'm strong enough for him to take me back.

Just keep it together, I tell myself.

Just a little while longer.

I don't have to deal with Shush. Not yet.

I have to get through dinner with my parents first. One thing at a time. Just take it one thing at a time. I don't have to do it all at once.

I don't have to fight both battles at once.

It's fine.

I'll be fine.

I am fine.

Eric still won't look at me and I try to tell myself that's a good thing. Maybe he senses that if he meets my gaze, if he gives me any sign his arms are open to me, I'll fall apart. I'll let everything fall apart because he'll be there to hold me up.

Except he can't get me through tonight. I have to do that on my own.

So I can't fall apart now.

I have to make it until the end of class. Just a little while longer. I have to find something to distract myself.

I flip the page in my notebook back, back to what I wrote yesterday in Creative Writing.

I pick up my pen and slowly start to color over the words, burying them with more ink. Line by line, I fill in the entire page with black.

I bury the lines where I described the tail, long and muscular, with deadly spines running its length. The lines where I described the wings, massive and strong enough to knock down stone walls. The lines where I described the scales, black and glittering, and hard as stone. The lines where I described the claws, each one as long as my hand. The lines where I described the teeth, ready to rip apart flesh.

And the lines where I described the eyes.

Not black and stormy, like Shush's.

But blue, so pale they're nearly transparent.

My eyes.

It's not my fault, I tell myself as I bury the last of the words.

I'm not the dragon.

It's Shush.

She's the dragon.

She's the one that tore my life apart.

I'm fine.

TWENTY-FIVE

For the millionth time in the last hour, I open my phone to Shush's text message.

We have to meet about bio. Tomorrow?

I stare at the blinking cursor, trying to figure out what to say back. I haven't sent Shush a text in ages, the screen of our conversation is all one-sided, all her pleas for me to talk to her again. Now even those have stopped.

I have to text her back. I don't have a choice. Since Dr. Nelson won't let me change partners, there's only one good way to go about this. Meet with Shush exactly once, divide all the work between us, and never meet again.

Not ideal but I can survive it. Probably. My fingers hesitate over my screen.

"When are they supposed to get here?" Ella asks.

I glance over at where she's sitting at my desk, legs pulled up under her, scrolling through her phone.

We're waiting for my parents to arrive and take us to dinner.

"Soon," I say.

She nods, and that's when I notice her expression.

She's still scrolling through her phone but I bet she isn't

seeing anything on it. There's a dreamy look on her face that says she's a million miles away. I don't get it. The whole Jake-is-gay thing *just* happened. But the look on her face says she's definitely imagining a new prince.

Shush can wait. I'd much rather hear about Ella's new fairy tale than set a time to face down my dragon.

Leaning forward on my bed, I poke her in the knee with one finger. "Okay. Spill."

She jumps a little, looking up at me. "What?"

"You've got that look on your face."

"What look?" she asks, but even as she says it, her face turns a light shade of pink.

"Like you're twirling in a sparkling fairy dress under a full moon with a tall handsome guy that's got a sword at his belt."

She looks down at her phone and her face gets even redder.

"A new guy?" I ask.

"I mean… maybe."

This will be nice. A little reprieve from my own stresses. "Tell me about him."

Ella hesitates, which is a little strange, since she was always more than happy to talk about Jake. Maybe she's a little gun-shy after what happened with him. I give her time to decide, not wanting to pressure her. People should be able to keep secrets if they want to.

"Okay," Ella says finally. "He's… he's in one of my classes. And I think… I think maybe he's flirting with me."

"What's he like?"

"Smart. And funny. And absolutely gorgeous." She actually giggles and I feel something like a smile on my own lips as I remember what it's like to be that happy.

You're magic.

"I think he was flirting with me yesterday," Ella says. "And maybe kind of before too, except then I was kind of into Jake."

"That's great." I don't have to force it. I don't. I'm happy for her. I'm happy for her because I'm fine. Fine people are happy for their friends. And I'm fine.

I'm fine.

"What are you going to do?" I ask.

She frowns, chewing on her bottom lip. "I don't know. Wait, I guess? Flirt back? See what he does?"

"Let me know if you need to set up another casual encounter."

She laughs, her face growing red again. "I don't think I'll need that."

"Tell me—"

My phone starts ringing and I don't get a chance to ask anything else.

"Hey Mom," I answer. "We'll be right down."

Ella jumps up and we grab our coats. "Later?" I say to her.

"Later."

We head down to meet my mom and dad and I spend the small amount of time it takes to walk down the stairs and out into the parking lot forcing my mask into place.

I'm fine.

I can do this.

It's not that I hate my parents. I love them. Most days, I even *like* them. I don't know if I would say I'm particularly close with either one of them—I never went running to them when I had a bad day at school or when a guy broke up with me—but we get along well. In general, I enjoy spending time with them. We have an easy, simple relationship. We *had* one anyway.

I decided a long time ago my parents didn't need to know the more complicated parts of my life. My prayers. My notes. My investigations. It would only make them worry. They'd want me to explain, to give them answers I don't have. They'd want to take me to doctors and make me see a therapist. Parents are better left in the dark. In fact, I think relationships between parents and their kids should always involve a fair amount of secrecy. I don't need to know about their sexual history or hear about that time they smoked weed in high school. And they don't need to know about my sexual present or the fact that I got drunk last weekend. They provide for me and in turn I give them happiness and pride. It was always so simple.

Until it wasn't.

Until Shush broke everything.

I'm fine, I tell myself as we push out the front door into the bracing chill of the winter air.

I can do this.

I'm fine.

"Hi sweetheart." My mom's voice is cheery as she greets me in the parking lot, just a little too bright. She wraps me in a hug, which I return, careful to apply pressure so she knows I'm actually responding to her embrace, not suffering through it.

"Hi Mom." When she releases me, I force a smile onto my face. "This is Ella."

"Hello Mrs. Winterson," Ella says, reaching out a hand for her to shake.

"It's nice to meet you Ella. Glad you could join us."

My mom looks over my shoulder, like she's expecting someone to come out the door behind us. "So do we need to go pick up Shush?"

I steel myself. The first hurdle.

"She's got a test tomorrow so she can't come." I put a little sadness in my voice, as if I'm disappointed she can't make it. "She's got to study."

My mom hesitates for a second, but then I see her make

the choice to think nothing is wrong and she smiles. "Of course honey. I understand."

I get in the backseat of the car and say hi to my dad, who's driving. Ella gets in next to me.

"Nice to meet you Mr. Winterson," she says, and then leans in close to me. "Shush?" she whispers in my ear.

I squeeze her wrist. "Later."

I still haven't explained what went on at the party and she's kind of dropped it, in the midst of learning Jake's gay and getting over that. Maybe her new guy will distract her so she drops this too.

On the drive to the restaurant, everything seems almost normal. Normally I hate small talk. I hate it when people talk about things that don't matter in order to avoid talking about things that do. I don't understand making conversation for the sake of conversation. But when you're trying to pretend you're fine, small talk is necessary. People expect it. If you don't talk, they ask why you're quiet, they assume something is wrong. So I start the small talk.

I ask my parents about work. About the neighbors. About their drive up. Anything except all the things I can feel going unsaid. And my parents participate in the charade with ease. They ask questions about our classes and we tell them about what we're studying. They ask Ella all sorts of questions about where she's from and what her interests are. They're delighted to hear she's helping me with math and Ella avoids telling them I failed my test last week. The drive to the restaurant goes so smoothly I start to think the whole thing will be okay.

It isn't until we're at the restaurant and everyone has ordered that it starts to go sideways.

"So how's Shush?" my mom asks, taking a sip from her wine glass after we all hand our menus back to the waiter.

"I'm sorry she couldn't make it tonight. I was looking forward to seeing her."

"Not that we aren't happy to meet you of course," my dad rushes to reassure Ella.

"Oh of course, of course," says my mom. "It's just we haven't heard you talk about Shush much lately. And we like to keep up with *all* your friends."

She takes a sip of her wine and looks at me expectantly.

Here we go.

Keep it together

You're fine.

Ella glances sideways at me and I will her to keep her mouth shut and her expression innocuous. I should have briefed her about what was going on with my parents and Shush, should have told her to help me steer the conversation away from this topic. But then she would have asked questions. She would have wanted to know what happened between me and Shush.

And I can't tell her that.

Ella is still looking at me so I reach my foot over and press my heel down into her toe until she gets the message and looks away.

"Oh Shush is good," I say. "A bit stressed with all the work she's got going on at the newspaper right now, but she loves it." I can't make everything seem too rosy or my mom will suspect something.

That was good.

My voice sounded normal.

I'm doing fine.

I'm fine.

"Well with all the news lately, I can't blame her," my dad says.

Seizing the opportunity, I bring up the latest scandal

224

from the news cycle, quickly changing the topic. "Have you heard he's still lying about the crowd at his inauguration?" "It's such a ridiculous thing to lie about," says Ella. My dad shakes his head. "Not if you're a narcissist. He wants everyone to think he's incredibly popular. He doesn't want people to remember he lost the popular vote by three million votes."

"Do we really have to talk politics?" asks my mom.

"Politics are everything," I say, and it's Shush's words in my mouth. "Politics are people's lives."

"Maybe if more people talked politics and more people participated, our democracy would function a little more like a democracy," says my dad.

"Maybe." My mom takes another sip of her wine and turns to me. "Anyway. Have you picked a major yet?"

I'd rather talk about politics.

"Not yet."

"When do you need to declare by?" asks my dad. I shrug in response. Being grilled on my decisions isn't really what I want to happen right now.

"Did you hear we're supposed to get a big storm next weekend?" I say. Please go for the subject change. Come on. My question hangs in the air but then my mom answers.

"Yeah ten inches of snow. Maybe a foot in some places."

"You know," says Ella, "I have relatives in the UP. Up there when you visit someone, you take a couple days' worth of clothes, just in case you end up getting snowed in."

The conversation spins from there and then the food comes. Everything seems like it's going to be fine. No more hard topics come up and I'm doing alright with my small talk. Again, I let myself think the night might be okay. I let myself buy into the hope that everything won't fall apart around me.

It's all going to be okay.
I try to ignore the looks that occasionally pass between my mom and dad. The way my mom keeps looking at me when she thinks I'm not paying attention. As if she's waiting for me to break.
I tell myself everything is fine, hoping if I believe it hard enough, it will be true.
And it lasts a good long while. The fine-ness.
I think I'm actually going to make it through dinner unscathed, think my Fine Kara mask is actually going to hold up.
Until the end.
We've eaten our main courses, kept the conversation on safe topics, even laughed a little. We're nearly finished with dessert. The waiter is probably going to be bringing the check any second. I'm almost to the end.
And then Shush walks in.

TWENTY-SIX

At first, I think I must be wrong. It's just that I'm thinking about her all the time now. That can't actually be her walking through the door in front of a few other students, smiling at the hostess and asking for a table.

It can't be.

But it is.

Shush.

I shrink a little in my chair.

I don't understand.

How can she be here? How can she be here right *now*?

My questions shrink behind the urge to hide under the table. To get up and run to the bathroom. To do something, anything to prevent her from seeing me.

You can't avoid me forever.

Please, don't bring her this way, I pray to the hostess. Take them to the other side of the restaurant. We don't have to make it long without running into each other. Just another twenty minutes. Until we finish dessert. Until my parents pay the check. Until we get out of here. Please not this way. Not this way, not this way, not this—

The hostess starts leading them straight for us.

Oh no.

What am I supposed to do?

My parents still think we're best friends. And maybe, before this past weekend, Shush would have played along because she still cared about me. Even after what she'd done to destabilize my relationship with my parents, she would maybe have at least tried to not make it worse.

But *after* the party?

You're what's wrong with me.

Leave me the fuck alone.

I never want to speak to you again.

Enjoy the spotlight.

There's no way she's going to try to help me now. I haven't even texted her back about meeting tomorrow. For all she knows, I'm planning to leave all the work to her.

Shush sees me and her steps falter, the smile fading from her face. The person behind her bumps into her and she starts walking towards us again. My dad is saying something to me but I have no idea what. All I can see is Shush, coming closer with each step.

I think, just for a second, that she'll keep going. That she'll walk right past our table without saying a word. I hope, just for a second, it will be fine.

And then my mom sees her.

"Shush," she exclaims, a smile bursting onto her face. "Honey how are you?"

"Hi Mrs. Winterson," Shush says, taking a step towards my mother and then turning to her friends. "I'll be right there." They move off without her, going to a table on the far side of the room.

This can't be happening.

I look from Shush, to my parents, and back again.

In all the ways I pictured tonight going horribly wrong—and there were a lot of them—this scenario never occurred to me. I hadn't imagined she would show up randomly at the restaurant.

This is worse than all the things I'd imagined.

Shush looks at me and I try to scream at her—tell her to leave—without saying anything at all. She hears me. I know she does.

But she stays anyway.

She always does what *she* wants.

"How are you Shush?" my dad asks. "Kara told us you were busy tonight. That you couldn't make it."

Shush turns to look at me, a smile on her lips but a hardness in her eyes that makes a cold jolt of fear shoot up my spine. "Did she?"

She's going to ruin it.

The fragile, fine world I've built for my parents.

She's going to tear it all down.

All she has to do is say, *Oh she didn't tell me you were coming.* And they'd both know I was lying to them about tonight. They'd both know something is wrong. They might even realize I've been lying to them for months about still being friends with her.

Don't do it Shush, I try to plead with her through my eyes while keeping my face a pleasant mask. Please please please don't do it. Please.

Ella taps my foot with hers under the table and I glance at her. She furrows her brow slightly, asking me what the hell is going on without saying a word.

I wonder if she can see the panic in my eyes.

Come on Kara, keep it together.

I try to push my Fine Kara mask back into place.

"Yeah Shush," I say. "I um, I thought you were busy studying for that test?"

Take the hint Shush.

Take it and leave.

Don't turn on me.

Just be on my side for once.

Help me.

She stares back at me and I can feel her making the decision. It feels like her claws curled around my neck, the pressure just light enough to make sure I know she's in complete control of deciding whether or not she shreds my skin or lets me go.

"I was," Shush says after a beat, and a relaxing wave of relief washes through me. But then there's silence.

And I can feel all my parents' questions surging up to fill it.

Say something. I have to say something or they're going to ask a question I don't want Shush to answer. She'll tell the truth. Whatever they ask, she'll tell the truth. I know she will.

I have to say something.

But what do I say?

I scramble but I'm coming up empty.

I don't have any words.

Come on Kara.

Say something.

Say—

"I liked your article Shush," says Ella. "About the Women's March."

Oh no.

She's only trying to help but she's said exactly the wrong thing.

"Thank you," says Shush.

"That school paper of yours has been making quite a splash," says my mom.

"We read about it in the city paper," says my dad. "When that anonymous story about the professor was published."

I rub my hand over my thigh. I prayed this morning. Pain, pain, pain. Please, please, please let this end.

This is exactly where the conversation shouldn't go.

"Is it true?" my mom asks, and there's a little concern in her voice.

"I always err on the side of believing women," says Shush, a hard layer under her light tone.

"Oh of course," says my mom. "I just… I'm sure that kind of thing doesn't happen here. That… that kind of thing happens at bigger universities."

Shush's voice loses some of its lightness. "Sexual predators exist everywhere Mrs. Winterson. Being a smaller college doesn't keep bad things away from here." She looks right at me, and I feel her claws digging a little deeper into my neck. "It just means people all know each other. So they don't want to admit it when someone does something terrible."

I want to be angry. I want to be furious at her for dangling her Lie over my head like a threat. Like she's thinking about telling my parents.

But I can't feel anything except fear.

Please let this end.

I don't know who I'm praying to but I send it up to whatever is listening, pressing the heel of my palm into my thigh until the separate stinging pains turn into one large ache.

Please let this be over.

"Do you know who wrote it?" Ella asks, leaning forward and pulling Shush's gaze away from me. The hint of eagerness in her tone makes me sick to my stomach.

Shush glances at me, a slight look of surprise on her face. I can tell she thought I would have told Ella all of this. Or at least some of it. Enough to make Ella hate her the way I hate her. But how can I tell Ella anything? I can't betray Eric. I won't.

I don't betray the people I care about. I'm not Shush.

"It was submitted anonymously," Shush tells Ella.

"So there's no way to know if it's actually true," Ella says, and I look at her. This is a different point of view than she had when the article first came out. Back then she was just determined to figure out which professor it was talking about.

I want to agree but I don't want to push Shush any farther. She already looks like she's on the verge of telling everyone she's the one that wrote it. Maybe she can put up with everyone else pushing back against her but if I do it, it will be different. It will push her too far.

I don't say anything, barely moving, as if any movement from me will be too much.

"Just because people don't want to be dragged into the spotlight and through the mud doesn't mean they're lying," says my dad.

"Exactly. Thank you," says Shush.

"Do we really have to keep talking about this?" asks my mom, putting her fork down a bit too hard on the table. "At dinner?"

"It's him that would be dragged through the mud," says Ella. "Not her."

"Do you really think that?" asks Shush, her voice raising a bit. I can hear her getting ready to step up on her soap box. "After everything that happened with the election?"

"Oh Shush, let's not bring politics into it. We were having a nice dinner," says my mom.

"There are still people that don't believe it," says Ella.

"Them," Shush corrects. "People that don't believe *them*. Over twenty women."

"I'm curious," says my dad, "why do you think that is?"

"People believe what they want to believe," says Shush. "They don't like to see bad things, even when those bad things are right in front of them."

She looks from my parents and back to me.

I freeze, pinned.

She sees it.

No one else sees it, but she does.

The edges of the mask.

Fine Kara.

She knows it's all a lie.

I lean slightly away from her, as if she's going to reach out any second and dig her claws under the edges of it. Rip it off. Reveal me to everyone.

How do I get her to leave? I have to get her out of here. Before she decides to stop playing nice.

"Hi," says a waiter, coming up to our table. "Will I get you another chair?"

No. She doesn't need a chair. She isn't staying. Leave Shush. Tell them you have to leave. Just end this already.

She holds my gaze for another long second, torturing me, and then smiles at the waiter. "No, thank you." She turns back to my parents. "I've got to get back to my friends. It was nice seeing you Mr. and Mrs. Winterson. Ella. Kara. I'll talk to you later."

Part of me wants to be grateful, as she walks away, that she implied in front of my parents we're going to be hanging out later. But there's still a cold knot tightening in my chest.

You can't avoid me forever.

I'll talk to you later.

It isn't an olive branch. It's a threat.

"Well that was… nice," says my mom, straightening in her chair. "Nice to see Shush again."

"She doesn't hold back, that one," says my dad, and there's a genuine smile on his face.

"Mark," my mom sighs, shaking her head slightly. "Can we get the check?" she asks a passing waiter. Then she looks back at all of us and forces a smile. "I don't know about you, but I thought that chocolate cake was delicious."

I unclench my jaw in an effort to smile back at her, and the taste of blood blossoms on my tongue. I hadn't realized I was biting the inside of my cheek so hard I broke the skin. The ride home is awkward. My dad tries, talking to Ella about her family, but my mom is silent. I can feel her worry, big and suffocating, in her stiff silence. I don't know what to do. I should say something but I don't know what to say. I try to interject a few words here and there into my dad and Ella's conversation, but they sound hollow to my ears. Like I'm faking.

Come on Kara, keep it together.

You're almost there. Almost fine.

After we drop off Ella, the car falls silent. My dad drives back to my building and stops the car. I want to get out and run inside, where they can't reach me. But the night isn't over yet.

Both of my parents get out of the car to hug me goodbye. First my dad, who wraps me up and kisses the top of my head.

"Hang in there," he says, and for just a second I think maybe he sees more than he lets on. But I don't have time to think about it, because then my mom hugs me, and when she pulls back, I think I'm safe.

I'm nearly back in my tower, nearly safe behind my tall stone walls.

And then my mother takes a deep breath and jumps into the freezing water she's been avoiding the whole night.

"So… so about the… about what we talked about over Christmas… You're… you're really doing okay? Right?"

The worry and hope warring in her expression could fuel a small country as they spin in circles. My dad, hanging back just slightly, meets my gaze and I can tell my mom's not the only one who's been worried.

Come on Kara, you can do this.

I just have to make them believe me. I have to make them believe me like I did that first night.

I remember how, after Shush and the parking lot and the long drive home with my mom, my parents had made me have a big talk with them. I remember how, after, my mom came around the kitchen counter and took hold of my face, one hand on each cheek. "Kara Jean, you promise me? You're okay?"

Now, standing in the parking lot outside my dorm, I take hold of her face in my hands, and I repeat the same words to her that I'd said then.

"I'm fine Mom. I promise."

I don't check my phone until I get upstairs, even though I felt it vibrate a while ago, because I know what I'm going to see.

Shush's name.

Just a simple message.

11 tomorrow, group room.

I manage to text a reply.

Ok.

And then I head for the shower.

I'm fine.

I promise.

TWENTY-SEVEN

Keep it together Kara.

I push through the library door and walk inside.

As I uncurl my fingers from around the strap of my bag, I realize I've been clenching them so tightly they've lost most of their feeling. I open and close them a few times, feeling blood flow back to the tips, bringing them back to life.

Keep it together.

I take a deep breath and start walking.

"Hey Tom," I say, waving a small hello as I go past the front desk.

Tom glances up from his computer and offers me a smile. "How's it going?"

"Good. It's good."

Lies. Lies lies lies.

If things were good, I wouldn't be walking like I'm on the way to be hanged. If things were good, I would be going to see Eric.

Instead, I have to meet Shush.

I keep going, walking slowly away from Tom and into the library, towards the group rooms. I'm not in a hurry to reach my destination, not in a rush to reach Shush. I take my time, meandering through the bookshelves. When I round the final corner, I stop in front of the group rooms and let out a breath.

She isn't here yet.

Good.

I walk instinctively into group room three. The first place I was ever alone with Eric. I imagine I can still see him, sitting there, smiling at me.

Anything else you want to ask me?

I take the same seat he was in that night. As if I'll be able to draw strength from his memory. I take out my textbook and my notebook and then glance at my phone. I still have a few minutes. I'm early. Shush is never early. Never even on time.

Breathe, I tell myself.

It's fine.

I'm fine.

Splaying my hands out flat on the table, I force myself to sit still. Force myself not to dig my fingernails into my forearms. Force myself not to reach for the sharp point of my pen, for the tip of the metal wiring in my notebook.

This morning, I spent time preparing for this meeting. I wrote down notes about the project, making a list of everything we would have to do, trying to minimize the amount of time I'd need to be alone in a room with Shush.

And I wrote notes to remind myself to keep it together.

To remind myself I'm fine.

I had to move from my hip bones to my knees. I'm running out of writing space. But the knees are nearly as good as the hips. The bone is close to the surface. In the winter, knees are always hidden and by the time spring comes, the scars will be healed and easily explained away.

It's fine.

I'm fine.

It's all going to be okay.

Come on, I tell myself, forcing a deep breath into my lungs as I watch for Shush through the clear glass wall. It's not like she's a real dragon. Even so, all I can picture is her burning me to a crisp the second she walks through the door. Opening her mouth and just burning me alive.

And then she comes around the corner.

She hesitates at the sight of me. But then she squares her shoulders, a determined look on her face, and walks towards me.

"Hey," she says, walking in, her tone light and normal.

And all my fear vanishes.

All my fear drowns under a wave of rage. Under all the anger I couldn't feel last night because we were in front of my parents and it was eclipsed by my panic.

I can't *believe* her.

She pulls up a chair and starts taking out her own things and it's all I can do not to throw my textbook at her.

She's acting like nothing has changed.

This could be last year, back when we were still friends, back before her betrayal. Before she turned my life with my parents into a lie. Before she ripped Eric away from me. Before her story made him too afraid to be with me.

Because that's what it is.

The more I've thought about it, the more certain I am that fear of Shush is why he broke up with me in the first place. He knows I'm friends with her. That I *was* friends with her. He works with her on the paper. He knows her. He must have known she wouldn't approve. Must have known she'd do anything and everything to keep us from being together, including lying. Including tearing both our lives apart.

And then she did.

She wrote that story.

All his worst fears confirmed.

Which is why he's barely looking at me.

I clench my jaw. "Let's get this over with," I say, and

there's a bite to my voice that makes her expression harden. She crosses her arms over her chest. "Fine."

It's a strange parody of all the times we used to sit together in the library and do homework. Before, we might have put on some quiet music, sharing funny social media posts to alleviate the boredom of the work we were doing. We would have lost track of time or made excuses to leave early and go to lunch.

Now, I just want to get the work done as soon as possible and get out of here.

I sit up a bit straighter, looking down at the information I'd prepared this morning. I don't want to give her the chance to take the lead, don't want to let her stretch this out any longer than it needs to be.

"I've picked a topic," I say. "I figure we divide the work and at the end you give your half of the presentation and I give mine."

"So we don't ever actually have to see each other?" Her voice drips with sarcasm.

"Obviously."

She stares me down and I fight to hold my ground. Her nostrils flare and for just a second I think I see fire swirling around the edges. But then she breaks away, rolling her eyes.

"Whatever. What topic do you want to do?"

I allow myself the smallest respite, let myself breathe for just a second. She's agreed. Good. This will be okay.

It's all going to be okay.

"Bones," I say. She arches her eyebrow at me. "I've written it all down," I tell her, ripping a piece of paper out of my notebook. I've already made up a list of the tasks. All we have to do is split them up.

For a minute, as I watch her scan what I've written, I think she's going to fight me on it. Demand we do a different topic. But then she sighs.

"This looks fine."

"Glad you're happy," I deadpan. "Pick what parts you want to do. I'll do the rest."

This is going perfectly. Well, as perfectly as it can go, considering I'm stuck in a room with Shush. Minimal talking, quick action. I'll be out of here in less than half an hour. Shush goes down the list, naming off the things she wants and copying them down into her own notebook.

It isn't until she hands me back my notebook and I start to pack all my stuff up, that she looks at me again and this time I know I'm not going to get out of here without being burned.

"God you can't even stand to be in the same room as me, can you?" There's a slight disbelief in her voice. An incredulousness that sets my blood boiling.

Good.

I need the anger.

It's a shield keeping everything else from getting in.

"No," I say simply. I get to my feet and turn around before she can say anything else, reaching for the door handle. I'm not going to stick around and let her lecture me.

Fuck.

The door doesn't open. Group room three.

Shush laughs—actually laughs—out loud. "Oh my god."

I don't wait. I pull out my phone and text Tom.

Stuck in GR3. Come get me out?

"Oh come on," Shush says. "You have to admit that's hilarious."

I sense it, as her laughter dies down.

Danger.

Silence seeps into the room, filling with all the things we aren't saying to each other. Shush doesn't do well with silence. With not saying what's on her mind.

240

I'm not going to escape unscathed.

But even though I'm bracing for it, gathering my rage around me brick by brick to keep me safe, her attack still manages to knock the air from my lungs.

"Are you still cutting?"

My gaze shoots up and locks with hers. She calmly stares me down, her expression expectant, awaiting an answer. As if this is something we talk about all the time. As if she just asked me if I was still reading a particular book.

And just the question, just the words, hanging in the air, so bold in their simplicity, knock all my walls to pieces.

Are you still cutting?

I'm defenseless. Naked. Caught.

I press back into the wall, praying for Tom to get here so I can escape.

Because I can't do this.

I can't I can't I can't.

She can't ask me these things.

She was never supposed to know.

I never told her. I never told anyone. The only people who had ever seen my scars were the guys I'd been with, and they found out by default. When you want to talk the language of skin, you can't help but read the secrets I've written there.

Shush found out by accident. She's always barging through doors without waiting to be invited.

When she walked in on me, I was naked.

That, in and of itself, was bad.

I'm not a person who lets other people see me naked. I never change my clothes in front of my mother or in front of other female friends. I've never changed in front of Shush, even though she's changed in front of me. When your skin is etched with prayers in a language you know no one will understand, you keep it hidden.

When she walked in on me, I was naked. But I wasn't *just* naked, standing there so she could see my scars. That might have been better. If you have to see something that scares you, it's always easier to see it already complete, rather than see the creation of it. It's easier to see the ghost than to witness the murder.

I can't even remember why I was cutting that day. I can't remember why I wasn't in the shower like I usually am. I might have been in a hurry or having a bad day. But when she walked in on me, my foot was up on my desk chair.

And I had a silver razor blade held between two fingers, halfway through writing a prayer on the skin of my thigh.

I think it was the first time I ever saw her speechless.

Immediately, I ran to the door—which she was still holding open, frozen in place—and pushed it shut. I put the blade back into its box, as if hiding it would make her forget what she'd seen. I rushed to pull on a pair of sweats, a shirt, to hide my naked skin from her shocked gaze.

Only then, when she could no longer see the evidence of what I'd done, did I finally meet her gaze. Only then did I say something.

"Shush it's not what you think."

Her voice escaped her like a breath she'd been holding, all at once in a soft woosh. "Oh my god Kara."

She looked at me like I was a stranger. She looked at me exactly the way I knew she would. Not just as if I was a friend hiding a secret or even a person she thought she knew and found out she didn't, but as if I was an entirely different species.

The silence stretched between us for a long moment as we stared at each other. All I wanted was to go back in time, to lock my stupid door. All I wanted was for her to forget what she'd seen.

"Look…" I stopped then, not knowing what to say. I'd never been in this situation before. I didn't know how to explain. "Can we just pretend you never saw that?" It was a desperate plea. Even as I said it, I knew it wasn't going to happen. This was Shush. She didn't pretend. She told the truth. Even when she shouldn't.

And then she did all the things that were all the reasons I'd never told anyone.

The first thing she asked me was if I was suicidal.

"Of course not," I said. To me, the idea was ridiculous. A cliché. A stereotype.

"Is there… is there someone I should call?" She sat on my bed, looking small, looking helpless. Wide eyes and a closed mouth that somehow made her look younger, look like she didn't know what to do. It was an expression I'd never seen on her face before. "A… a doctor or a therapist?"

I leaned against the wall, crossing my arms over my chest, and shook my head.

"What about your parents?"

At this, I took a step towards her, as if I might need to physically prevent her from doing that. "Shush you can't tell them."

Her eyes widened. "They don't know?"

"They don't *need* to know."

"Kara… I… *Of course* they need to know." She was still looking at me like I was something she didn't recognize.

"Shush please." I had to make her understand. I could hear the tinge of desperation in my words. I'd spent my whole life keeping my parents in the dark about this one thing. I couldn't let her change that now. "Shush you can't tell them."

She stared at me for a long time then. I could see the wheels working behind her eyes, trying to figure out what to do, trying to figure out what to say. Finally, she spoke, and then she said just a single word.

"Why?"

"It'll just make them worry."

"No... Kara. I mean... *why?*"

I knew what she was asking. But I didn't know how to explain it. I'd never known how to explain it. Not in a language she would be able to hear.

"You won't understand," I told her. Taking her hands between mine, I looked her straight in the face. She had to understand at least this part. "Shush, promise me you won't tell anyone. Promise me you won't tell my parents."

She hesitated, but she—eventually—nodded, and when I pressed, she agreed out loud. "I promise."

But she didn't let the subject drop. She pestered me for weeks to talk to her. She said if she couldn't tell my parents and I didn't want her to take me to the campus counseling center, then I had to at least talk to *her* about it. She even threatened to report it to her supervisor, which, technically as my RA, she was supposed to do.

But I couldn't talk about it.

I stare back at her now, trapped in the group room in the library, incredulous that she would ask me that now, after everything she'd done.

Are you still cutting?

She has no right.

To ask me that as if we're still friends.

To ask me that at all.

But I should have expected it.

After she first found out, it took me a few weeks to realize she wasn't going to give this up. In the midst of all her politics and her journalism, I was her new mission. I'd thought maybe if I gave her time, she would move past it, but she didn't. Any time we were alone together, she eventually brought it up. Asking me if I was still doing it. Asking me why I'd started. Asking me to talk to her about it.

When Winter Break finally rolled around, I was grateful. I knew I was going to have to slip out of my friendship with Shush, and I was hoping I could do it as easily as we had entered into it.

I'd been pulling away for weeks, spending more time on my own, refusing some of her invitations to hang out and not offering any of my own. I planned on ignoring her for Winter Break and hoping she got the message.

But she just couldn't leave well enough alone.

Just like now.

"How…" I'm not sure what question I was going to ask but it dies in my throat. I swallow, hard, and straighten, grasping back some of my anger. "We aren't friends anymore Shush."

"Kara—"

"No," I cut her off. "We. Are. Not. Friends."

Her look of concern morphs into one of stubbornness. "I'm not going to apologize for what I did. It was the right thing. I did the right thing."

I shake my head. Because she's wrong.

She's so wrong.

She's ruined everything.

When my mother came to pick me up for Winter Break, I should have guarded her. I should have never let her leave my sight. Shush wasn't supposed to be there. Even though I trusted Shush to keep her promise not to tell, I knew my mother would sense the wrongness wafting off her.

I knew she would ask questions. Questions Shush would answer whether or not she opened her mouth to actually speak.

I packed up everything I wanted to take home before my mom showed up, so when she arrived all I had to do was take my bags and meet her at the car. I wanted a quick exit. But then I forgot my purse in my dorm room and I left my mom waiting outside in the car. I was only gone for a minute. Just a minute.

When I came down, Shush was with her.

And my mother was looking at me as if she'd seen a ghost.

As if *I* was a ghost.

As if I was a monster.

As if I scared her.

I looked at Shush, and I knew. She'd told. She'd broken her promise.

She'd betrayed me.

And as she walked past me, leaving me in the parking lot with my mom, she didn't even apologize. "Eventually you'll forgive me," she said.

And I couldn't say anything. Didn't know what to say. Just like now.

At my silence, Shush leans forward over the table, her presence suffocatingly large in the small group room. "Kara you can still talk to me. Just tell me. Are you still cutting?"

I don't say a word.

I can't lie, because she'll know.

But I'm not going to talk to her about this.

Not back when we were still friends. Not now. Not ever.

Cutting is mine.

It belongs to me.

She wouldn't understand and I have no obligation to tell her about it anyway. It's my business.

She can stay out of it.

My phone buzzes in my hand. Tom texting me back.

On the way

I breathe a sigh of relief and lean against the wall, putting myself as far away from Shush as possible. She's still looking at me. I can feel her gaze burning a hole into my face. But I keep my eyes trained on my phone, staring at Tom's text message. He'll be here soon. I don't have to put up with this much longer.

I can do this.

I'm fine.

"Oh fuck you," Shush says, obviously exasperated.

At this, I can't help but look up. She's glaring at me, sitting rigidly in her chair.

"God Kara, what's your problem?"

I open my mouth. *My* problem? My *problem*?

After everything she's done, she has the audacity to pretend she doesn't know why I can't stand to be around her?

"Come on Kara, say it. Say *something*. Or do you need a little alcohol to tell me how you really feel?"

The dig hurts, but not nearly as much as the rest of what she's done to me. I press my lips together, refusing to give in to her goading. I'm not sure what I'd say even if I did want to speak to her. I glance at the door.

Come on Tom.

"You're not going to make me feel bad for trying to help you."

I probably could have taken it if she stopped there. I know she thinks she's trying to help me. Even if she's wrong, I know that's what she thinks. And somewhere inside me there's still the girl who stayed up all night comforting Shush as she cried and raged the night after the election.

I could have taken it if she stopped there.

But she didn't.

"You're not going to make me feel bad for telling the truth," she says.

White-hot rage lances through me. When I speak my words come out hard and razor-blade-sharp.

"The *truth*?" I feel like I could spit fire. I take a step towards her. "You don't *know* the truth Shush! You *can't* tell it!"

"I told your mother the truth," she says stubbornly.

I shake my head, pulling at my hair.

She doesn't know.

She doesn't know anything.

"I told the truth to your mother," she says. "And I told the truth about *him*."

"Jesus Christ Shush, you—"

"I told the truth!" She's on her feet now, leaning on both hands across the table, like she might jump across it and attack me. "I told. The *truth*."

"You don't know the truth Shush! You don't know anything about me and Eric! You—"

"It's not about you!"

I stop, frowning. I don't understand.

I thought she'd taken the details I'd given her about Eric—before she knew I was talking about Eric—and twisted them into her horrible story. Twisted them into what she thought had happened between us. Twisted them into something terrible.

"What...?" I don't know how to ask the question.

"It's not *your* story Kara."

"I know that, of course I know that. Eric would never—"

"He would! He would and he did and he's not the man you think he is."

"God Shush, get over yourself," I scoff. "You're not some savior come to rescue poor little me. Eric—"

"It's *my* story Kara."

I don't understand. "What?"

"It's my story." She stands up straighter. "He did that to *me*."

Everything stops.
I'm not breathing.
I'm not feeling.
I'm not thinking.
Eric did that to me.
He's not what you think.
It's my story Kara.
He's not what you think.
Eric did that to me.
He's not what you think.
"You're..." I shake my head. "You're lying."
She has to be lying. I don't understand why she would
do this. Why she would make something up like this. Why
she would insert herself into it. I don't understand why but
she *has* to be lying. She has to be.
The door opens behind me.
Tom's voice breaks through the rushing sound in my head.
"Hey Kara. Sorry it took me so long. Locked in again huh?"
Shush is still looking at me. When she speaks her voice is
quiet, but firm. She isn't letting me escape. "Did he say you
were magic too?"
No.
You're magic.
No.
No no no.
I have to get out of here.
Did he say you were magic too?
I push past Tom.
Did he say you were magic too?
I run past the bookshelves.
Did he say you were magic too?
I run outside.
Did he say you were magic too?

I run to my dorm room.
Did he say you were magic too?
I run to my shower.
Did he say you were magic too?
I run to my blade.

TWENTY-EIGHT

The first time I had sex with Eric, we went to his house.

At first, I was nervous. He picked me up in his car off the edge of campus and when he parked inside his garage, I hesitated to get out. It felt like we'd taken a fork in the path through the woods and I couldn't see exactly where we were going.

But Eric knew.

His movements were sure and steady as he walked around the car and opened my door for me.

I trusted him.

He took my hand and helped me out, carefully, since I was wearing the only dress I owned. A light, summery thing. He pulled me inside the house and shut the door behind me, and then he lifted my hand above my head and twirled me in a circle.

"I love it," he said. "You look beautiful." He pressed me up against the closed door and kissed me until I felt my nerves melt away.

It was the first time I'd ever actually been in his house, and it was exactly like I expected. Full of books. Single bookshelves, floor to ceiling bookshelves, a small stack on his desk. The walls were filled with artwork that made me want to stop and look at it. It was his castle, through and through.

I reached out to run my fingers along his bookshelves, along the edge of a picture frame. I wanted to soak it all in through my skin. I didn't ever want to leave.

He poured us glasses of wine to drink while he made me dinner, refusing to let me help him cook. I was torn between wanting to explore his house and not wanting to leave his side. I wanted to remember it all. Every little thing.

The angle of the knife as he chopped peppers.

The exact arrangement of books on the shelves in his living room.

The way he laughed when I said something funny.

I wasn't nervous anymore. The more we talked and laughed, the more I felt like I actually was this character he thought me to be, the more I felt like I wasn't pretending. As if his belief was making me real. I was intelligent and interesting, offering smart comebacks and insightful comments. I was beautiful, the kind of girl who caught your eye from across a room and held it. I was someone worthy of a prince. I was a princess.

I never wanted the night to end. Time passed so slowly and too quickly at the same time. After dinner I helped him with the dishes—he washed and I dried—and it felt so delightfully domestic, like we'd finally started our real life together. Like we'd pulled up the drawbridge and now we had the castle all to ourselves. Exactly the way it should be.

When he kissed me he tasted of wine, a dark rich red that tasted bitter from the glass but somehow sweet from his lips.

When he kissed me, we were at the center of an enchanted forest, and no one was there but us.

When he kissed me, I felt like he wanted nothing more than to be my prince.

When he kissed me, I felt like the center of his whole world, like I was a story someone could get lost in.

I felt like a different person.
Someone whole and unbroken.
Someone new.

Someone magic.

I could have kissed him forever, pressed against his kitchen counter, but he stopped. He looked down at me, brushing my hair away from my face, as if he couldn't bear not to see every inch of me.

Then he took me by the hand and led me to the bedroom. We hadn't planned it. I hadn't come over expecting it. Except, when he stood me next to the edge of his bed, and kissed me again, I knew the night couldn't have gone any other way.

This is how the story always goes.

I knew, somewhere in the back of my mind, that I was supposed to be afraid. I'd been told this story before. Don't stray off the path Little Red Riding Hood. There are dangers waiting in the dark.

It hurts when the wolf comes in.

But his hands were warm and gentle. He went slowly, taking off my sandals first.

And I wasn't afraid. I wasn't even nervous.

Until he started to lift up my dress.

I stiffened as his hands slid up my thighs, taking the dress up with them. He stopped, coming up to kiss me softly until the tension melted from my muscles.

But my fear had nothing to do with sex.

I couldn't remember the last time I'd been naked in front of another person. Eric still didn't know the extent of the words I'd carved into my skin. If anything was going to make him turn away, it would be seeing them all at once.

He wasn't in a hurry. He took his time pulling my dress up over my head. Unhooking my bra. Sliding my underwear off my legs.

And I waited. I waited for the fear. The anger. The decision to ignore the scars he saw on my skin.

But none of that happened.

He was gentle when he pushed me back onto the bed, when he lifted me up until my head was on the pillows. Standing at the edge of the bed, he looked down at me, laying there, opened to my last blank page, spread out on his bed to read.

He might have spent a year just staring. But still, I wasn't nervous. Because of the *way* he was looking at me. As if I was the only thing he could see. The only thing he wanted to see.

He wasn't looking at me with fear. There was no pity in his gaze. No heartache as he read the book of me.

There was only fascination. Only desire.

He wasn't afraid of my scars. He wasn't afraid of me.

That was when I knew he loved me. And I loved him.

When he took off his clothes, and moved over me, my scars were the first things he kissed.

He read me out loud.

Each scar a murmured magic word, a translation from something I'd never been able to read. I closed my eyes and let his voice wash over me, memorizing each word so I could keep them forever, finally a key to understand myself.

"You're magic," he said.

Over and over.

As he kissed the scars on my thighs, my hips. As he climbed the ones I had made like a ladder up my side, moving up the rungs of my rib cage until he reached my heart.

"You're magic. Absolutely perfect magic."

Over and over.

Until I believed it.

~

I can't sleep.

Every time I close my eyes I see Eric or Shush.

I see them with me. I see them separately. I see them together.

Did he say you were magic too?

When I'm unable to resist the siren call of insomnia, unable to lash myself to the mast and listen to it while sailing past, when I must dash myself upon the rocks, there are two types of melodies I hear. The first is nebulous, vast and unknowable, like the sea. I can search and search, sail for days and weeks, dive for minutes and hours, and still I won't get to the bottom of it. The second is shallow water on a clear, sunny day. I can see straight through to the bottom, make out the exact edges of the shipwrecks beneath the waves, where I will soon join them.

It's the second melody that drives me from my bed tonight.

I know exactly what I'm doing.

I have to see him.

The need has whispered quietly under my skin for weeks and weeks. Ever since he broke up with me. Ever since Shush wrote her article. I've been ignoring it. Forcing it back down until I knew it was safe to go see him again.

But it isn't whispering anymore.

It's screaming.

Eric Eric Eric.

What do I do now?

I shove my hands deep into the pockets of my coat as I head out into the cold. Tonight the familiar paths I walk through campus are traitors, lined with words I can't stop seeing.

Eric did that to me.
You're safe with me.
Kara you have to tell someone.
You're magic.
He's not what you think.
It's all going to be okay.
Did he say you were magic too?
I can see them on the sidewalk, so thick and dark I have to step over them. I become superstitious, walking slower, taking care to only step on unbroken, blank pavement, in case something should break.
It's all going to be okay.
It's late, but there are still students walking around. I try to ignore them, but at this time of night, voices carry.
"Come on Natalie, come over."
"It's late."
"You're safe with me."
I forgot my headphones. All I want is to drown out all the words.
"But what about—"
"Hey, hey. It's all going to be okay."
I walk faster, shoving my hands deeper into my coat pockets. The cold is bitter tonight, but it isn't enough to drive out all the words in my head.
You can't avoid me forever.
Do you know the fairy tale behind the invention of the kiss?
Did he say you were magic too?
It doesn't matter. I don't care.
All I can think about is Eric.
About seeing him. About what Shush said. About what Eric said. I just want it to stop. I want it all to be quiet.
So I can sleep.
So I can breathe.

Eric will know how to fix it. He'll know how to fix me.

And I know I shouldn't be going to his house. Not now. Not this late at night. This isn't what a princess is supposed to do. This isn't waiting in my tower for him to come and call me down.

But Cinderella went to the ball. Ariel gave away her voice for legs.

It's fine, I tell myself as I cross the street that takes me off campus.

It's all going to be okay.

Eric will know what to do.

Eric did that to me.

He'll know how to fix the hole Shush has ripped in my world.

Did he say you were magic too?

He'll make everything okay.

And then, I stop.

I'm here.

This isn't the first time I've come to Eric's house in the middle of the night. Keeping our fairytale world all to ourselves involved a lot of sneaking around. But it's the first time I've felt this nagging sensation at the back of my neck, like someone taking hold of my collar and tugging.

Kara he's not what you think.

I shouldn't be here.

But my feet stay rooted to their spot on the sidewalk.

I can't move.

I picture it happening the way it had before.

Me walking up to his front door and knocking. Him opening the door and tugging me inside, swallowing my laugh of delight by sealing his mouth over mine. Him quickly shutting the door behind us, shutting out the world.

I take a step towards the front door.

Then I stop.

I picture it happening differently.

Me going around to the backyard and knocking on his bedroom window. Him turning on the light, illuminating me standing there, waiting for him to save me. Him letting me inside, folding me into his arms, letting me cry, all the while whispering, "It's not true."

I take a step towards the backyard.

Then I stop.

I picture it happening differently.

Me going around to the backyard and knocking on his bedroom window. Him turning on the light, illuminating me standing there, waiting for him to save me. Him shutting off the light and closing his blinds, leaving me alone, out in the cold.

It's over.

We can't do this anymore.

I take a step back, away from his house.

What do I do now?

He's the core of my world. A solid, fully formed gravitational center. Now I'm spiraling off into space with nothing keeping my path steady and true. Nothing to give me an orbit, a path to follow.

I'm standing in the middle of my castle, wondering where to go from here. Because who is a princess without her prince?

The girl they find in the woods. The tragedy in someone else's story.

That's how the story goes.

I take another step towards his front door.

Then I stop.

Exhaustion comes over me in a wave, making my legs feel weak.

258

I can't do this.

I can't take it.

I turn and head back to campus, walking like I'm expecting dragons to come out around every corner. Shush. Eric.

Around and around.

Wanting to burn me alive.

You're magic.

Eric did that to me.

It's all going to be okay.

I want to walk into the trees and lay down in the snow. Just curl up and sleep until I'm not tired anymore.

But I don't.

I keep walking on the sidewalk. I head for something else familiar. Something to help with the exhaustion.

I'll just let out a few of the words. Spend some time releasing them from where they're trapped under my skin.

Maybe then they won't be screaming.

Eric did that to me.

Maybe then I'll be able to sleep.

You're safe with me.

I just need to rest. That's all.

Did he say you were magic too?

I'm fine.

TWENTY-NINE

There's a scuff on the wall of my dorm room.

Just to the left of my desk. A slightly black smudge that's just this side of too dark to be a shadow. I know its dimensions, its shape. I know what it came from, the exact time it was made. One day when Shush came over to study, she kicked her shoes off, throwing them into the corner, the black rubber sole of her boot scuffing the wall in the process. And I'd never cleaned it off.

Get up, I tell myself, curled on my side beneath my blanket. I have Biology in fifteen minutes.

Maybe the scuff will come off with water.

I don't have time for a shower, I don't have time for anything other than getting up and heading out the door. I can see myself doing it. Throwing off the covers. Taking off my pajamas. Pulling on the jeans and the sweatshirt that are still on the floor from yesterday. Grabbing my bag and leaving. I can see myself doing all of it. But I don't move.

Maybe I'll need soap to get the scuff off.

I can't move.

Get up.

The voice gets louder in my head.

Get up.

Get up.

Get up.
And still I don't move. What's the point anyway?
It's over.
Will it make a difference if I never leave this bed?
Eric did that to me.
I can't find any reason to get up.
Eric did that to me.
I know I should feel angry.
You can't avoid me forever.
Or maybe I should feel sad.
You're magic.
Or maybe even disgusted.
Did he say you were magic too?
But I don't.
Fuck
I don't feel anything.
Eric's face flashes through my head. Then Shush. Princes
and princesses and dragons. A castle wall. A drawbridge.
Pull it up and keep me locked in here.
I don't care.
Some days I am made of paper.
On these days I feel nothing. I watch the world. I watch
things happen to other people, I watch things happen to
me. I am not a player in this game. I am the paper doll you
move around the board. And I don't care what happens to
me. I don't want to win. I don't want to lose. I can't see how
it matters.
Some days I am made of paper, but I am not light. I am
heavy. I'm so heavy, my bones so full of absolutely *nothing*, I
don't think I'll ever be able to move.
Get up.
Get up.
Get up.

The edge of my tabernacle is showing. I hide it on my desk, in the little bookshelf on top, behind a few of my favorite books. I can't remember not hiding it properly. I've been taking special care to conceal it ever since Shush found out about my prayers. She threatened to take my razor blades, so I lied and told her I threw them all out, but I don't think she ever really believed me.

I need to color it back in. The original box was clear plastic, but I colored it in with a black permanent marker to hide its contents. The black is starting to fade. I'll have to redo it.

Get up.

Get up.

Get. Up.

I can't even summon the desire, the energy, to grab my laptop off the floor and put on something to watch.

I roll over and close my eyes.

I'm not going to class today.

~

"You okay Kara?"

I blink at Ella, who's looking at me with a wrinkled forehead, a slightly worried expression overtaking her usually cheerful face.

"Yeah I'm fine, just tired."

Jake looks up from his textbook and eyes me. "You getting sick?"

I shrug and try to focus on the math problem in front of me. We're sitting in the cafeteria, finishing up our Calc homework while we eat breakfast. Or while they eat breakfast. I haven't done much more than take a couple bites of toast.

"More coffee?" Jake asks.

"Yeah, thanks."

"Ella?"

Ella shakes her head. "No thanks."

I hand Jake my mug and he goes to get the two of us more coffee. I should have gone to get it instead because the minute he's out of earshot, Ella turns on me.

"You sure you're okay?"

"Yeah. I'm fine."

"You said that already." She's squinting at me and I focus on not collapsing under her gaze. "Is it Shush?"

What little energy I had drains out of me and I sink deeper into my chair. "No. I'm just tired." It isn't a total lie. I haven't been sleeping. I am tired. It's just that Shush is the main reason why.

"You still haven't told me what's going on with you two."

"I..." I can't. I can't explain the whole twisted mess, I'm not even sure I understand all of it. I don't have the energy to sort through it. I don't even have the energy to figure out these stupid math problems. "I know," I manage. "Sorry, I just... can we just work on this right now?" I tap my pencil on my notebook.

For a second she looks like she isn't going to accept that answer. But then she looks down at my paper. "That isn't right," she says, pointing at the problem I'm working on. "Here, let me show you."

I try to focus on what she's saying as she explains what I've done wrong, as she tells me how to fix it, but all her words run together. Still, I nod, make the appropriate sounds to indicate I get it. Ella doesn't buy it.

"You need me to go through it again?"

I sigh. "Sorry. It just doesn't make sense." I don't tell her it won't ever make sense. I don't tell her nothing makes sense now. I just sit there as she shows me how to do it again. She's taking me through it a third time when

Jake comes back with our coffee.

"I had trouble with that one too," he says, looking at my paper.

I drink my coffee, letting it burn my tongue and the roof of my mouth. I try to pay attention to what Ella is saying, and I don't tell her what I'm thinking. I don't say she's wasting her time because I'm never going to understand. I don't understand anything. But it doesn't matter. I know it should matter. That I'm going to fail Calc and have to leave. But I can't bring myself to care. I don't have the energy.

"You sure you're okay?" she asks again as we pack up to head to Calc. And I wish she hadn't asked. Because it's taking everything I have to go through the motions and lying takes extra effort. I manage it anyway.

"I'm fine."

~

FUCK

The carving stares back at me as I sit and wait for Eric to get to class. My eyes are open out of habit, not out of any actual desire to keep them open.

My bones are heavy. Too heavy to sit upright in this chair.

FUCK

Slouching over the table, propping myself up with my elbow and resting my chin in my hand, I dig my nail into the desk. I imagine I'm digging into one of the fresh cuts I made on my side this morning.

Eric did that to me.

Some days I cut to prove to myself I'm strong. I push

deep, I cut hard, I grit my teeth against the pain.

See? I tell myself. If you can withstand that without crying, without even flinching, then surely you can take whatever today throws at you.

The bright red marks stand out like war paint, preparing me for the battle to come. It doesn't matter that only I can see them, I know they're there.

Today is one of those days.

I haven't slept since Saturday. Since Shush.

Did he say you were magic too?

But I had to go to class. I had to see Eric.

So I needed to keep it together. I couldn't fall apart.

See? I told myself as the blade sliced into the skin of my side this morning. You're fine. You're strong. You can handle this. You can do this.

And I did. I'm here.

FUCK

Eric walks in. Starts class the way he always does.

"Hello class. How's everyone doing today?"

I don't understand.

I don't understand why everyone is acting like the world is still spinning. Acting like everything is still the way it was before.

Kara he's not what you think.

It's strange. Like I'm watching it. Watching the world spin on without me, while I sit here, not moving.

Did he say you were magic too?

I can see Shush's face as clearly as if she was sitting across from me, hear her voice as if she was the one speaking instead of Eric.

Dr. Callahan, I remind myself.

FUCK

I watch him as he lectures.

I watch him with Shush.

"Please pass these out," he says to Zoey. But it isn't Zoey. It's Shush.

Smiling up at him.

Or it's me.

Brushing the tips of his fingers with mine in plain view of everyone. The only physical affection I'm allowed to show him in public.

"That's an excellent point," he says to another girl, a girl whose name I don't know.

And it's Shush.

Beaming at the compliment.

"Can you elaborate?" he says. "I'd love to hear more."

And there she goes. Wowing everyone. The center of attention.

Just like always.

The center of Eric's world.

The book he wants to read. A fairy tale, not a tragedy.

FUCK

I look away from him, digging the point of my pen into the wood of the desk, adding my ink to what others had written.

FUCK

I can hear the word, whispering over my skin, curling into my hair the way his fingers had done. The way he'd said it that first night I spent in his bed, and many nights after.

FULK

At the beginning, as he had risen over me, my scars still warm and humming from his reading, I had him. "I've never…"

And he'd smiled and kissed me. "We don't have to do anything you don't want to do."

FULK

"It's all going to be okay," he said. And I believed him.

FULK

He'd whispered it into my ear as he came apart above me.

FULK

As if I had stolen the very concept of speech from this man for whom words were everything.

I had done that to him.

You're magic.

Me.

Did he say you were magic too?

And suddenly it isn't me spread open underneath him. It isn't my blonde hair his fingers tangle into.

It's Shush's dark curls.

FULK

My pen breaks, snapping in half. Several students turn to look at me. Eric meets my gaze. And for the first time, I can't read the blackness of his eyes. Instead I see Shush's dark ones, looking back at me, piercing into me.

Eric did that to me.

It can't be true. It's not. If Eric did that, then he can't be a prince.

Did he say you were magic too?

If he's not a prince, then what am I?

Nothing.

I'm nothing.

He looks away from me, and I look back down at the desk. I use my fingernail this time, wondering how hard I will have to scrape to rip off my nail, to draw blood.

FUCK

This isn't me. It isn't my life. It's someone else's. She doesn't even look familiar.

Did he say you were magic too?

I get up, not looking at anyone.

Not the other students. Not Eric.

I leave.

Go back to my dorm room.

TRIGGER WARNING

The following section contains graphic depictions of self-harm. If you are not in a place where you feel up to reading that, please skip to the next section.

Remember, you're not alone. Mental health resources can be found at the back of this book. Take care of yourself.

THIRTY

Some days I am made out of paper. On those days, I cut to make sure I'm real. On those days, I cut to feel the pain. To know that I can still feel it.

The only thing saving me, the only thing keeping me moving, is the fact that I have done this all before. It's muscle memory. I don't have to think about it. I can make the water hot and take off my clothes and get into the shower all without really telling myself anything beyond—You need this. Do this.

I take the blade up between my fingers and look at my skin, searching for where to write this time.

My forearms. They're pale. Smooth. Blank. Like paper.

I've never written on my arms before. It's so difficult to hide there, and it's where everyone looks for scars. The skin there is smooth and clean. I see no stories there.

Maybe, I think vaguely, trying to form a thought inside my brain made of paper, this is what I need. To snap me out of it.

To get rid of the nothing.

I just need to feel. To make sure I'm still real.

I make a cut across my wrist, pressing just deep enough to draw up red blood. To release some of the pressure, some of the nothing making my bones so heavy. Making it so hard to think, so hard to move.

And when the blade digs into my skin and that first sweet sharpness takes away my breath, the relief that washes through me is so thick I nearly collapse under the weight of it.

I'm still here.

I'm still real.

I'm still alive.

And then it all crashes down on me again. Because now, I am made of flesh and bone.

And I *feel*.

It's my story Kara.

Eric did that to me.

Did he say you were magic too?

For the first time since she said those words to me, I start to cry. I shake with the force of it, sobs tearing through me.

Stop.

I sink to the floor of the shower, hugging my knees to my chest.

Stop crying.

Stop crying.

Stop. Crying.

But I can't.

I can't breathe. I can't breathe I can't breathe I can't breathe.

It's too much. It's too heavy.

God Shush get over yourself.

It's my story Kara.

You ruined everything.

Eric did that to me.

Enjoy the spotlight.

Did he say you were magic too?

Blood drips from the cut on my wrist and I wonder how much I would have to lose before the words stop. What would it feel like? To cut so deep I never have to cut again? To release so many words that the inside of my head was silent?

Would it feel like breathing?

I put the blade to my wrist again, pushing in the point, gritting my teeth through the pain.

I'm still here.

I'm still real.

I'm still alive.

But I'm not sure I want to be.

THIRTY-ONE

Kara you have to tell someone.

I lean against the brick wall, the winter cold seeping through my clothes.

The cuts I made yesterday on my wrist are deep. Fresh and throbbing. Keeping me here.

I shift my gaze from the students wandering the sidewalk to the sign outside the building across from me. The building I've been staring at since the sun came up.

Student Counseling Center

I'm twenty feet from the door I need to push through to go inside. I imagine a small woman with glasses and a kind face, dark hair streaked with just the right amount of gray, pulled back into a professional bun. She would have a clipboard and a personalized pen with a gold tip, ready to make sure my words were recorded.

"So, why don't you tell me what brings you in today?" she would ask, her pen at the ready, her brow furrowed with just the right amount of care and concern, a motherly smile on her lips.

People who slit their wrists go to therapists. Right? That's what I'm supposed to do.

But I wouldn't say that.

"I haven't slept in four days," I would respond, shrugging

273

as if it was nothing.

Always best to use facts, things I can stand on. Things that won't turn slippery or crumble beneath my feet like all the actual reasons I haven't been sleeping. All the words that won't stop racing around my head since I saw Shush in the library.

Eric did that to me.

I wouldn't talk about that. Just, I haven't slept in four days. Simple. Easy.

I wouldn't mention the cutting. Never in any of the scenarios in my head, do I mention the cutting.

"And why do you think you haven't been sleeping?" the kind woman would ask, her tone at just the right pitch.

"The dragons."

"Dragons? What dragons?"

This is where it starts to get complicated. Because they keep blurring together.

First there's Shush. It's been her for a long time now. It's supposed to be her.

Except she says it's Eric.

He's not what you think.

And if he's the dragon and not the prince, then who am I?

I never thought you'd ruin my life for a little attention.

What have I done?

Enjoy the spotlight.

None of it makes any sense. My eyes are open as I look at the door to the counseling center, but all I can see is Eric's face.

You're magic.

I rub my eyes even though I know that won't make Eric's face go away, won't make any of the words disappear. How long has it been since I've slept?

You're safe with me.

Has it only been four days? Has it been longer?

It's all going to be okay.
"It's all going to be okay." I whisper the words under my breath, but they don't sound the same as when he said them.
They don't sound *true*.
"It's all going to be okay."
The shape isn't solid, the words can't hold it, they keep slipping through my fingers.
Did he say you were magic too?
I reach out and try to grab onto them.
You're magic.
But when I open my fist, there's nothing but air.
Absolutely perfect magic.
Nothing.
It's all going to be okay.
I stare at the building, and I know I can't go in. I have nothing to give them. They'll want a story, something with a beginning and a middle and an end.
Once upon a time…
But how can I tell a story if the characters keep changing?
The prince. The princess. The dragon.
Here isn't where I need to be. Here they'll only have more questions. I start walking away. The last thing I need is more questions.
I need answers.
Can you tell me what I say?
And he's where I go for answers.
I check my phone, looking for the time. He's always in his office this early in the morning.
The first time I went to his office, I found it empty and open. I went in wanting to memorize every detail. The deep cherry wood of his desk. The coffee pot in the corner. The books lining the walls.
I wanted to read him. The order of his books, the place-

ment of each framed diploma, the angle of his writing on the papers on his desk. I poured over his books, reading the titles, running my fingers over the spines like I might be running them over his skin.

The first time I went into his office, I filled it with my imaginary scenarios. Us laughing in the corner, drinking coffee as early morning light spilled through the window. Us sitting together at his desk, heads bent low over a book.

This time, when I walk in, it's filled with memories. The way the spines of his books felt on my back as he pressed me up against them. The exact location he was standing when he broke up with me.

We can't do this anymore.

It's over.

Eric isn't here but he'll be back soon. He never leaves his office open and unlocked for long. I push the door partially shut so no one will be able to see me in here if they walk past. I gaze at the walls, his bookshelves, the window, searching for evidence of my existence in this place.

There. On his desk.

A coffee mug.

I saw it in a store window one day and picked it up for him. It's black, like his hair. Like his eyes. There's white writing on one side. *Once upon a time...* Etched in the same white scrawl on the opposite side is the rough outline of a castle.

I pick it up, cradle it between my palms. As if I can still feel the warmth from the coffee staining the bottom, or the warmth of his hands as he held it.

I bring it, gently, to my mouth, where I know his lips have curled over the side. Maybe I can taste him, lingering there on the porcelain rim.

"Kara?"

I nearly drop the mug, spinning to face the now-open

door. Eric's standing there, a look of surprise on his handsome face.

As if he never expected me here.

As if I never belonged here.

As if I was never naked on this desk.

I set the mug down.

Eric glances over his shoulder, out into the hall, and then closes the door.

"What are you doing here?" He moves past me but doesn't sit down. As if he doesn't plan to stay long. Or he doesn't plan for me to stay long.

I search his face for a hint of something I never saw before.

Eric did that to me.

I try to picture it.

The fingers that traced so gently over my scars causing fear. The arms that made me feel so safe being used as a cage. The mouth that made me feel so loved being used to violate Shush.

It happened here, she said. In his office. I'm standing exactly where she was.

Did he say you were magic too?

"Kara?"

He's waiting for me to do something, to tell him why I'm here. But I don't know how to ask what I came here to ask. The words knot up inside my throat and all I want is to fall to my knees and beg him—

Tell me it's not true.

Tell me she's a liar.

Tell me I'm magic.

—but I can't. As if saying it all out loud will make everything Shush said true.

"You kept the mug," I say, because it's all I can manage.

His expression softens then. "Of course I did. I love it."

Something in me falls away.

I take a step towards him, waiting for him to open his arms and welcome me in the way he has so many times before.

But he doesn't.

He moves past me and sits down at his desk, glancing at his computer screen before looking back at me. "Why are you here? Do you need something?"

"I..."

I look around the office, searching for the words to say.

I have a sudden vision of myself on his bookshelf, beside his books and the other beautiful, broken things he's collected. Maybe I'm just another thing he wanted to keep on his shelf.

But I don't care.

Maybe I'm not his world.

It doesn't matter.

Because he's mine.

I look back at him, sitting behind his desk, and remember the times he had opened me on top of it.

I want to beg him to do it again.

Can you tell me what I say?

Maybe I'm just an inanimate object, but it doesn't matter.

I want to tell him I don't care.

You don't need to pretend with me. Just tell me what I am.

Am I a magic spell that gives you strength to keep going? Am I what gets you where you want to go? Or am I the reward at the end of your quest? Will we ride off into the sunset? Am I the princess trapped in a tower until you set me free? Am I the pretty damsel in distress riding behind you, my arms wrapped tight around your waist so that I do not fall off?

I'm accessory, not necessity.

But I don't care.

I. Don't. Care.

Just tell me what I am.

Just tell me where you want me.

At what angle shall I sit on your bed? Your desk? Your shelf?

Do you want me clean? Kept behind glass, a collectible to be admired but not touched? Put on the white gloves so the oils on your skin don't damage my delicate pages, wear off my magical words, make me lose value.

Do you want me dirty? Am I the book with the broken spine and the bent pages? Have you read me so many times that I no longer hold surprise? Am I a favorite to be tucked away between others, only to be taken out on dark and stormy nights to provide a bit of entertainment? The fire crackles in the corner and your whiskey glass is sticky with its alcohol but my pages are smooth and worn from your touch.

"Kara?" he presses, leaning forward.

Anything else you want to ask me?

"Dr. Callahan." His name lodges itself against my teeth, making it harder to breathe.

Can you tell me what I say?

Can you teach me how to read the pattern of scars on my skin? Are they Braille to read or are they lines of text I've cut away? Are they something I have made or something I have lost? Do I read them, or the blood that comes from making them?

I've been looking, I want to tell him.

I've tried.

I've tried to do what you did. Tried to look at myself and see what you see.

You're magic.

But I can't find it.

I don't belong to my skin, to my body, to my name.
And I can tell you all the different ways I know how to
say red. But I can't speak this language.

I want to place myself in front of him, hold out my arms
so he can see. Tell him I'll be an A plus student, I'll wait until
he has time for me. I'll wait with my thin, red wrists and
I'll wear a Catholic schoolgirl skirt if you want, just please
please please tell me what this says.

"Eric…" I say his name like it will be the key to unlocking
all of this.

Can you tell me what I say?

I close the distance between us, sitting sideways on his
lap, curling my fingers into his hair. His arms come around
me and when I press my mouth to his, slip my tongue
between his lips, his fingertips dig into me.

He moans.

And I can hear it.

You're magic.

This is what he wants.

I can give him what he wants.

TRIGGER WARNING

The following chapter contains graphic depictions of self-harm, sexual assault, and attempted suicide. If you are not in a place where you feel up to reading that, please skip to the next section.

Remember, you're not alone. Mental health resources can be found at the back of this book. Take care of yourself.

THIRTY-TWO

I reach for his belt.

But he grabs my hands.

"No." He pushes me away, pushes me off him. "Kara, I really don't have time for this right now."

And suddenly I don't want to *hand* him the book of me. I want to *hurl* it at him.

I want to shove everything off his desk, tear off my clothes so he can read my dark red words. I want to beg him until he digs into me with his nails, his teeth, until he has ripped every page from me and made me plain to read. I don't care about the pain—hurt hurt hurt me just do *something*. I need I need I need, please please please—

I wrap my arms around myself, pressing into my fresh wounds. Pain. Bright pain shocks my body back to itself. I take a shaky breath.

"Eric…" I look up at him. "Please."

Please stay.

I'm here.

It's all going to be okay.

Please don't leave me here. Please don't leave me here alone.

He sighs. And when he stands up and takes me in his arms, my knees weaken with relief. He pulls away slightly, looking down at me. I gaze up at him and remember him rising up over me in his bed, looking at me like I was a pool of magic he could drown himself in.

"It's all going to be okay," he'd said. And when he kissed me, I believed him.

I believed him.

Now I gaze into his eyes, searching for what I'd seen then. That reassurance. That surety.

I'm here.

You're safe with me.

You're magic.

It's all going to be okay.

"Eric please…" I say again.

And all I want is for him to kiss me. For him to whisper the words against my lips so they sink into my skin, through my flesh and into my blood. I want him to kiss my cuts, red openings to the inside of me, whisper the words into me so they sink into my blood and into my bones, so my body will make more of them without him.

Anything else you want to ask me?

I want to hold out my forearm, fresh with aching cuts, and beg him to tell me again.

Can you tell me what I say?

You're magic.

What do I do now?

It's all going to be okay.

Instead, he looks at me with pity. "I'm sorry Kara. I told you. It's over. What we had… What we had was beautiful. But it's over." He takes my face between his hands. "You understand, right?"

I find myself nodding. Even now, I want to make him happy. Want to make him believe I'm intelligent enough to understand what he's telling me.

You're safe with me.

I'm here.

The words slip away like he never said them at all. I don't have anything to hang onto.

"God... you're really something," he says. He brushes the hair back from my face, as if smoothing a cover away from an old, favorite painting. "You're magic."

I close my eyes and lean into his hand, trying to let the words in. This is, after all, what I wanted him to say.

You're magic.

But they wash over me like water, refusing to sink in.

All they do is *hurt.*

My eyes feel hollow when I open them, looking up at him. I remember a time when just him holding me like this would have been enough to keep the words at bay for days.

Can you tell me what I say?

I move away from him, covering my mouth with my hand, trying to keep the words in.

What do I do now?

"Kara?" He takes a step towards me. "Are you... are you okay?"

That might be concern at the edges of his vision. This is okay. I know what to do with this question. I take my hand away, move it back to my side. This question only ever has one answer.

"I'm fine." My voice doesn't sound like mine, but he doesn't seem to notice.

"Okay, good. Good." He nods to himself. "And you won't... you're not going to tell anyone?"

I look up at him blankly. The counseling center sign flashes in my head. Shush's face. Ella's face. Who would I tell? Why would I tell?

"No."

What would I say?

284

"Good. Okay, that's good." Again, he nods, and I can already see him retreating, his mind going away to something else. He goes back to sit down at his desk, moving papers around, signaling he has to get back to work. Signaling I should leave.

And that's when I see it.

Ella's name.

At the top of one of the papers.

Ella's name. And below it, a sticky note graced with Eric's handwriting. You're–

No.

No, it can't be. It can't it can't it can't this can't be happening.

I think back to when Ella told me about her prince. What exactly did she say?

I have class with him.

And I realize she never told me the name of her new prince.

Oh god.

I look up at him. And I see it.

His black hair turns to scales. His teeth grow into points. His fingers turn to claws. There is fire in his eyes as he looks at me.

"I'll see you in class," he says, dismissing me.

And I run.

I run across campus and all I can see are his eyes. I can see it, what Shush has been saying all along.

Kara he's not what you think.

It's all hollow.

You're safe with me.

You're magic.

It's all going to be okay.

It's all lies.

He's not a prince.

I try, reaching, to get back the fairy tale. To tell myself the story.

Once upon a time…

But it's wrong. It's all wrong. Nothing is how it's supposed to be.

Kara you have to tell someone.

I run past the counseling center, but I don't even feel the pull to go in this time. What would I say now? I can't talk about dragons. About princes and princesses and fairy tales.

I can't tell Shush. She knows already. And she hates me now.

I can't tell Ella.

Oh god.

Ella.

Ella and Eric.

He's not what you think.

Eric did that to me.

There is no prince and princess here. No happily ever after. There never was.

What would I tell them?

Anything else you want to ask me?

Can you tell me what I say?

That I have no idea who I am? That I can't read my own skin, that I need him to read my story for me? None of it makes any sense.

I can't breathe.

The words wrap themselves around my throat, choke me, fill my ears so I can't hear anything but them, blanket my eyes so I can't see anything but them.

Fuck

I want to claw the words out from behind my eyes, dig out their blackness with my fingernails.

Kara he's not what you think.

Memories of my time with Eric rush through my head.
The first time he kissed me.
The first time we had sex.
All the times after that.
And in each one, Eric starts out as the prince, tall and
handsome and gallant. And then his black hair morphs into
black scales. His hands become claws. His teeth lengthen
into sharp points. His words twist and turn, become black,
become poison.
Eric is the dragon.
And I don't fight him.
I invite him in.
Hold out my wrists for his teeth to sink into.
Shudder as his forked tongue tastes my blood.
Come back for more.
Can you tell me what I say?
My fingertips find and sink into the cut on my wrist.
It's not true.
It's not true.
It's not true.
You're magic.
I went back to him. Again and again I went back to him.
In the library, in his office, in his house.
I wanted him. I wanted what he gave me.
And I knew all along.
Anything else you want to ask me?
I never asked.
Am I the only one?
Because I knew. He was too sure of himself. Everything
he did, he knew exactly how to do it. I wasn't the first. I
wouldn't be the last. I knew.
Sometimes if you tell yourself a lie enough times, you
can start to believe it's true.

You're magic.
But I can't lie anymore.
Did he say you were magic too?
There is no fairy tale. No prince. No princess. No dragon.
There's just me.
And Dr. Callahan.
And what I'd done to feel like I was worth something.
What I'd done to feel like a princess instead of a tragedy.
What I'd done to feel like I was magic.
What I'd done to get answers. Even if they were only lies.
The day I brought him the mug, he fucked me in his office.
He lifted me up onto the desk, pushed himself between
my legs, slid his tongue into my mouth so deep I couldn't
breathe.
I tried to kiss him back but he was moving so fast. Faster
than he ever had before. Pulling off my clothes. He put his
hands on my shoulders and pushed me to my knees.
And I wanted to give him what he wanted. But I still
gagged as he pushed himself hard into my mouth, still tried
to pull away because he was going too fast and I couldn't
breathe but he had hold of me. One hand on the back of my
head, again and again and again.
And then he was pulling me up, turning me around,
bending me over the desk, kicking my legs apart.
I whimpered as he forced his way inside me, and he
covered my mouth with his hand.
"Fuck," he said. "Fuck Kara."
And then he gave me what I wanted.
Once upon a time…
"You're—" He pushed hard. "—magic."
He said it over and over.
Until I relaxed.
Until I believed him.

Fuck
I feel sick.
The words climbing and clawing their way up my throat.
Kara you have to tell someone.
What would I tell anyone, if I told them?
Do you know the fairy tale behind the invention of the kiss?
I reach my dorm room and fumble with my key in the door in my rush.
You're magic.
I have to get them out.
Eric did that to me.
I can't stand it anymore.
Did he say you were magic too?
They're suffocating me.
You can't avoid me forever.
The water is scalding and I don't care.
Eventually you'll forgive me.
The blades are blunt, so I press harder, cutting into the skin at my hip.
Kara you have to tell someone.
What would I say?
That I fucked my professor? That I went back to him over and over so he would fuck me and tell me I was magic? Again and again and again?
You're magic.
Again and again and again I cut into my hip, trying to make the words stop.
Can you tell me what I say?
What do I do now?
You're safe with me.
It's all going to be okay.
Kara you have to tell someone.
Eric did that to me.

Did he say you were magic too?
This isn't a note, it doesn't have a message.
This is destruction.
This is shredding the paper until I can't read the words anymore.
The razor slips from my hand and clatters to the floor of the tub. I hold up my hands and find that they are shaking.
He's not what you think.
I sink to the floor of the bathtub, curling up against the wall, the water pounding down on me.
You're magic.
He's lifting me onto his bed, crushing me into his mattress. He's laying me down on his couch. He's carrying me to his kitchen counter. He's pushing me up against the wall in the library stairwell.
Fuck
I can't breathe. Again and again and again I went back to him.
You're magic.
You're safe with me.
I'm here.
It's all going to be okay.
I pull at my hair, remembering all the times his fingers had tangled into it. I want to rip it out. Maybe my skin will come with it. Maybe that will be enough to get the words out of my head.
It's all going to be okay.
I can remember how those words felt on my skin, how they looked in the air, coming out of his mouth and moving to rest on my lips.
You're magic.
I believed him. I opened my mouth and my body wide, wanting to swallow those precious words whole.
Wanting to feel them in my bones.

I wrapped myself around him, aching for those words to become real. And now they're dissolving into nothing.

"It's all going to be okay." I say it out loud so I can watch the words come out, watch the sentence form in the air like it had when he said it, a blanket moving over my skin, warming me, protecting me. But it doesn't look right.

I try again.

"It's all going to be okay."

The words are slick with desperation, like the blood at my hip. They won't stand up straight.

"It's all going to be okay."

They were a magic shield when he said them. They protected me.

But now, they wrap themselves around my ankles, my wrists, creeping in between my lips to fill my mouth as if he'd tried to gag me with them.

You're safe with me.

You're magic.

I curl my fingers around my wrists, digging my nails in.

Anything else you want to ask me?

It had only ever been the one question.

Can you tell me what I say?

And I wanted so badly to believe the answer he gave me that I hadn't stopped to consider it might be a lie.

I bang my head back into the shower wall, again and again.

I'm fine. I'm fine I'm fine I'm fine.

It's all going to be okay.

It's going to be okay.

Going to be okay.

Okay.

Okay.

Okay.

Then I'm standing to my feet. I have to get them out. I
have to get them all out.

I reach not for the razor but for the razor blade. This time
it's different.

I want to reach into my veins, into my bones, and rip out
all the words until there aren't any left. Until I am a blank
page. Until I can begin my story again.

I put the razor blade to my wrist.

You're magic.

Kara he's not what you think.

Fuck

What do I do now?

You're safe with me.

Eric did that to me.

It's all going to be okay.

I don't want to release the words, the way I've been
doing for years. That hasn't been working. It's not enough.
This isn't a peaceful surrender. I'm going to war. I want to
feel the words die in my hands, feel their blood gushing
over my fingers.

I drag the blade in one long line, cutting open my
storyline.

I bite my lip so hard against the pain that I taste blood.
When I pull the blade out, there's resistance, as if my flesh
wants to keep it in.

It's all going to be okay.

I drop the blade, slick with my blood, with all these
words, and watch them all come out.

The blood comes out fast, covering my arm in red, falling so fast over my fingers. For long seconds I stand there,
mesmerized.

Once upon a time…

We can't do this anymore.

Kara you have to tell someone.
Did he say you were magic too?
Anything else you want to ask me?
Can you tell me what I say?
Eric did that to me.
You're safe with me.
You're magic.
It's all going to be okay.
It's working.
They're leaving.
I'm lighter now. Freer.
A wave of exhaustion washes over me.
And I realize the blood isn't slowing down.
It's so thick the water can't turn it pink before it washes down the drain.
I hadn't thought there would be words I'd want to keep. But my fingers wrap around my wrist so tight, trying to keep them in.
"Eric." His name comes to my lips without me really thinking about it.
I get out of the shower, getting blood all over the bathroom floor. I nearly slip and fall. Out in my dorm room I try to search my coat pockets for my phone without letting up pressure on my wrist.
Eric will come.
He'll help me.
I get blood on the screen of my phone as I find his name. The phone slips out of my hand and I follow it down to the floor, kneeling, clutching my wrist and bending down over the phone as it rings, as I drip blood onto the carpet.
It's okay.
It's all going to be okay.
Eric will come. He'll help me. He has to.

When he answers, I sag with relief.

"Eric please—"

"I already told you Kara," he says, and this time his voice is thick with annoyance. "This is over. No more calls. No more anything. It's over. Goodbye."

And then he's gone. And I'm alone. Again.

The blood is still flowing. I can't keep pressure on my wrist. I need more hands. I need help.

I'm calling Shush before I realize what I'm doing. It's only after the phone starts ringing that I think she might not answer. She hates me now.

But then—

"Kara?"

"I need help. Shush I need help. I'm in my dorm room, I need—"

"I'm coming. Hang on. I'll be right there. What's going on? Kara? Kara are you there?"

Am I?

I'm laying on the floor now, curled around my phone, staring at it, and I can hear her saying my name. But she sounds so far away. Muffled. Underwater.

I think back to the first time I went swimming. How scared I was when all the sound went away. Back then I broke the surface of the water screaming.

This time I sink deeper.

I don't want to scream.

I close my eyes.

And the words fade away.

Just like I wanted.

I can't hear myself anymore.

There's only the dark.

And the silence.

THIRTY-THREE

Some days I feel like a someday.

I'm the sense of deja vu I haven't yet felt. I'm the word I've lost on the tip of my tongue. I feel like something that has yet to happen, something that's waiting for tomorrow or the next day.

Like everyone around me is alive and I'm not. Like I'm constantly on the edge of cresting a hill and if only I could get to the top I could see where I'm going, see where I am.

But I never actually make it there.

I never make it to the someday.

I never happen.

But that's okay.

It's quiet now.

I feel light.

Like I'm flying.

It's all okay.

I don't want to leave this place.

It's nice here.

Quiet.

Peaceful.

~

Someone is shaking me.
I open my eyes.
Shush.
Shush is here.
She looks worried.
She's saying something, but I can't hear her. She's muffled and far away. I'm still underwater.
And then I surface.
"Kara, Kara, Jesus, Kara, fuck."
She keeps talking. It sounds strange.
"Say something. Fuck Kara say something. Say something. Kara, talk to me."
"Hey." The word sounds wrong. It feels wrong in my mouth. I say it again. "Hey."
"Jesus Christ I thought you were… fuck. Fuck Kara."
I can see her wrapping a shirt from the floor around my wrist, where—oh—there's a lot of blood. It's everywhere. It's going to stain the carpet. That's going to be a big mess.
I can see it but I can't feel it.
Not really.
Is that *my* arm that hurts?
It feels like someone else's.
"It's going to be okay," Shush says. "It's all going to be okay. Don't worry. You're fine. You're going to be okay."
Someone giggles.
I think it might be me.
I blink, expecting Shush to disappear. But she stays where she is.
"Shush? You… you came?"
"Of course I did," Shush says. "Hang on. I'm calling 911."
"No. No Shush don't." I grab onto her wrist with my good hand, surprised I can move at all. "Just… just help me."
"Kara we have to go to the hospital."

I shake my head. Or I try to. I'm not sure if it moves.
I'm tired.
So tired.
"No 911," I say. "Just help me. I'll... I'll tell you every-thing. Promise. Just help me."
Static creeps in at the edges of my vision. Flickering black and white boxes like an old TV screen when the cable's out.
"Kara? Kara stay with me. Come on Kara. Kara say some-thing. Kara—"
There's a word there, hanging in the air. An image. Imprinting on the insides of my eyelids.
Students in classrooms raising their hands.
A title.
A name.
Kara.
Was it ever really mine?
Silent, sweet blackness swallows me whole.

~

Some days I feel like a someday.
I feel like I'm forever driving down a road trying to get home but I have no idea where I'm going. I can't read the signs and even if I could, I don't know the destination I'm trying to get to. I don't know where my home is. The town where I know all the cracks on the sidewalk, all the names of all the people who owned the houses before the people living there now, and the neighbor's dog who died when I was a kid.
The place where I belong.
I'm not one of those people who remembers their child-hood. I can't tell you if I knew who I was back then—a girl who wore dresses and played with dolls or maybe a girl with

scrapes on her knees and dirt on the bottom of her bare feet—
or if I was always just pretending. Just following the story I
thought I was supposed to be living, even if it wasn't mine.

I never knew how to know which was which.

A home is the beginning and the end of a story. The place
you start and the place you go back to.

If you don't know your story, how do you recognize your
home?

~

When I wake up, it's to the sound of something ripping.

I open my eyes, just a little. I don't have the energy to
open them all the way.

I'm in my bed, laying down. Shush is ripping duct tape
off my wrist, off the shirt she's tied around it.

I don't say anything. I can't. My tongue is heavy. I'm not
flying anymore. There's just weight and fog and pain and
tired on top of tired.

She unties the shirt and fresh pain spikes in my wrist,
piercing through the already existing ache.

I wince.

"Hey hey hey. You're awake," Shush says, but she doesn't
stop what she's doing. She wraps a hand towel around my
wrist quickly, staunching the fresh blood that flows out.
Then she pulls fresh duct tape off a roll, wrapping it tight
over the towel, around my wrist.

"It's okay," she says. She pulls my hand up over my head
and starts duct taping it to the wall. "You didn't cut as deep
as I thought. It's going to be okay."

Oh no.

I didn't finish it.

I didn't get them all out.

The words.
They're going to come back.
I can't fight them again.
I can't.
I'm so tired.
I just want to sleep.
Just.
Want.
Sleep.

∼

I've never been one half of a whole.
I used to think this feeling that pulls me under—this someday feeling—was because I was incomplete. I was missing a piece of myself. My other half. My better half.
That's how the stories go right?
You're not somebody until you've got somebody.
You're not a princess without a prince.
So I did what I thought I was supposed to. I looked for my other half. I dated boys in high school. Looking.
But none of them fit. None of them made that feeling go away.
And then there was Eric.
You're magic.
And I realized I'm not missing my other half.
That isn't what this feeling is.
I don't feel incomplete.
I feel unknowable.
All this time I've spent searching, I've been looking for the wrong thing. I don't need a puzzle piece to complete my picture.
I need a compass. A key. A legend. A way to read myself.

Someone to translate.

I need a map to all my pieces so I can find them, so I can put them together.

Can you tell me what I say?

Because I don't know.

I don't know who I am.

I don't know who I am and I don't know how to know. I don't understand people who know who they are. Who told them?

Because I've been looking. I've been searching under my skin for years. And I haven't found any answers.

I can't find myself. I'm not anywhere to be found.

I don't exist.

~

When my eyes open again, it's dark outside. Shush has my desk lamp on, and she's sitting next to it, looking at something on her phone.

What time is it?

How long have I been sleeping?

I shift my position slightly and realize I can't feel my fingers. Or my arm. Except for the dull ache trying to escape from where Shush has duct taped me closed, trapping the words I still need to let out.

I tug a little, but I can't pull my arm down. I tug a little harder.

Ouch.

A sound escapes my throat. Something between a whimper and a groan.

It hurts.

Not just my arm but my head.

It's screaming at me. Angry at what I did.

God it hurts. Everything hurts.

"Hey," Shush says. "Hey."

She stands up and comes over to crouch down by my bed. "You're awake."

I look at her and I know my mouth opens but I can't make words come out.

"It's nearly seven. You've been asleep for a long time."

Seven.

That's... I went to see Eric this morning. I slept through a whole day.

And still, all I want to do is sleep again. My eyelids feel heavy.

I try to swallow, try to say something. But nothing comes out. Just air rasping over my vocal cords.

"Here," Shush says. She brings a water bottle to my lips. "Drink."

The water is cool and soothing. I drink it too fast and end up coughing. Over and over, pain chases every cough.

"Just breathe," Shush says. "Breathe."

I try to do what she says. After a minute, the coughing passes. I look past Shush, look around the room. There's a bottle of cleaning solution on the floor, next to a large dark red stain on the carpet.

I see last night in flashes.

The blade falling to the floor of the bathtub.

The blood coming up from my wrist, spilling over my fingers.

The way it soaked through the towel.

What did I do?

I look up at Shush because I want to ask her.

Why am I still here?

She's saying something, but I can't tell what. The blackness pulls me under.

~

I am not hollow.

I am hollowed out.

The difference is that one has never known what it is to be solid, to be full, to feel sturdy like the next gust of wind will not go through you.

I can feel where my insides have been pulled out, the scrapes from blunt metal tools on the insides of my ribs where I have been excavated. Like an old mine shaft left vacant and abandoned, ready to collapse beneath my feet.

I've just been trying to finish the job. To break through my egg-shell skin encasing nothing but what used to be, covering what I'm missing, hiding the fact that if I peel my skin away there will be nothing to see.

I can feel it even without a mirror. The emptiness leaking out of my eyes. On better days this makes me hungry. Ravenous for stories, adventure, to be filled up.

On worse days this makes me a non-person.

And I can't bring myself to want anything at all.

~

When I wake up again, Shush is taking my arm down from where she's taped it to the wall.

"Sorry," she says. "I think the bleeding is slowing down and I want to clean this."

I want to say thank you.

I want to ask her why she's helping me.

Why she's helping me after everything I did.

But I just lay there. I can't say anything.

"Oh, Ella kept texting you," she says, almost like an after-thought. "I said you were sick. That you went home."

Ella… Ella… and Eric…

No.

"She doesn't know, does she?" asks Shush. "About the cutting?"

I shake my head and the world wobbles at the edge of my vision.

Ella doesn't know.

Ella doesn't know *anything*.

"Figured," says Shush, her mouth a tight line.

I let her change my bandages. When she takes off the duct tape and removes the towel, my arm starts to bleed again, but it isn't as bad as it was before.

She squirts something that smells strongly of antiseptic on it and I wince at the stinging pain. But it's familiar. Like water from the shower washing out a fresh cut.

She rewraps my arm in a new towel and puts on the duct tape again.

"I didn't know what else to do," she says, seeing me eye the duct tape.

I shake my head. Or I try to anyway.

Everything is heavy again.

This time she doesn't duct tape my arm to the wall. She just lifts it up over my head, letting it rest on a pillow there.

I should do something. Say something.

But I don't know what to say.

And my eyes are already closing.

"Just rest," she says. "I'll be here. I'm here."

And it's nice. For a second. Just for a second.

To feel like I'm not alone.

∾

I can't remember what it felt like to feel solid. To feel real.

I can't remember a time when I knew who I was, when I didn't feel this gaping hollowness of questions inside me. All I know is it existed. A full, solid, real me existed once upon a time.

Sometimes I wonder if it would be better if the real me had never existed at all.

If I was just hollow. Instead of hollowed out.

Because I can feel it. Feel me. The me that's missing. Like someone has ripped out all my pages and left me with nothing but a hardcover shell. Just my name *Kara* embossed on the front. And nothing but the ragged remnants of a story that used to be left inside.

Maybe if I couldn't run my fingers over the jagged edge of the torn pages, couldn't feel the thickness of my spine and know that something is supposed to be here, then I wouldn't care. I wouldn't spend all my time feeling like a question without an answer. Feeling like a book without a story. Feeling like a tragedy. The girl they find in the woods who has been broken beyond recognition.

Maybe then I wouldn't spend all my time feeling like I'm constantly about to turn a corner and discover myself standing there. If only I can go just a bit faster, just a bit farther.

Maybe then I wouldn't feel like a someday.

Maybe then I wouldn't feel like something that isn't ever going to happen.

∼

I sleep forever. I want it to be forever.

When I wake up, Shush cleans my wrist and changes my bandages. She makes me drink water. She makes me eat food, things she's gotten from the vending machines downstairs.

She doesn't say anything beyond what she needs to take care of me.

"Drink this."

"Eat this."

"Rest."

I've never seen her so quiet.

She puts on Netflix but I couldn't tell you what we watch.

I do what she says and then I sleep.

I drink.

I eat.

She cleans my wrist and replaces my bandages.

And then I sleep.

Over and over.

Eventually I start to feel a bit stronger. I don't sleep as much. I can sit up in bed on my own. I can even talk.

"Why are you doing this?" I ask Shush as she cleans my cut again.

"You won't let me take you to the hospital so someone with real medical training can. YouTube and Google only get you so far." She frowns in concentration, and I wince as she dabs antiseptic over my cut. "Really you should go to a doctor. You might need stitches or something."

"No Shush, I mean… Why are you helping me?"

"You think you can do this on your own?"

You didn't want to help Shush. You wanted to get your way. You wanted to make it about you. Just like you always do.

She should hate me. I don't know why she doesn't hate me.

"I… I called you a liar. I…"

Shush clenches her jaw. "Yeah that wasn't the highlight of our friendship really."

"I'm sorry," I say. "For… for everything."

"I know." She wraps another towel over my wrist. "Me too."

I give her a look.

"I shouldn't..." She sighs. Securing my makeshift bandage with duct tape once again, she stands up straight. "I shouldn't have told your mother like I did. I just... I was worried about you. It's not an excuse. It just... It is what it is." She crosses her arms over her chest and I wait to feel a spark of the anger I've been holding onto for so long. She betrayed me. She did the one thing I asked her not to do.

But I don't feel angry.

I just feel... hollow. Empty.

Like I let out all my anger when I tried to let out all the words.

Somewhere in between calling Shush for help and now, I stopped being mad at her.

"So... what now?" I ask.

"Do you..." She hesitates. "You're still covered in blood. I can... I'll get a washcloth, if that's okay?"

No, I want to say.

I want to pull the blankets up to my chin.

But I'm not sure what use there is in hiding anything from her anymore. She's seen it all already. She's seen the worst of it.

So I give her a slight nod.

She gets a washcloth and comes back. She starts with my arm. Dabbing with the washcloth, wiping off the dry blood around the makeshift bandage she's rigged. She works down from there. Moving down my arm, over my shoulder, up my neck.

She frowns, pushing my hair back.

"We'll need to get you in the shower eventually," she says, almost to herself.

I want to close my eyes. I don't want to watch as she pulls the blanket down. I'm still naked under the blankets, and even though I haven't looked, I can feel the blood dried over my skin.

"We'll need to change these sheets too," she says.

I don't want to watch as she starts to wipe the blood off my ribs. I don't want to watch her look at all the cuts I've made there.

But I can't look away.

She tries to hide it.

She tries to keep her expression blank. Clinical. Like a doctor.

But I can see it.

In the slight furrow between her eyebrows. In the tensing of her jaw. In the sadness in her eyes.

Pain.

Pain because of what I'd done.

I want to close my eyes. Want to close it out.

But I can't look away.

It's like a blade, slicing into my skin.

Over and over.

As she cleans the blood off my ribs, my hips, my thighs. As she sees the extent of my prayers.

She has to get up a few times, rinse out the washcloth, come back with it newly dampened with warm water. I don't know how long it takes, but eventually she's done what she can. Then together, we manage to get one of my extra large sleep shirts on me.

She runs a hand through her hair. "Now, I need to go back to my dorm. I've got to get some homework and some fresh clothes and supplies. Something other than vending machine food."

When she looks at me again, there's worry in her gaze.

"Are you... are you okay here alone? Just for a bit?"

I nod. "Promise I won't slit my wrists or anything."

A smile cracks her grim expression. "Fucking Christ Kara. Too soon."

But she seems to feel a bit better as she puts on her shoes

and her coat and heads out the door. She makes me talk to her on the phone the entire time she's gone. I don't actually talk. I listen to Shush breathing on the phone and every so often she says, "Hey, you there?"

And I respond. "I'm here."

She's only gone a half hour, and still I say it so often I feel like the words are carved into my lips.

I'm here.

I don't know what it means.

But I know it's true.

I'm here.

THIRTY-FOUR

"I think you should try to shower today," Shush says, looking down at me with a critical eye. "Honestly you're starting to smell."

I try to run a hand through my rat's nest of blood-encrusted hair and cringe. Even though she tried to clean me off with a washcloth, I'm still a mess.

"And I'm worried about infection," she says. "I've been keeping your wrist pretty clean but…"

She doesn't have to say it. I have plenty of other cuts that could get infected.

"Okay."

"You feel up to standing?"

I nod and she comes to help me up. When I'm fully upright, I sway a little, leaning against her.

"Okay?" she asks.

"A little light-headed."

"Take your time."

I wait for the world to stop spinning, trying to take deep breaths. I feel weak, like I can't trust my legs to hold me. But instead of sitting back down on the bed, I keep going. "I'm good."

Shush lets me go but she walks next to me as I walk around the dark red stain in the carpet. Shush has been trying to clean it and it's faded, but I don't think we'll ever be able to get it out.

"You need my help with the shirt?" she asks as I step into the bathroom.

"I… I think I can do it."

In all honesty I'm not entirely sure. My legs still feel shaky. But she's seen too much of me over the past few days. And even though she couldn't possibly see anything worse, I'm still grasping for some amount of privacy.

"Okay. Just… I mean I guess you won't be able to stop the bandage from getting wet. I'll change it when you finish."

"Okay."

I glance around the bathroom. It's spotless. No sign of the blood that had stained the shower, spattered on the floor and the countertop, streaked the walls as I stumbled out for my phone. No sign that I tried to kill myself. As if it never happened.

"I took your razor and your razor blades," Shush says, her tone matter of fact. "I'll be right outside if you need me. Don't shut the door."

She leaves, closing the door most of the way but leaving it cracked just a little. As if she's worried about what I might get up to in here.

Not that I blame her.

Getting off my shirt proves to be more difficult than I thought. But I don't ask for help. I can do this one thing. Just this *one thing* on my own. Besides—I pull my injured arm through the sleeve and grit my teeth—it's not like I'm not used to pain.

I don't look in the mirror until after I get the shirt off. I know it's going to be bad and I just want to see it all at once. When I do, the force of what I see makes me take a step back.

I suck in my breath at the stranger in the mirror. She

looks like she's been through a war. Like she's been tortured. Like she hasn't seen the sun in months. Like she's hardly been fed. She's covered in scars and cuts, some still fresh and bright red, some older and scarred over. There's a spot on her hip that still seems angry and small red lines on her thighs, trailing like so many ladders up her sides.

And then there's her wrist. Wrapped in its makeshift bandage.

It's her eyes that get me though. More than the cuts. It's the dark shadows under them, the way they look hollow.

Abandoning the mirror, I get into the shower.

Slowly, I wash the blood off myself. My fresh cuts cry out against the hot stinging spray.

The skin is ragged at my hip from where I'd tried to dig out all the words, cutting over the same place again and again. The water opens it up, just a little.

And there's blood.

Fresh and red and bright against my pale skin.

I dip my finger into it and hold it up, staring at the blank white shower wall.

Write something.

Say something.

Get the words out.

But nothing comes.

There are no words.

The hollowness washes over me in a wave.

Just... empty. I'm empty.

The urge comes quietly, naturally.

I'm looking for my razor before I even realize what I'm doing.

I want to feel. I need to feel something. To know I'm still here. That I'm still me. That I'm still real.

But my razor is gone. Shush took it. I'm saying her name before I can stop myself.

"Shush." I didn't mean to call her, but she comes anyway.

"Hey." Her voice comes from the other side of the shower curtain. "You okay?"

"I…" I can't say it. I want to ask her for my razor, but I know that's wrong. It's all I want but I know I shouldn't want it. And she definitely won't give it to me anyway.

"Do you need help?"

"My hair," I manage, even though I haven't tried to wash my hair yet.

She pushes aside the shower curtain. And maybe it's something she sees in my eyes, in my face. But she starts moving me, her hands on my shoulders, instructing me as she goes.

"Just move back a little. Okay. Tip your head back."

I do what she says. I can't think of anything else to do.

And when she starts talking, I don't say anything.

I just listen.

"I met Eric when I was a freshman. Introduction to Fairy Tales. That's what you had right?"

She doesn't wait for me to respond.

"I wasn't… back then I wasn't like I am now. I grew up in a house with six siblings and I was always the one that could take care of myself. My parents didn't have to worry about me, so they didn't pay as much attention to me as they did to everyone else. And that's fine, that's not—it's not like they did anything wrong. But Eric, he paid attention to me. He… saw me. You know?"

I don't say anything and I don't think she expects me to. But I know what she means. Eric looks at you like you're the center of his world.

Shush keeps talking. She works shampoo into my hair and tells me about how she flirted with him. How she stayed late after class, how she worked with him on her papers in the library. And it all sounds so familiar.

Until it doesn't.

"When I went to his office that night, I... I knew it was a bad idea. I just, I thought we were both on the same page. I thought we were flirting. Flirting with each other. With this... this line. Between what was okay and what wasn't. Because it was fun.

"I never wanted to cross it, I... He was handsome, you know? And he was clever and he made me feel... he made me feel special. Like—" She scoffs.

"Like magic," I say softly, and she nods.

"That's all I wanted," she says. "Just that feeling. I didn't want to cross the line. I didn't realize until that night that he did."

She moves me out of the stream of warm water and a chill settles over me as she starts working conditioner into my hair, combing through it with her fingers, teasing out the knots.

"And then he touched me. He touched me and he kissed me and I... You read the story. And after he—" She takes a deep breath. "After he sexually assaulted me, I didn't tell anyone. I didn't tell anyone because I felt like it was my fault. I flirted with him. I knew how it would look. Like I'd dangled myself as a shiny red apple in front of him and how could he be blamed for taking a bite?

"But I was wrong.

"I spent weeks blaming myself, not talking to anyone. And then I went to an open mic night. I heard this girl perform this incredible slam poem about when she was raped. About feeling guilty. About figuring out it was never her fault.

"I decided I wasn't going to be quiet anymore. I was going to talk."

313

She goes quiet for a long minute and I start to ask a question. "Why…" But I don't know how to finish it.

"Why now?" She moves me back into the water and starts rinsing out the conditioner. "It wasn't because of you. I mean it was, but it wasn't. After what happened with the election, with all those women who came forward with stories about him and no one believed them? No one believed them. Because we'd rather call all those women liars than imagine one man as a bad guy. Because it's easier to believe women are liars—easier to think what we say doesn't matter—than to picture a guy we like doing terrible things." She takes a shaky breath and when she starts up again there's a little less rage coming out in her tone.

"I thought, maybe if more of us told our stories, more of us would be believed. And I owed it to them. I owed it to you. I owed it to myself. So I told the truth."

I don't say anything. I don't say anything as she finishes washing my hair, as she shuts off the water and helps me dry off. I don't say anything as she helps me into clean clothes.

I don't say anything until I'm back in bed, tucked under my covers.

And then I tell her.

I tell her about Eric. The library. Dinners at his house. His office. How he understood my cutting. I tell her about the magic.

And she listens.

She listens until I don't have anything else to say. And then, she pushes. She pushes at the parts I left out.

"You're not planning on stopping are you? Cutting?"

She's looking at me with her hard gaze, her journalist's gaze, and I know I can't lie to her. But I can't tell her the truth. So I say nothing.

"Kara please. After everything—fuck after you almost *died*—you think this is good for you?"

I press my lips together, sealing all my words inside.

I know all the reasons cutting is bad for you. I'm not an idiot. I know I use it to cope and I know it's self-destructive. Self-harm, they call it. I know it isn't healthy.

But I don't care.

There are so many types of self-destructive behavior it's hard to name them all. And still cutting is what people find so offensive. Celebrities will admit to being addicted to drugs or alcohol or say they've been starving themselves but when's the last time you heard of one that went to rehab for cutting?

You'd laugh about your hangover and how you don't remember the name of the person you fucked last night, but you wouldn't ruefully smile and shake your head at your best friend as you lift your shirt to show the cuts on your ribs and say, "I did something bad last night."

Even with the wider acceptance of mental illness like depression, cutting is never mentioned. You might casually mention seeing a therapist during lunch with colleagues. But would you ever casually bring up cutting? Show the scars and talk about how this one is taking a while to heal?

Why is that? What is it about cutting in particular that's so terrible. So shocking and outside the norm that you'd never mention it.

Something about the blood. Something about the blade.

Such an obvious way to hurt yourself instead of all the more deceptive ways.

It scares people.

I mean, is it really so bad to do self-destructive things? As long as they aren't hurting other people? There are plenty of examples where a little tearing down results in a much

stronger and more beautiful final product. The pruning of
a rosebush. A fire in an old forest making way for new life.
Removing a tumor and then the uterus that housed it.

Why is what I'm doing any different?

I'm removing the poison. I'm removing the words.
Taking out all the terrible words that make my head so full
I can't think straight and make my bones so heavy I can't
bring myself to get out of bed.

I know it looks bad.

The cuts and the scars and the secrecy and the lies. But it
will look better when I finish. I'm not sure how to find my
story but I know I need to find it. So I've been ripping out all
the pages that don't feel like mine, trying to find a story that
fits. Trying to find a story worth living.

And if my hands are scraped and bloody—if I've killed
too many darlings—it's only because I'm trying so hard to
do it well, to do it *right*.

"Kara?" Shush presses softly.

I shake my head. "You don't understand."

"Explain it to me then."

I don't say anything. I close my eyes, leaning my head
back against the wall.

I can't do this.

One true sentence.

I can't talk about this.

"Kara don't stop now. Just tell me. Tell me why—"

"Why is it so bad? Why is cutting so much worse than
everything else?"

The words burst out of my chest so hard it hurts, leaving
a hollow sort of aching in the center of me. Shush stares
back at me, and I know I should stop talking now.

But I can't.

Something's been ripped away.

316

I can't keep it in.

"Come on Shush, how many different types of self-destructive behavior are there? How often do people do things that aren't good for them? People drink a bottle of wine after a hard day. People fuck people they shouldn't. They eat things they shouldn't or they don't eat things they should. "Don't you think cutting is one of the better ones? At least if I come home and cut after a hard day, I'm not going to drive my car drunkenly off the road and murder some innocent bystander. I'm just…" I take a deep breath, drawing my knees up to my chest and hugging them. "Nobody talks about cutting. But it isn't as bad as everything else. It isn't as bad as you think."

Shush is quiet for a long time. Just sitting there, looking at me. And when she finally speaks, she sounds determined.

"Kara I can help you. I can get you help."

"Shush, stop." I dig my fingernails into my arms, wanting to disappear inside my skin, wanting to get as far away from her as possible.

"Have you ever tried to stop? There's so much out there Kara. Online support groups, people who've done it before, people who know how to help you stop. If you just—"

"I don't *want* to stop."

I stare at her, breathing hard, and realize as the words hang in the air, that they're true.

I'm not stupid. I know cutting isn't what you call normal and it's certainly not what you call healthy. I know I could have gotten help at any time. From a counselor. From a friend. From my parents. I knew if I wanted to stop I needed to tell someone. I knew I needed to get help.

Sure, I didn't tell people because I knew it would hurt them. But that wasn't why I didn't tell. Not the real reason anyway.

Because the internet exists. I could have gotten help from

strangers. From books. I could have researched techniques and tips. I could have tried to stop. But I never had.

Because I didn't want to stop.

I *don't* want to stop.

Even now, the thought of giving up cutting is scarier than the memory of all the blood pouring out of my wrist. It's scarier than thinking I was going to die.

Can you tell me what I say?

Cutting is the only thing I really know about myself. I know why I do it. I know it helps me. Cutting is the only thing I have that makes me *me*. It's the only thing I can hang onto that differentiates me, that gives me structure, gives me solid lines. It's what I know. It's all I know.

"It's all I have," I say to Shush, my voice so small I can barely hear it. "It's all I have."

Shush comes over and sits next to me on the bed, wrapping me up in a hug.

"No," she says. "It's not."

I don't move. I don't return her hug but I don't push her away. Eventually she lets go, but she doesn't move from where she's sitting next to me.

"Just tell me *something* Kara. Talking about it will help."

One true sentence.

"I… I don't know where to start," I say.

She shrugs. "At the beginning."

I pick at a loose thread on my comforter, not looking at her.

The first time I ever cut, I was fourteen. My boyfriend had just broken up with me. We'd only been together for six months but I was already writing my first name with his last name in the margins of my notebooks, already giving up part of my identity for him. Everyone did that back then. Planned for a future as if we could actually see it and not some illusion our child-brains dreamed up based off Disney movies.

I wasn't sure I saw it the way everyone else did. They seemed so sure. They seemed to take delight in their certainty. For me, the image was hazy, a mirage drifting up from pavement scorching in the sun and the closer I got, the more it seemed ready to disappear.

I think that just made me hold onto it all the harder. The prince and the princess. The fairytale castle and the Disney dreams.

So he broke up with me and the thing I'd been holding onto so tightly vanished in an instant.

And it hurt.

I just wanted to see the pain is all. I didn't want it to be invisible, the way everything else was. I wanted it to be something I could hold onto. Something I could see.

That's a nice story isn't it? I got into cutting because my boyfriend left me. It has a beginning and a middle and an end. It has hard plot lines that make sense. Action and reaction. Solid and substantial and real.

There's just one problem.

None of it is true.

Well, it is. Just not the way I want to tell it.

I was dating a boy at fourteen who broke up with me. But I didn't start cutting because he'd broken up with me. I was already cutting when we started dating. No solid cause and effect relationship there.

I'd told this imaginary story in my head before, figuring eventually I'd need a simple explanation to placate whoever I told it to. Everyone understands teenage heartbreak. And that was a nice little fairy tale everyone would understand.

The truth is harder to explain. The truth is I can't remember the first time I cut.

Everyone assumes it must be a big event, something you would never forget. But do you remember the first prayer you ever said?

When I don't say anything, Shush does. "Can you tell me why?"

How do I explain it? The prayers? The notes? The days I feel like paper? How do I explain feeling like I haven't happened yet?

I'd heard whispers at school about a girl who did it. The other girls called her a drama queen. Crying out for attention. But that isn't me.

I am not a cutter.

I don't consider myself part of that group. I'm not sure exactly when I began to differentiate myself from them. Maybe from the very beginning, when I chose to cut on my hip, where I could easily hide it, rather than my wrist, where anyone might see.

I didn't want anyone to know.

I wasn't a fourteen-year-old girl with open wounds on her forearms, baring her pain to the world, begging someone to see it, begging someone to listen. Desperate cries for attention aren't my thing.

And that's all cutters are doing right? Crying out for attention. At least, cutters as I always heard about them. That they're looking for attention. Not that they don't hurt, but that they want help. That they want someone to notice, someone to take pity and ask what's wrong?

I never wanted that.

If someone asked me what was wrong, I wouldn't be able to tell them.

If you need to scream out your pain into the world, is it real? Or are you just pretending? Over-exaggerating for the sake of the melodrama, hoping your boyfriend notices and realizes how much he hurt you, hoping he takes you back.

I don't scream my pain out into the world.

I hoard it. I hide it in the secret places of me, in case anyone would try to take it. No one will spread blue plastic tarps and demand I separate it out into pain to keep and pain to throw away and pain to deliberate over until all those closest to me are in tears and I'm ready to give up, ready to take all of my pain back into my collapsing house and hold it to my chest until I'm suffocating beneath the mass of it.

When I cut, I'm not asking for attention without words. I'm not *begging* for someone to notice my pain.

I'm *waiting*.

Not for someone to take my pain away but for someone to love it. For someone to see my wreck of a castle and want nothing more than to explore my ruins. Eric was the first. He didn't try to rebuild my crumbling stone walls. He ran his fingers over the jagged edges and admired the pattern of destruction. He didn't try to make me different. He saw the brokenness of me and wanted me anyway.

And I know it's wrong.

But it's also true.

Shush is still looking at me.

"I'm not doing it for attention," I say, my voice raw.

"I know Kara. I know you're not. I know you."

Questions so desperate rise up in my throat that I have trouble not saying them. Do you know me? What do you know? What do you see that I can't?

Can you tell me what I say?

I know that doesn't make any sense. But it's all I can think of to say. What have you read on my face? In my body language? In the words I say? Can you tell me what it is? Can you tell me what you've found? What clues have you unearthed about why my castle is in ruins? What happened here? Why am I this way? Why am I broken?

"You won't understand," I say.

"Try Kara. Just try."

I stare down at my hands, wondering if my fingernails would be enough to dig the words out from under my skin so I could offer them to her. But she doesn't want more questions. She wants answers.

"It makes me feel better…" Even to my ears it sounds like a pitiful excuse. But it's all I have.

She's quiet for a minute, and then, she meets my gaze. "Do you feel better now?"

I stare back at her, feeling like her sad black eyes are pits to drown in.

Hollow.

Like me.

"No," I whisper, my lips trembling.

And then I start to cry.

TRIGGER WARNING

The following section contains graphic depictions of self-hatred and self-harm. If you are not in a place where you feel up to reading that, please skip to the next section.

Remember, you're not alone. Mental health resources can be found at the back of this book. Take care of yourself.

THIRTY-FIVE

This is how you punish yourself.

You do not cry out. You do not protest you have done nothing wrong.

You do not struggle. You do not strain to be free from your captor. You do not try to escape.

You walk to the whipping post with quiet resignation. You are the person about to be ripped open. And you are also the one about to swing the whip.

It's your duty to hold out your wrists and let yourself be tied to the post. It's your duty to tie the knots.

Except there are no knots. The rope is loose around your wrists and any time you want, you could escape.

But you don't.

You don't even want to.

Because you know you deserve it.

You swing the whip with no mercy and when it bites into your skin, you lean into the pain.

This is how you punish yourself.

You use the razor—three dull blades—and crush your skin against bone. The hip. The ankle. The knee. Places where the bone is already close to the surface, already trying to break through.

These are not neat columns of small red prayers or the

organized collection of sharp words in a note. Criss-cross cuts on top of one another, change the angle, push harder. Tear your skin ragged.

Because you deserve it.

You have been judged and found wanting. You are an awful excuse for a human being who has done terrible things and hurt the people who love you.

You deserve this pain.

And after, breathing hard, collapsed against the post, fingers still curled around the leather handle of the whip, you feel better.

Because you have restored balance to the world. You have carried out justice.

Bad people are punished.

People who hurt people are punished.

But even as you're congratulating yourself on carrying out the sentence, you're circling back to the whipping post.

Because people who hurt people are punished.

And you've torn yourself bloody.

Look down. A rope is tied tight around your ankle, lashing you to the whipping post.

And it's your knot but you don't remember tying it.

You look up and see the tracks you've worn into the dirt, an ever-tightening spiral as you circle the post again and again, digging yourself deeper with your never-ending quest for justice.

You can't get out.

There is only you.

And the post.

And the whip.

This is how you punish yourself.

THIRTY-SIX

I cry until I run out of tears. My sobbing stops, and still Shush doesn't let me go. She's been holding onto me, just holding onto me, letting me cry, holding me together.

I'm exhausted. Like I've been running forever and I have to keep going except I don't know where to go.

"What do I do now?"

I don't realize I've said the words out loud until Shush responds.

"What do you mean?"

"I just…" My fists open and close at my sides, clutching at the fabric of my comforter. "What do I do now?"

Shush gives me one more squeeze and gets up. She goes to my desk and all I can think is she's taken my razor blades—what else could she be getting?

She plucks a black permanent marker from my pencil holder.

"I read somewhere," she says, "that if you feel like you want to cut, you should draw there instead."

"What?"

She must hear the skepticism in my voice because she laughs. "Don't knock it till you try it."

Stretching out her hand, she tries to give me the marker, but I hesitate. I don't see how using a marker will help anything. Markers won't help me punish myself for losing control in front of Shush like I just did. Markers don't cause pain. Markers won't let me release the pressure building up under my skin. Markers won't help me breathe.

"Okay," Shush says. She plops down on the edge of my bed and holds out her hand. "Foot."

"What?"

"Give me your foot."

Again, I hesitate, but she just waits, her hand outstretched, until I stretch my foot out and rest it in her palm.

She starts at my toe and works her way up, slow and methodical, drawing short, horizontal lines. There's some pressure with each line. But no pain. Instead it feels a little cold, a little damp, as the marker presses to my skin.

"Want to know what else I read?" Shush asks, not looking up, her gaze intent as she works her way up over my ankle bone, covering the old scars I've made there with lines of marker one by one. She avoids any newer cuts, and still somehow finds so much skin to write on.

"Okay," I say, watching as more and more of my skin is covered with black marker.

"Most people who self-injure are teenagers or young adults. It's not as uncommon as you think. Eighteen percent of people have cut or self-injured at some point."

She doesn't say it, but I hear it anyway.

You're not alone.

She's moving up my shin now. Rotating my leg as needed. Making neat rows and columns of small black lines.

"People who cut aren't necessarily suicidal."

"Shush I—"

"But people who cut *are* at a higher risk for suicide." Shush pushes on with her facts. She must have been reading up on this a lot. "There are a lot of different reasons why people cut. People who cut are very critical of themselves so they might be punishing themselves. They might be trying to take away or feel emotional pain. They might be trying to get some control. They might be trying to stop themselves from feeling numb."

It's strange to hear all of this out of Shush's mouth. Everything I've been feeling, so close it's almost as if it's something I told her. It's strange to hear her talk about it as if it's normal. As if it isn't something that changes absolutely everything.

It's strange to think other people feel the same way I do.

"Most people cut in secret. They're not doing it for attention. Most people aren't trying to kill themselves. They're just trying to feel better. And just because—"

She looks up at me.

"Just because the cutting isn't always bad doesn't mean it isn't serious. And it's addictive. It's not easy to stop."

She lets that hang there for a second, and then she lifts the marker from where she's drawn another line on my thigh.

"I think you can take it from here," she says, pointing the marker at my shorts. "You and I spent a lot of time getting way too close already."

It's like a bubble of tension in the room bursts. I laugh and take the marker from her.

"Yeah I don't think you need to see me naked again anytime soon."

She gets up off the bed and stretches.

"Listen, I need to go back to my dorm, okay? I've got to get some clothes, take a shower. You gonna be okay here on your own?"

She says it casually, but I can see the hint of worry in the corners of her eyes. I can't blame her for the way she's looking at me. Like I'm going to shatter the second she turns her back. Part of me is worried about the exact same thing.

"We can talk on the phone like we did before?" she says.

I shake my head. "It's okay, I'll be fine. I'll just... I'm just going to sit here and watch Netflix."

She looks at me another long minute, and then starts pulling on her boots.

"Alright. Try the marker Kara. Just try it. Please."

"Okay."

I don't say it until she has her hand on the door.

"I thought I was the only one. I thought... I thought I was the only one who felt... lost."

Shush grins. "You're great and unique and wonderful and all that but you're not *that* special. You're not the only one who doesn't have any idea what the hell they're doing."

"You do."

"Me?" Shush laughs. "I'm making this shit up as I go along."

Then she leaves.

And I'm alone.

I do what I said I was going to do. I put on something to watch and settle in with my water bottle and my snacks.

It doesn't hit me all at once.

Instead it creeps in slowly, one thought at a time.

My whole life is different now.

I've spent the last year revolving around two things. Eric. And cutting.

And now I don't have either one of them.

I don't have Eric to tell me I'm magic and I don't have cutting to help me when I feel like I can't take it anymore.

I have to figure out an entirely new person to be now.

And I don't know where I'm going to start.

Because I never knew. I never knew how to know who I was.

And now I'm not Eric's princess.
And I don't have my religion.
I'm back to square one.
It's okay, I tell myself. It'll be fine.
It's all going to be okay.
Automatically I look towards my desk, where my razor blades used to be.
But I'm not supposed to do that anymore. I'm not.
I'm supposed to…
The marker.
It's next to me on the bed.
Stupid. It's so stupid. There's no way this is going to help.
I just have to be strong. I have to wait it out.
But…
Picking up the marker, I pop the cap off and draw a line on myself.
It looks solid and black against my pale skin, covering an old scar on my thigh, tucked in between fresh ones in various stages of healing.
It looks… like something. Like the beginnings of a word.
I draw another line. And then another and another and another.
When I write the first word, I don't intend to. I put the marker to my skin intending to draw another line and instead I find myself writing a word I recognize.
Once
I pause, and then I keep going. I lose track of time, writing on every inch of skin I can reach. This is what they look like. This is what the words look like. All the words inside me.
This is what they look like.
Once upon a time…
We can't do this anymore.
It's just us.

No one else matters.
Come back to me.
Kara you have to tell someone.
I'm lost.
What do I do now?
Do you know the fairy tale behind the invention of the kiss?
You can't avoid me forever.
People wouldn't understand.
You're safe with me.
It's over.
Let me in.
I trusted you.
One true sentence.
I don't know who I am without you.
Kara he's not what you think.
Eric did that to me.
Did he say you were magic too?
Anything else you want to ask me?
Can you tell me what I say?
You're magic.
It's all going to be okay.

And somewhere, I'm not sure where, the words start to change. They change from things Shush said, things Eric said. They change to things I've never told anyone.

This is how you write a note.
Some days I feel like paper.
This is how you punish yourself.
Some days I feel like a someday.
I don't know who I am.

When my dorm room door opens and Shush sees me, standing there in a sports bra and shorts, writing on the last bit of available space I can reach on my side, she looks scared for a second.

My first instinct is to hide. To put my shirt back on. To apologize.

But I don't.

I just stand there, and let her look at what I have to say.

After all, is it really worse than seeing me bleed out on the floor?

After a second she just nods.

"Damn," she says. "That's some powerful art right there. You want to order pizza?"

~

They start out bold on my pale skin.

All the words that have been racing around and around inside my head, sinking into my bones. There for me to look at in the mirror.

But gradually, they start to fade.

I don't try to scrub them away, I don't spend time in the shower trying to scrape off my skin, hoping the words come with it.

I just let them slowly disappear. Shower after shower. I keep track of their progress. They go from bold and black to being nearly invisible. Until one day I'm looking in the mirror and they're gone.

And my skin is still scarred. Some of my deeper cuts are still healing over.

But just the absence of the words makes it look… cleaner somehow.

Lighter.

Like a blank page.

And for the first time, instead of that thought filling me with fear, it fills me with something else.

Anticipation.

Hope.

~

"Do you want me to come in with you?" Shush asks.

"No," I say. "I think… I think I want to do it on my own."

She nods and gives me a little smile. "Good. Good for you. Text me when you're done."

"Okay."

I take a deep breath, feeling the cold winter air fill my lungs. "See you in a bit," I tell Shush. And then I walk forward, past the sign that says *Student Counseling Center*, and push through the front door.

"Can I help you?" asks the student behind the desk.

He's smiling at me and I open my mouth to say something, but nothing comes out. My feet are rooted to the spot, my hands shoved deep into the pockets of my winter coat, and even though there are a million words swirling around inside my head, I can't say them.

I can't say anything because all I want to do is get out of here. I want to go back to my dorm room now that Shush isn't there. I want to find something sharp and I want to open up my skin. And even as I want to do it, I see the expression on Shush's face as she saw the extent of how I've hurt myself. I caused her pain.

And somehow instead of that making me want to stay here, it just makes me want to leave even more. I need to find something sharp. I need to balance the scales.

People who hurt people are punished.

I hurt her.

I hurt myself.

I don't deserve help.

I didn't deserve Shush's help and I don't deserve to be

here now, asking for more help from someone else. I don't deserve any of it. I deserve the pain. I deserve what I've done to myself.

I deserve all of the pain and the suffering and the hurt. I deserve to be punished.

Turning, I start to head out the door but I stop short. Shush is still outside. Standing across the sidewalk, leaning against another building. She's waiting. Waiting to make sure I get help. And I know instantly that if I leave she might not force me to come back today. But eventually she'll make me come back here. Eventually she'll make me get help. Whether I want it or not.

Oh.

It hits me all of a sudden. The truth of it.

There's a difference between crying out for attention and trying to ask for help without knowing how. If you don't think you're worth the help, then how do you ask for it? Is that what I've been doing? Screaming silently and hoping someone will hear me anyway?

I knew I wasn't supposed to be screaming for help. I knew I wasn't supposed to be that girl. That broken tragic crazy girl who throws her pain in everyone's faces.

I was supposed to be a pretty princess trapped in a tower awaiting rescue. Sure something might be wrong, there's always something wrong in the fairy tales, a reason the princess is in trouble. But the princess can't show that any of that wrongness has affected her.

My hair had to stay perfectly braided and my complexion smooth as glass. I had to say please and thank you and act as though nothing was wrong and still somehow ask for help.

And maybe I thought I didn't need help because I told myself there was nothing wrong with what I was doing. But maybe I've been lying to myself. Maybe I was trying to ask

without knowing how. Maybe this is what I needed.
I meet Shush's gaze and she gives me an encouraging smile.
Maybe someone who loves me isn't someone who accepts me as I self-destruct, someone who admires my brokenness. Maybe someone who loves me is someone who tells me I don't have to be that way. Someone who tells me I am worth more. Someone who tells me I deserve help.
I take a deep breath and turn back to the guy behind the counter.
"Yeah I need... I need to talk to someone. I need help," I say. And it feels good to say it.

THIRTY-SEVEN

I don't know how to do this.

Get up.

My ceiling looks the same above my bed as it did before. My blood never stained its white surface. But it feels different. Like it's a different ceiling. Or like I'm a different person. Everything feels different.

Get up.

I don't know how to exist in this world now. I don't know how to get up and go to class with Shush and act like everything is normal when she's seen me with my wrist cut open. When she's scrubbed my blood out of the carpet and washed it off the bathroom floor. When she's seen all the damage I've done to myself. When she's seen all the secrets I've kept for so long.

"Get up." Shush tugs the covers off me and holds out her hand. I let her pull me to my feet. "We're gonna be late."

It's like last week, with Shush taking care of me, happened in some alternate world. As I start to get ready for class, everything feels like I'm doing it for the first time even though I've done it all a million times before.

Getting out of bed. Washing my face. Brushing my hair.

It's all harder now.

Like someone told me to walk on my hands.

I'm still in the same place, doing the same things, but the whole world is upside down. No one's taught me how to walk this way. I don't have the balance. My muscles aren't used to it. I don't have the strength to hold myself up.

But Shush is here, keeping me moving.

"You know," she says as she does her makeup in my bathroom mirror, "I think we should move you into my house."

"What?"

She hasn't left me alone for longer than an hour since she saved my life. Even when I went to the counselor, she waited outside the whole time.

I want to tell her I don't need her to babysit me anymore.

But I'm not sure if it's true.

"I'm not sleeping on your dorm room floor again, I'm just not." She has a big bed in her room, big enough for the both of us. And I try to tell her it isn't necessary, but she won't hear it. "Shut up. Let me take care of you."

I bite my tongue.

I don't know how to do this.

She keeps helping me but I don't know how to keep letting her without trying to balance the scales. I don't deserve this.

I don't deserve her help. And I don't know how to tell her. Telling her will only make it worse because then she'll feel bad. She'll feel bad that I think so little of myself. She'll try to convince me I'm worth it. That I'm worth *something*. That I'm a good person. But she hasn't been inside my head. She's only seen the aftermath.

Even after talking to a counselor, even after asking for help, it's hard to keep accepting it. More trying to walk on my hands, trying to force myself to do something I'm not used to doing. I'm already exhausted and I'm not even dressed yet.

I stare at my closet and wonder what a person wears their

first day back to school after surviving cutting their wrists.

Shush comes over and pushes past me to grab a pair of jeans, a t-shirt, and a sweater. "We'll pack you up later," she says, leaving no space for argument. "You can stay with me. Just until you get back on your feet."

I want to tell her she's got that all wrong. She doesn't want me to get back on my feet. Back to walking through the world the way I did before. She wants me to walk on my hands. And I don't know how.

I don't know how to do this.

"Hey." Shush pokes me in the center of my chest, making me look up from where I'm staring at the clothes she put in my hands. "One thing at a time yeah? Just do one thing at a time."

Slowly, I nod.

That, at least, I know how to do.

I can cut up—

Deep breath.

I can break down each day into its parts, and just make it through each of them on their own. Except before, when I made it through the small stretches of living, I could go back to cutting. I could escape to breathe. Or write notes on how to do better. Or punish myself for what I'd done wrong.

What do I do when I make it through them now?

Shush is still looking at me so I start moving. I put on the clothes she gave me, and I walk with her to class. I go through the motions of what used to be my life, except it's all different now. Like a parallel universe. Everything just a little off.

When I walk into Biology, the room looks the same. But I'm not scouting for Shush so I can make sure she isn't waiting to ambush me. I'm walking next to her. And when the professor starts her lecture, I'm not thinking about how to get through this and get out before Shush can burn me.

Instead, I'm thinking about Patricia.

Patricia is my new counselor. Or therapist. Psychiatrist. Shrink. I'm not sure what the difference is.

"So what do you want to talk about today?" she asked when I first sat down. Strange because there wasn't a couch I could lay down on and talk about my mother or whatever it is you're supposed to do. Just a big armchair. I wanted to tuck my feet up under me, take up less space. But I was still wearing my winter boots, wet from the winter snow.

"What brought you here today?" she asked softly, as if asking the question a different way might give me an answer.

But I knew the answer.

I clasped my hands tight in my lap, because everything in me wanted to hold out my wrist and yank up my sleeve, showing her my bandaged wrist. And still everything in me wanted to run out the door without showing her anything. Without saying a word.

Because I didn't know what to say.

One true sentence.

I don't know how to talk to people about cutting.

I don't have the words, the language, for this secret I've kept buried for so long. I don't know how to dig it up. I left the shovel somewhere else, so I've been trying to unearth it with my hands. My nails are broken, my fingers streaked with dirt, but I've still only scratched the surface of all the parts of it I've buried. The holy items of my religion. Instructions for how to write a note. The whip.

There's still so much to bring into the light but I'm exhausted.

I don't know how to do this.

Patricia looked at me with kind eyes and a patient smile, as if she had all the time in the world to wait. But all I wanted was to crawl into the hole and bury myself with my secrets instead.

I got up, and purposefully turned away from the door so I wouldn't be tempted to run away. I had to do this. I promised Shush I would try to get help. And after all the pain I caused her, I had to do this one thing.

I had to try.

No matter how much it hurt.

Maybe this would be my new whipping post. Revealing all my horrible secrets.

I started looking at the books she had on her shelves. Reading the titles, running my fingers over the spines like I might climb inside one of them and run away.

Of course these weren't my usual books. Fantasy and fairy tales. With dragons that were always defeated in the end. These were different. These were reality. With dragons that didn't ever seem to go away.

Then I found one I could use.

I pulled it off the shelf and flipped through it until I found the page I needed. Cutting as a form of self-harm.

One true sentence.

I handed Patricia the book. "This," I said. "This is why I'm here."

~

"Hey," Shush hisses in my ear. "Take some notes."

And then I'm not in Patricia's office anymore. I'm back in Biology, with Shush elbowing me, and I pick up my pen.

Just this one thing. I can do this one thing.

I put my pen to paper and write down one thing.

And then another.

And then another.

~

At lunch, we meet Ella.

She sees us sitting in the corner of the cafeteria and waves, immediately heading over.

"Hey," she says, smiling at me with her fairytale princess smile. "Feeling better?"

I nod, because it's what I'm supposed to do. Not because I actually am.

I still don't know what I'm feeling.

Ella gives Shush a look and leans in to whisper in my ear. "I kind of thought we didn't like her?"

And I know I should tell her. I should explain. But it's so much story and I can't pick it up and carry it right now. I'm barely standing as it is.

I'm upside down, my whole body aches from the strain of keeping myself upright.

I still don't know how I'm sitting here calmly putting forkfuls of food into my mouth instead of curling up in a ball in the far corner of the room, rocking back and forth and screaming just to make sure I can still hear myself.

I should tell her. I have so many things to tell her. About Shush. About me. About Eric.

But I can't.

They're buried, all the secrets are buried deep and they're so heavy. I can't lift them right now. I can't even dig out the dirt around them.

I can't.

So I say, "We uh... we're okay now."

After a second, Ella shrugs, and throws down her stuff on the table next to me. "I'm getting pizza. I'll be back."

"Talk to me," Shush says, as soon as Ella is out of earshot.

"I can't... I can't do it." I shake my head and dig my fingernails into the table so I don't dig them into my skin.

"Can't do what?"

"I can't tell her." I look up at Shush and I can feel the misery on my face, see it reflected in the concern on hers. "I know I have to but I can't Shush. I just—"

Shush holds up a hand. "Slow down. Hang on. Take a breath."

She waits until I follow her instructions.

Inhale.

Exhale.

"Don't be so hard on yourself. You don't have to do the whole thing in a day okay? You can tell her when you're ready."

"But then… I'm lying to her."

Shush shrugs. "Yeah but you're holding yourself together. You're trying. Baby steps. Baby steps are okay."

Shush still doesn't know. About Ella and Eric.

She doesn't know my cutting isn't the only secret I'm keeping from Ella. But maybe that's okay. Maybe the principle still applies.

I'm holding it together.

Kind of. I think. Maybe.

I haven't cut. That counts. It has to. It's all I have right now.

So I keep going.

I make it through the rest of the day the way I always did before.

With masks.

With Fine Kara.

Fine Kara is fine. I'm fine. I'm just fine.

And no one else can see I am literally tearing apart at the seams.

It's forced, like I'm just going through the motions. But Shush doesn't think that's a problem when I tell her.

"Fake it till you make it," says Shush as she walks me to Creative Writing. As if she can see the edges of my mask now.

She's hovering over me. She's been trying to make it

seem like she's not, but she is. I don't mind, really. It feels like she's taking a little of the weight. She might not be helping me dig up all these secrets but she's handing me water and food, trying to keep my strength up.

And that's better than doing it all alone.

∾

I make it through to the end of the day. To packing up my essentials and going with Shush to her house, where she makes us soup and grilled cheese for dinner. We watch trash TV with her roommates and it's different from the evenings I'm used to. It's louder. But there's laughter and warmth and it's really not so bad. It's almost kind of nice.

It isn't until the middle of the night that it all starts to get bad again. I can't sleep because every time I close my eyes I see all the words again. I see all the words and I see all the things I did with Eric.

Do you know the fairy tale behind the invention of the kiss?

Can you tell me what I say?

You're safe with me.

You're magic.

It's all going to be okay.

And tomorrow I'm supposed to face him.

I'm supposed to go to class and put on my Fine Kara mask and expect it all to be okay.

But it won't be.

I know it won't.

I'm going to get to class and he's going to be there and I'm going to fall to pieces in front of him and everyone.

Everything is spinning so fast inside my head that I feel like I can't catch my breath. And all I want is to cut.

To slow the world back down to that one instant with

that small action and that manageable pain.

I get out of bed and head for the bathroom.

Shush finds me there a minute, or maybe an hour later. But she doesn't have to clean up my blood this time. She doesn't have to pull a razor blade from my fingers.

Instead she eyes the black marker, and the name I've written over and over in small, neat letters on my leg.

Eric.

She shuts the door behind her and slides down it until she's sitting on the floor across from where I sit, leaning against the tub.

She's looking at me, waiting, but I don't know how to do this. I don't know how to talk to people about what's in my head.

But I try.

One true sentence.

"What do I... what do I do about tomorrow?" I ask, my voice small in the hollow hours of the morning.

Shush shrugs. "Don't go. Just do all the assignments and email them," she says. "That's what I did. Asshole still gave me an A."

I nod, sagging a little, feeling like I might just fall asleep here on the floor. But Shush pulls me up, makes me get back into bed.

"Get some sleep. Sleep is good for you."

And maybe it's because she's there next to me. Or because I've done nothing but follow her instructions for a week, but when I close my eyes, I don't see words this time.

I just sleep.

~

Another week passes before I finally decide I'm up for

telling Ella. Not about Eric. But about me. About my cutting. The sleepover is Shush's idea.

"Then you'll have the whole night to find the right time," she says.

But when is the right time to show fairytale princess Ella all the ways I've hurt myself?

I can picture the whole night. From the time the three of us walk from campus to Shush's house, to the time we'll all fall asleep together in Shush's bed. There will be movies and pizza and Shush even got us wine. I've had sleepovers with friends before. They are light-hearted things. They're places for secrets. But not secrets like these.

They are meant for confessions of crushes and admissions about who it was that left period-stained underwear in the bathroom trash in the seventh grade. They are meant for secrets that evoke laughter and agreement.

"Oh my god I think he's cute too," and, "I totally would have done the same thing."

They aren't meant for secrets like mine.

For confessions of the ways I have punished myself.

They aren't meant for pain.

I can't figure out when to bring my pain into it. After the wine is gone or before we've started drinking it? Will it be easier for Ella to learn I cut myself open while she is eating pizza, filling herself with something good, or will it make her sick? Should I interrupt the laughter of a romcom by tugging up the sleeve of my shirt and showing her what I've done to survive myself? Would it be better to do it while light is still fading or should I keep it a secret whispered into the dark?

I don't know how to do it and I don't know when to do it. But I know I have to.

I can feel it, the words rising up to my lips every time there's a beat of silence. As we walk to Shush's house. As we spread out in the living room, all sweatpants and hair tied-up and prepared to pick away at our homework without really worrying about finishing it. As we start the first movie. As we decide what we want on our pizza.

And I want to escape this room with the two of them and go into the bathroom. I want to drown myself under hot water and carve the words into my skin.

But I can't do that.

I don't do that anymore.

And still I can't say the words.

I press my lips together and Shush catches my eye as she sees me digging the point of my pen into my hand, harshly tracing the lines of my palm in black ink.

I switch to writing on the notebook page.

I'm a cutter.

I'm a cutter.

I'm a cutter.

Over and over and over again.

And the name feels somehow wrong and right at the same time. Like someone's offered me a home but I just don't know if I can accept it.

One true sentence.

I've gone to see Patricia three times and she's told me all about cutters, confirmed what Shush told me and more. And she has tried to tell me I'm not alone, that I belong to a group of other people who know what it is to feel this way. As if I can't breathe for the need to get up and find something sharp to release this pressure. To preemptively punish myself for the way I'm about to hurt Ella. For the way I'm about to stain her fairytale world with my tragedy.

I'm a cutter.

I'm a cutter.

I'm a cutter.

And then I can't keep the words in any longer.

"I'm a cutter," I say. There's a beat of silence. Like the air stops moving in the room.

"What?" Ella asks, her voice barely audible.

I glance at Shush, who gives me an encouraging nod.

"I'm a cutter," I say again, louder, over the volume of the funny dialogue coming from the TV. This time the words come a bit easier.

And then, because I don't know what else to do, I lift up my shirt so she can see the ladder of scars on my side. As if I was trying to get somewhere. Or climb out of my own skin. Most of the cuts are healed now, but there are still a few where the new skin hasn't covered the red trying to creep out from inside me.

They keep reopening when I move, not quite ready to heal.

Ella reaches out towards me, towards my scarred skin, as if she's going to touch it. But then she stops, her hand falling back to her side.

And when her gaze meets mine, I curl my fingers into fists, letting my nails dig into my palms.

Because it's there in her eyes now.

The tragedy.

The pain.

And it's my fault.

This is not the sweet bite of the blade breaking my skin. It's the gaping chasm of pain I run away from. The one I think is so deep that if I let myself fall into it, I worry I won't ever get out.

And I wait for her to look at me in horror. For her to pull away from me as if I will infect her with my blackness.

But she doesn't.

"Does it... does it hurt?" she asks.

Yes, I want to say.

But that's why I do it.

I do it because it hurts.

And I don't know how to explain that. How do I tell fairytale princess Ella that sometimes it feels good to hurt? How do I explain that even as it hurts, it doesn't hurt as bad as everything else? How do I tell her that even as it hurts, it feels good. And still it's like having too much of something you like. After it stops feeling good, it makes you feel sick.

Guilt.

Shame.

That this is how I feel better. That this is what I need to feel better.

But I can't say any of that.

"Yes."

And then I tell her about my wrist.

"I'm getting help now. Because... because of this."

And I pull up my sleeve.

She reaches out her hand to curl her fingers around my wrist, the same way I had done when I apologized to her after the party. She does it as if she wants to hold me together where I'd tried to tear myself apart.

And then she squeezes.

"Ah." I wince as pain shoots through my arm.

"Sorry sorry sorry," Ella says, a look of alarm on her face as if she might have broken me.

Shush is the first one to laugh. And when I join her, it's in disbelief that laughter can find space in this room right now. Ella's face turns red but she starts laughing too.

After the laughter dies down, the silence comes back. And I don't know what to say now. I don't know if I should tell her more or if I've said what I needed to say.

But Ella speaks first.

"Are you… are you okay?"

My automatic response rises to my lips. The response I've used for so long.

I'm fine. Fine Kara is fine.

But I don't say it.

Patricia's words come back to me. "It's okay not to be okay," she'd said to me after our second session. "Everything won't fall apart if you admit you're struggling."

And still I want to say it.

I'm fine.

I want to hold it up like a shield, so she won't see how exhausted I am from all this digging up of secrets.

Except.

Except I'm not exhausted. Yes, this was difficult, one of the most difficult things I've ever done. And yes, I am tired. But I feel lighter somehow. Like I had to dig up the secrets but once I release them into the air, I'm no longer holding all their weight.

I meet Ella's questioning gaze. *Are you okay?*

I take a deep breath.

One true sentence.

"I'm… working on it," I say. And then I smile.

Because, even if it's terrible, it feels good to tell the truth.

THIRTY-EIGHT

"You need to tell them," Patricia says, looking at me over her notebook.

I pick at a loose thread in my sweater, not meeting her gaze.

"You know you need to tell them."

I do. I know she's right. It's just that I don't want her to be. I don't want to tell them. We've been talking about this for a few weeks now. At first she was gentle with her suggestion, but now she's getting more insistent.

"Why do you think telling them is going to be so difficult?"

My gaze snaps up to meet hers. I have to see if she's serious or if she's just trying to provoke a reaction. Telling them this secret is going to be the hardest thing I've ever done. She knows that. After everything we've talked about, she has to know that. And I can see it, in her open expression, that she does. She just wants me to talk about it. Typical therapist.

"Kara? Why is telling your parents about your cutting, about your suicide attempt, going to be difficult?"

I feel sick. I feel the words coming up into my throat and choking me. I know I need to say them, to get them out so I can breathe again.

But I can't.

I look down, going back to picking at the loose thread in my sweater.

~

Some days I cut because I hate myself.
Because I can't stand to be around myself anymore.
Everything I do makes me irritated and angry. I'm a
pathetic, pitiful girl who not only won't live up to her
potential but won't do anything good or important with her
pathetic, pitiful life.

It didn't start that way. As a raging, out of control fire
burning my world to the ground. It started as an ember of
discontent smoldering in my gut.

It started as:

Some days I cut because I shouldn't feel sad.

I grew up in a good, happy family. I was never abused,
my childhood wasn't difficult, my parents didn't ignore me
or push me to perfection. They were loving and supportive.

I'm not particularly unattractive according to conven-
tional societal standards and I've always done well in
school. I don't have any reason to feel like a gaping chasm
of misery is constantly waiting to swallow me whole. But
I'm exhausted from fighting to escape it.

It started as:

Some days I cut because I shouldn't feel lonely.

I was never one of the kids sitting alone at the high
school lunch table. Maybe I was never popular, but I
always had friends. And still sometimes I feel so lonely that
all I can do is cut myself open to try and feel some of that
pain on the outside.

It started as:

Some days I cut because I don't like myself.

Because I don't feel the right way and I don't do the right
things and I can never say what I'm supposed to. Because
I shouldn't be sad. Because I shouldn't feel lonely. Because

I'm ungrateful and no matter how much I have, I always feel like something is missing. I always feel like something is just off. Like something is wrong. Like I don't fit in my skin. Like this life isn't mine.

And somewhere along the way, it changed.

It turned from a small smolder into something burning me alive.

Some days I cut because I hate myself.

Because I believe I deserve to be miserable. If I feel that way anyway, then at least now I have a reason. If I won't just enjoy my happy life then at least now I have something to cry about.

Some days I cut because I hate myself.

Because I believe I deserve to be scarred. If I feel all alone, then I should give myself a reason to keep people away. A secret to hoard. A shield to keep them at arm's length.

Some days I cut because I hate myself.

Because I believe I deserve to be broken. Something in me has always felt broken. Something I can't find. At least now I can see it on the outside. At least now it serves as a warning to others.

Some days I cut because I hate myself.

Because I feel like a waste of space. Like I am using valuable resources—food, water, air—when they should be used for someone else.

I feel like I shouldn't exist.

And when I break myself open, I'm mad even then. Because the pain isn't enough. The cut isn't deep enough. As long as there is blood in my veins, it isn't deep enough.

Because I don't deserve to be alive.

But I'm too much of a coward to actually do what I need to do.

I couldn't even do that right.

Some days I cut because I hate myself.
And I don't know how to say that to the people who love me.

~

My mom's smile is unsure as she looks across the table at me, her hands secured around a mug of hot coffee. My dad's face is a little puzzled, but not quite as unsteady. He hasn't sensed the earthquake I'm about to unleash on their world. We're sitting in the café, them on one side of a booth and me on the other, sandwiched between Ella and Shush like support beams to keep my roof from caving in. I asked my parents to come visit. So I could tell them. So I wouldn't have to keep this one secret.

But I don't know how to do it.

I thought it would be easier, after telling Ella.

But I still don't know what to say.

I don't know how to tell them the truth after lying to them for so long.

Both Shush and Ella are trying to keep the conversation going while I drink my coffee and try to get my courage up.

"So how are you, Mr. and Mrs. Winterson?" Shush asks.

"We're doing just fine honey. How are you all doing with school?" At this my mom looks at me.

"Good," I say, because I know I should.

"Calculus?"

"Oh we're kicking some Calculus butt Mrs. Winterson," Ella says, smiling.

I look down at the table, at my mom's coffee, my dad's, mine. I remember the first time my dad caught me drinking coffee at fourteen, how he'd said I shouldn't start so young. How my mom had come into the kitchen and applauded me for liking it black instead of needing to add creamer and sugar like my dad. After that drinking coffee together in the morning had become a routine, something we did as a family, something to say we loved each other.

I take a large swallow of coffee. It's too hot. It burns my tongue, the roof of my mouth, my throat as it goes down. The pain feels good. Familiar.

I meant to tell them right at the start, so I wouldn't have to spend all this time worrying about it. But all I can think about is the last time we talked about my cutting. The only time we'd ever talked about my cutting.

After Shush told my mom and abandoned the two of us in the parking lot, neither of us said anything. She didn't ask me questions and I didn't offer any explanations. We spent the drive home in silence and when we got to the house, I ran upstairs to my bedroom, trying to pull myself together before I went down to face my parents.

I came down from my bedroom in pajama pants and a tank top, as if the reason I raced up to my room was to change. When I saw my dad's face, I knew my mom told him what Shush said to her.

I smiled at them, trying to pretend like nothing was wrong. I leaned over the counter, purposefully displaying my wrists, free from cuts or scars, and saw them both glance down to check. I'd worn a tank top for this exact purpose.

The arms are where everyone thinks to look.

"Kara…" It was my mom who started it. "Kara we need to talk to you."

"What's up?" I injected a note of cheer in my voice, keeping my face carefully blank, as if I had no idea what they were talking about.

I could see my mom turning over the words in her mouth, deciding what to say, how to start, which words to use.

"Sweetheart, Shush… Shush told me." I said nothing and

my mom bravely pushed on, holding my dad's hand for support. "She's worried about you."

I frowned, as if this was news to me. "About me? Why?" They didn't hear it. The Fine Kara tone I put on my voice. But of course they wouldn't. It was the same one I'd used for years.

"She says she saw... she saw scars from... from where you've been cutting yourself." When she said the word cut, she gripped my father's hand harder and both of them stiffened. As if the mention of the word had actually caused them the pain I feel from the action.

Relief washed through me. Shush hadn't said she saw me cutting. This was okay. I could handle this.

I took a deep breath to prepare myself. Everything hinged on me pulling off this moment, on me keeping my story intact. I was their happy and put-together child. There was nothing wrong with me.

"Oh that." My tone was light and airy, like I was brushing it all away as nothing. "Don't worry about that. I'll have to talk to her. She must be confused."

"Confused?" My dad frowned then. "Do you have scars Kara? Are you—" His jaw clenched. "Are you cutting yourself?"

"No, of course not." Relief crossed both of their faces and in that instant I knew I could do this. I could keep this story going. "She must have seen scars from ages ago. From high school."

I'd decided on a partial truth. I'm terrible at lies. This way, I wouldn't be making anything up from scratch.

"So you... you were cutting in high school?" my mom asked. I could hear the hurt in her voice, but it wasn't as pronounced as it had been before, when she'd thought I was still cutting now.

"Just a couple times. It's not a big deal, really. Everyone was doing it back then. It was like… it was just what the girls were doing you know? Some… some emotional thing I guess." I tried to make it sound childish, like it was so long ago and so stupid that there was no way I would still be doing it.

"Kara that's…" My dad took a breath, tried again. "Why didn't you tell us?"

Because you'd never understand.

"Because it honestly isn't a big deal. I swear."

They wanted to believe me, I could see it in their faces. That's what happens when the lie is something you want to believe and the truth is something that would hurt you.

That's why it's been so easy to lie to them for all these years. Because that's what I've been doing. Telling them a story they want to believe. Telling them a story about their happy, fairy-tale daughter instead of the tragedy they really have.

I've been lying to them for years.

And now I'm supposed to somehow tell them the truth.

I don't realize the conversation at the coffee shop has slowed to silence until Shush gives me a nudge under the table.

Ella presses her leg against mine.

"I umm…" I can't look at my parents.

I want to get up and run away and never look back. I want to disappear. Just vanish into the air and find a new home in one of the books on the walls around us.

"What is it honey?" my mom asks. I take another drink of coffee so I don't have to look at her. I can't do this.

~

Patricia let the room fill with silence. Her question hanging in the air.

Why is telling your parents going to be so difficult?

I could wait her out. I've done that before. Waiting until

she tries to come at the subject a different way and I can twist out of answering. Or waiting until she changes the subject altogether, deciding getting me talking about something—even if it isn't this—is better than me not talking at all.

But I know I need to answer her eventually. I can't avoid this forever. I dig my fingernails into my palms.

"Because..." I start and then stop. She just looks at me, waiting. "Because it's going to hurt them."

I meet her gaze and my voice breaks. "I'm going to hurt them."

~

"Kara?" my mom says gently.

And I still can't look at her. I can't look at either one of them.

How do I look into the face of someone who taught me to tell the truth and tell them I lied about hurting myself?

How do I look into the face of someone who raised me and tell them I've been doing this for years?

How do I look into the face of someone who taught me how to take care of myself and tell them I do it not just in spite of knowing it isn't good for me but *because* I know it isn't good for me?

How do I look into the face of someone who gave me so much and tell them some days I feel so much *nothing* I have to cut myself open just to feel *something*?

How do I look into the face of someone who taught me to walk and tell them I am so exhausted from the vast emptiness inside me that some days I can't move?

How do I look into the face of someone who kissed my scraped knees better and tell them I hurt myself in order to feel better?

How do I look into the face of someone who taught me

right from wrong and say that yes it makes me feel guilty but that only makes me want to punish myself more?

How do I look into the face of someone who taught me to speak and say I didn't ask for help because I don't think I deserve it?

How do I look into the face of someone who loves me and tell them how much I hate myself?

How do I—

"Kara," Ella says gently. "You can do this."

Shush reaches down and takes my journal out of my bag. "Just read it."

Still not looking at my parents, I open the journal to the page I've marked.

~

"That won't stop them from loving you," Patricia says. "They can take it. Parents are tougher than you think."

Even if she's right, that still leaves a problem. A huge problem.

"What do I… How… What should I say?"

Patricia smiles and takes a spare notebook from her desk, handing it to me.

"Why don't we try writing some of it down? It will be easier if you spend time finding the words first. So you don't have to worry about finding them in the moment."

I look down at the blank piece of paper. And I still don't know what to say.

"Just take it one word at a time," Patricia says.

One true sentence.

"You can do this. You've done so many hard things already. Just start. Write down one thing. One sentence. Start there."

I take a deep breath, and I put the pen to the paper.

~

It doesn't feel like me. The person sitting at this table between Ella and Shush, staring down at the words I wrote over and over, spending pages editing and rewriting, trying to find the words. Trying to make them right.

Just do it, I tell myself. It's just reading. You know how to read.

They taught you how to read.

See Jane run. Run Jane run.

See Kara lie. Lie Kara lie.

My throat closes up and I have to swallow a few times before I manage to start.

"Mom, Dad, I have to tell you something."

I hear the words come out of my mouth but I'm not saying them. I wouldn't be saying these things. I wouldn't be saying any of this.

"I know I told you I wasn't cutting anymore. I know I told you it wasn't a big deal." I bite the inside of my cheek. *Lie Kara lie.* "But I lied."

I hear my mom's sharp intake of breath. I feel my dad stiffen. But I still don't look at them. I have to keep going. These are secrets I've kept buried for as long as I can remember. To say them like this feels wrong. But I know I have to say them.

"It was a big deal. It *is* a big deal. And a few weeks ago everything... everything got really bad and I..."

I can see the words on the page but I don't know how to say them. They lodge in my throat.

I can't breathe.

I can't move.

I feel my parents staring at me, urging me to look at them. But I can't.

Shush presses her knee against mine, solid and steady. I

can hear Patricia in my head, telling me to keep going all the
times we practiced this.

You can do it. You lived it. That's the hard part.

Except somehow it isn't. Somehow the fact that I
survived it doesn't make telling the story any easier. And I
know it should.

But some part of me would rather be bleeding out on my
dorm room floor than talking to my parents about it.

And I know that's terrible.

But it's true.

How do I look into the face of someone who gave me life
and tell them sometimes I don't want to be alive?

"Kara…?" My mom turns my name into a question. And I
don't have an answer for her. I am a question. Not an answer.

Or at least not the answer she's looking for.

One true sentence.

"I tried to kill myself." The words come out in a rush
and I keep going. I can't let them hang in the air, can't give
them time to wrap around my throat and choke me. "But
it's better now. I'm better now. I'm getting help. I'm seeing a
counselor. I just…" Finally, at the end of it, I look up. "I just
wanted to tell you the truth."

"Oh honey…" It's like my mom's face has frozen and then
shattered. She's trying to keep it together and that only makes
it worse. Like she's trying to pick up the broken pieces of her
heart and all I can feel are the cuts it's making on her hands.

My dad's face reveals nothing. The only hint he heard me
at all is a ticking of the muscle in his jaw, pulsing just under
his skin.

"I'm sorry," I say. Because what else can I say?

"How?" my dad asks, and my mom presses her lips
together so hard all the blood drains from them.

"I… I cut my wrist." I don't show them, the way I did Ella,

even though it's still bandaged. I don't want to break them. Not any more than I already have. So I tuck my arms under the table. Ella grabs my good wrist and squeezes it.

"Why?" My mom says it but she doesn't look like she really wants answers. She looks like she's terrified of them.

Terrified of *me*.

I shake my head. "I'm sorry." Tears sting at my eyes and I swallow, trying to force them away. "I'm getting help," I remind them, trying to make them feel better, trying to give them a solid fact to hold onto.

"Are they licensed, these people?" my dad asks. "Do they want you on medication? Do we need to take you to a professional?"

"Why… why didn't you tell us?" my mom asks. And in her voice is that small, broken echo of betrayal. Of disappointment. "Why couldn't you just tell us?"

"I'm sorry," I say again.

I say it over and over as I answer their questions. All the questions I actually have answers for. No, I never went to the hospital. Yes, my arm is healing. No, I'm not on medications yet. Yes, I will go to a psychiatrist. No, I don't need to come home. Yes, I want to finish this semester. No, I haven't cut since.

Over and over.

I'm sorry.

I'm sorry for not being the daughter you raised. I'm sorry for letting you down. I'm sorry for hurting you. I'm sorry for not being everything you taught me to be.

I'm sorry I am broken.

Over and over.

I'm sorry.

I'm sorry.

I'm sorry.

As they get up to leave, I'm still saying it.

I don't know how long we've been sitting here but my coffee has gone cold. I tried to give them what few answers I could but it isn't enough. I know it isn't enough.

It will never be enough.

So I say it again.

"I'm sorry," I tell my dad as he hugs me goodbye. He holds me a little tighter, a little longer than usual. Like I'm falling apart and he can hold me together if he tries hard enough. He wants to be able to *do* something.

"What do you need? What do you need us to do?" he asks. And I don't have any answers for him. I can't give him a task. Pick up the hammer and nails and build me a treehouse so high nothing bad will ever hurt me again. There isn't anything he can do. And so I say it again.

"I'm sorry."

"You don't need to apologize," he says, hugging me harder. "This isn't something you apologize for."

Still the words rise up to my lips.

I'm sorry.

But I swallow them back down.

When he lets me go, my mom wraps me up tight. She doesn't say anything, just holds me until I feel her start to shake with the effort of holding back her sobs.

Then she lets me go, and without looking at me, rushes out of the coffee shop. My dad gives me an apologetic look and then follows her out.

"You did it," says Ella.

I feel like I might fall over.

"You survived," says Shush. And I can tell she means it as a joke, gallows humor. But I can't laugh. Her words hardly even register.

My world is darkening at the edges and all I see is my

mom rushing out. She couldn't even look at me.
Like I am the monster from all of her nightmares. Everything she ever prayed wouldn't happen.
In the flesh.
In *her* flesh.
I never should have told them.
I never should—
And then she's back, pushing through the café doors in a rush. Taking my face between her hands.
"We're not mad at you," she says. "Okay? We are not mad. We're... we're glad you told us."
She wraps me up in her arms. "We love you. We all love you so much. It's all going to be okay. We're gonna get through this. It'll be okay." She pulls back and looks me in the eye. "Okay?"
Tears start to fall down my face.
She doesn't let me go, her eyes searching mine for a response.
But I can't speak.
I can't say one more word.
Instead, feeling her arms around me, I nod.
Okay.

THIRTY-NINE

This is how you keep going.
   You try to get the basics right. You get up. Shower. Brush
your teeth. Put on clothes. Eat something for breakfast. Go
to class. Eat something for lunch. Go to work. Eat something
for dinner. Do your homework. Go to bed. Sleep.
   This is how you keep going.
   You do all the things you know you're supposed to care
about. You don't have any desire to eat, but you eat anyway.
You don't really care if you're alone or with your friends,
but you spend time with your friends anyway. You can't
bring yourself to worry about passing your classes, but you
study anyway.
   This is how you keep going.
   You try to find things you want to do, even when the
concept of wanting anything feels like it drained out of your
wrist onto the floor. So you find things you don't hate doing.
Reading. Writing. Spending time outside in the sun. Spending time with your friends.
   You feel like you're faking it. Like the inside of you is
hollow. Like you're an actress in a play you didn't write,
and you're just playing a part. But you play the part anyway.
   This is how you keep going.
   When you want to cut, you don't.

You talk to your therapist. You talk to your friends. You write on your skin with black marker. You scribble down all of your words in a journal until they go away.

This is how you keep going.

One moment, one hour, one day at a time.

You don't know what you're doing but you do it anyway.

And sometimes when you're with your friends, you're even interested in the conversation.

Sometimes when you talk, you mean the words you say. Sometimes when you laugh, you feel like it's real. Sometimes, you even feel happy.

This is how you keep going.

~

The last time I went to Eric's office, I was running. I was desperate. I was breaking apart and I wanted him to save me. I needed him to save me. To tell me I was magic.

This time I'm walking slowly. And I don't know how I feel. I don't think I'm falling to pieces but I'm not really together. I don't know what exactly it is that I need from him. I just know it's something.

I need *something*.

I don't have to think about where I'm going. I've walked this path so many times before. I know the way from my dorm to his office as well as I know the pattern of scars on my skin.

There's a hint of summer in the air, the sun warm on my face. The weeks that passed since I talked to my parents have gone by in a blur. Now it's the first week of May. Finals week. And I've just been checking things off my list.

First, the Biology presentation with Shush.

That went smoothly. We spent ages preparing. I don't like getting up in front of people but after all the spilling of

365

secrets I've been doing, talking to people about bones was almost easy. We haven't gotten our formal grade back yet, but Dr. Nelson gave us a thumbs up and an approving nod when we finished.

Then Calculus.

I've been doing better. Ella's been helping me a lot and Dr. Howards gave me some extra credit assignments to help make up for the test I failed. I landed a B on the test a few weeks ago. Still waiting to get the grade back for the final, but I think I did well. Well enough not to fail the class and lose my scholarship.

I leave the sidewalk and head onto a dirt path through the trees, the ground softer but still firm beneath my feet. I'm almost there now. Deliberately, I slow my steps.

My days have been getting better.

I'm seeing Patricia regularly, and she's been giving me techniques for coping. When I can't breathe, I put on a song that makes me feel like I'm walking through a meadow beneath mountains. When I feel everything all at once, I go for a run. When I can't feel anything, I hold an ice cube, tight, in my hand, until the pain of it brings me back to my body.

She's been encouraging me to journal a lot, which is helping the most. When I get stuck on something—a song or a scene or a sentence I can't let go of—I write about it. I try to figure out what it is that makes me get stuck on them. And I try not to get angry when all I'm doing is putting words to my questions instead of finding answers. Because even figuring out how to phrase the questions is better than nothing. So when I feel like I can't escape the words in my head, I try to write them down, try to figure out how to describe what it is I'm thinking, what it is I'm feeling.

Sometimes I just call Shush or Ella and ask them to talk to me. It doesn't matter what we talk about as long as we're talking. I've even connected with an online support group for cutters. It's nice to talk with Shush and Ella but it's different to talk with people who actually understand the way I'm feeling. I've never met someone else who cuts before. Sometimes one of them says something and I can latch onto it like that, *that* is how I feel. Having words to describe it makes it all seem… smaller somehow.

A few weeks ago I moved out of Shush's and back into my dorm room. The first nights were hard, but I've been getting better. I've been sleeping through the night. Journaling helps. Every night before bed I write down anything that's been bothering me during the day.

And then the words are out there.

They're down on paper where I can see them, where I can make them small and not so big they chase my sleep away.

There's only one thing left that feels so huge it might swallow me up.

Eric.

Once upon a time…

I stop at the foot of the stairs leading into the Letters and Arts Building. Pressing the pad of my thumb against the corner of the stone wall beside the stairs, I look up at the door.

I'm putting it off.

Climbing the stairs. Walking down the hallway to his office. Going inside. Seeing him.

I press my thumb just a bit harder into the sharp edge of the stone.

I've seen him a few times around campus since I cut my wrist. Always from a distance. And I always hid or left before he could see me. I've been handing in all of my assignments by email, and I could have done the same thing with my final paper.

But I want to see him.

I have to see him.

Ella and Shush offered to come with me. I could have had them here, one on either side, urging me up these stairs or saying it was okay to turn back. I could have had Shush calling him names and Ella looking at me with a grim but sympathetic understanding.

We told Ella a few weeks ago. Shush and I. We told her about Eric.

We were all in the café together, studying.

"So do you guys—sorry Shush, sorry—do you *ladies* want—"

Ella broke off as her phone buzzed. She picked it up to look at the message and my heart tried to sink into my stomach. Because I recognized the expression on her face.

You're magic.

A princess that's just received a formal summons from her prince.

"Actually I think I have to leave," she said.

"Ooh the mystery man awaits?" Shush's tone was teasing, but it was only because she didn't know. I hadn't told her Ella's prince was Eric. I'd wanted to but I knew Shush would take over, and make me tell Ella. I wasn't ready.

I'd been wanting to tell Ella ever since I first realized Eric was trying to pull her into his fairytale web of lies.

But I hadn't.

I couldn't.

The ground still felt shaky beneath my feet. What if telling Ella made everything fall apart?

He's not what you think.

When Shush tried to tell me about him, when she started hinting about the truth of him, it had been the start to breaking apart our friendship. What if I told Ella and she stopped being friends with me? What if she thought I was lying? What if she thought I was just jealous? What if she chose Eric over me?

The hard part was I couldn't even blame her.

That's what I'd done.

Chosen Eric and his lies over Shush and her truth.

Eric did that to me.

What if Ella was angry with me for waiting so long to tell her? The more days that passed, the worse that fear got. How far had he taken her along the path into his fairytale kingdom? What had he done that I could have prevented if I'd just told her sooner?

She would have every right to be furious with me.

I was furious with me.

But every time I opened my mouth to try and say something, the words died in my throat.

I could feel it happen, as she started packing up her things, getting ready to go meet him. Something else slipping away, something I should grab onto before it spun out of control.

"I'll see you later," Ella said.

She turned to leave and I grabbed her wrist. "Ella wait."

She looked at me, obviously expecting me to say something else. I didn't know how to say it. I hadn't practiced this. I didn't have anything written down.

But I had to say something.

She'd done nothing but help me. With Calc. With climbing my way back from wanting to die.

And now I had to help her.

I took a deep breath.

"Does he say you're magic?" I asked.

Ella's half-confused grin faded from her lips. "What?"

"Holy shit." Shush came to life next to me. "Kara, he—"

"Yeah," I said, not looking at her, keeping my gaze trained on Ella.

"Asshole," Shush muttered. "That *absolute* fucking asshole."

"What's going on?" Ella asked.

"That mother—"

I bumped Shush's knee with mine, cutting her off.

She'd had too much time to move past it, to move from seeing him inside the fairy tale to seeing him in the real world. She didn't really remember him as a prince anymore. She'd been where Ella was but she had both feet out of that story now. I still had one inside it.

It had to be me. I had to tell her.

"We know about Eric," I said gently, tugging her wrist so she sat down in the booth across from us.

"Dr. Eric *Fucking* Callahan," Shush said under her breath.

"Shush," I warned, still watching Ella, waiting for her to protest, waiting for her to bolt. I didn't know how far he'd pulled her in. I didn't know how hard we were going to have to work to get her out.

"I don't… I didn't…" Ella looked lost. A kite with her strings cut. "I don't understand."

"We were magic too," I said.

And I had to bite my tongue against the sudden wave of *hurt* that tried to pull me under.

"But he…" Ella started, shaking her head. "He said… I thought…"

"I know," I said, squeezing her hand. "He makes you believe it. That you're magic. But *he* isn't. He isn't a prince Ella." It was the first time I'd said the words out loud. *He isn't a prince.* They tasted strange on my tongue. I said them again. "He isn't a prince."

Shush snorted. "Got that right."

"Do you want to get some dinner?" I asked Ella. "And we can tell you about it?"

After a long minute, she nodded slowly, and we all packed up our things and got to our feet.

Shush walked in the middle, slinging her arms over our shoulders. "Yeah," she said. "We'll fill you in on just what an absolutely fucking pathetic complete and total asshole he is." The conversation had gone as well as it could have. We told her our stories, and she told us hers. And it was familiar. The way he started flirting with her, innocent touches and notes on her papers. The way he made her feel like she was the only person in the room. The way he started helping her with homework outside of class.

And I hated myself the entire time she was telling her story.

Because it *hurt*.

It still hurt, even though I knew it shouldn't, to think about him wanting Ella. Even though I knew it was wrong, it still hurt to picture him with anyone else.

And maybe that's why I put off telling her for so long.

Because I didn't want to face this part of myself. This part of me that still misses him. That still misses who I felt like with him.

You're magic.

And at the end of her story, when she told us she hadn't kissed him yet, I felt something else.

I felt *happy*.

Not because I saved her—or rather, not *just* because I saved her—but because that part of him is still mine.

Do you know the fairy tale behind the meaning of the kiss?

What he gave to me—the magic he whispered over my skin—I still have it. He hasn't given the fairy tale to Ella yet.

And I know all the terrible things he is.

I've seen the dragon hiding in the prince's skin.

The claws and the teeth and darkness behind his eyes.

And still.

I miss him.

I miss what he gave me.

Sometimes when I lay awake at night, all I want is to go to his house. To have him wrap me up in his arms and tell me everything's going to be okay. I want him to kiss the new scar on my wrist, to see how broken I became, and tell me I'm magic anyway.

Can you tell me what I say?

I want him to give me back my new character.

Princess.

Someone beautiful instead of broken. Someone worthy of rescue instead of being found when it's too late.

Anything else you want to ask me?

I know I'm supposed to get over him, but I don't know how. For the last year of my life, he was my prince. He was my everything. I've lived in this fairytale world for so long, it's hard to see past it. And I can't ask Shush how to move on. She's so far gone she doesn't remember the path she took to escape the woods. And I can't ask Ella because I'm supposed to be leading her out.

The only person I want to ask is Eric.

What do I do now?

How do I get over you?

How do I know if I'm over you?

And this is why I have to go back.

Why I have to see him.

I have to know for certain.

I have to face the dragon but more than that, I have to face the prince. I have to look into his eyes and feel whatever it is I'm going to feel.

I have to *know*.

Are all these feelings of wanting him just residual? Left over, half-faded memories of a story I lived but not a story I am still living?

Or do I really still want him? If he reached out his hand, would I take it? Would I turn my back on all the steps I've taken since trying to kill myself—turn my back on Shush, on Ella, on who I might become—to go back to who I was with him?

I want to say no.

But I don't know.

I want to run away, to turn around and go back to my dorm, email him my final paper and just forget this all ever happened. I could do it. I could go back to Shush and Ella and I could ask them to come with me. I know that.

Except I have to do this on my own. I know that too.

Sometimes there is nothing you can do.

I walk up the stone steps.

Back across the drawbridge.

To see if I've really escaped.

Or if I've just been pretending.

You're safe with me.

I can see it happening. I walk into his office and when he opens his arms, I collapse into them. He leads me back inside the castle and I let him. I hold out my arm and feel his dragon's tongue savor my suicide-scar. *What have you done?* he asks. I look at him and see the dragon, so I close my eyes and remember the prince. And when he holds me close, I let myself disappear inside his fairy tale, ignoring the way his claws cut into my skin.

You're safe with me.

I can see it happening. I walk into his office and when he opens his arms, I slap him across the face. I rip up my sleeve and show him where I cut myself open, screaming at him. *Look at what you've done!* I tear the castle walls apart brick by brick, throwing each one at his terrible dragon face. And then I set the rubble on fire, burn everything down with both of us still inside.

I hesitate, just outside his door.

Before, when I walked into his office, it was entering a castle. A castle filled with spells and secret doors. A place to find Eric. A place to lose myself. I sought out magic in the details. The color of his desk, the arrangement of his books, the scent of coffee in the air.

Now, when I walk in, I brace myself. I am prepared for the fairy tale to pull at me, to try and trap me back between its pages. I am prepared for everything to gleam slightly of gold, to give a haze to the air that makes it hard to see everything in its real light.

I am prepared for the sight of Eric, turned away from me, packing papers and books into a bag, to make me feel weak. I am prepared for my body, my head, my heart, to react to him as if he's still a prince.

I'm here.

I am prepared.

He doesn't hear me come in, so I clear my throat, and he spins around like I've ambushed him.

"Kara," he says, surprise evident in his tone. "What a... what a pleasant surprise."

His voice is different somehow. Thinner.

"We've missed you in class."

I don't look at him, letting my gaze travel around his office instead.

It's different than I remember.

There's no mystical hum of magic, no sunshine coming through the windows, highlighting dust particles floating in the air like the remnants of some spell. I don't feel strong stone walls rise up around me, protecting me, keeping me inside the fairy tale.

Instead, it's just an office.

Diplomas in frames on the wall. A bookshelf filled with

books. A computer. A desk covered in papers. A familiar mug on top of a stack of ungraded finals.

"To what do I owe the pleasure?" he asks.

Still, I don't look at him.

I reach into my bag and pull out the final paper I've printed, set it on his desk before he can try to take it from me.

"Good," he says, picking it up and starting to flip through it. "Good."

Part of me wants to walk out now.

I've faced him. I walked in here and handed him my paper.

But I don't have my answers.

I look at how he holds my words in his hands and wait for the longing to come. The longing to have his hands hold me that way again. Like I'm a book of magic spells he can't wait to read.

I reach for the mug. Pick it up, cradle it in my hands, wait for the memories attached to it to pull at me. Wait for them to burn me.

But it doesn't feel warm from his touch. It doesn't feel like a portkey to take me back into the fairytale memories I have of him.

It feels cold.

And hard.

Just a mug.

If I dropped it on the floor, it might shatter.

Gently, I place it back on the desk.

"This is excellent Kara," he says. "Well-reasoned. Insightful."

Simple words of praise that would once have made my skin flush with pleasure. Words I used to spend my nights awake replaying, watching them dance in the darkness, letting them pull me in like words to a magic spell.

But now, I just stand there. And still, I don't look at him.

Reaching out, he traces a finger down the edge of my palm, hanging loosely at my side. And I wait to feel the sparks, wait to feel the heat of him.

"Kara… look at me."

I don't move.

He takes my hand in both of his, twisting it so it's palm up, and traces the lines of my palm with his finger. The way he used to. The way that used to make my body pull towards his.

You're magic.

"I'm sorry," he says. "I'm sorry I've been… out of touch lately."

If he moved his fingers six inches up my arm, he would see what I'd done to myself. I wonder how he'd react. I wonder if I care.

If he pressed his lips to my deepest scar, would I let him pull me back in?

If he finally reacted like all the other boys, angry and scared, would it hurt?

He keeps talking. "I've just been so busy with every-thing."

Still I say nothing.

"I wish you would look at me," he says. "I've… I've missed the way you look at me."

I have to do it. I know I do. I have to look at him.

But I can't.

Will he look the way I remember him in my head? Will I still see the prince? Will I still see the fairy tale?

And worse, what if I don't? What if I see the dragon?

What if I want to keep him in my head as the prince? As the man who kissed my scars and told me I was magic? What if I want to keep him in the fairy tale so I can revisit it? So I can pretend it was full of light and laughter and none of

it makes me feel dirty, like I want to peel off my own skin?
"And really, if I'm being honest, I've missed everything...
everything about you."
Honest.
You're safe with me.
I'm here.
You're magic.
Was he ever honest with me?
Did I want him to be?
What if I don't want the truth?
What if I want the fairy tale?
He's still tracing the lines of my palm like he can unlock
the secret code of me. And I have to know. I have to know
if somewhere deep down I still believe he has the answers
I'm looking for. I have to know if I'll see the dragon or the
prince. I have to know which character he is so I know
which character I am. I have to know.
I look up at him.
What I see surprises me.
And, at the same time, it doesn't surprise me at all.
I don't see the Disney prince, with thick black hair and
shining eyes and a smile that would make any girl go weak
at the knees. And I don't see a dragon, with sharp teeth and
claws that would hook into me.
I see *him.*
Dr. Eric Callahan.
A middle-aged literature professor.
His hair is dull, not glossy, and it's streaked with more
gray than I remember. His eyes, still a deep black, are lined
with wrinkles and have dark circles under them as if he
hasn't been sleeping. His hands, which I remember as being
strong and sure, feel frail and uncertain as they hold mine.
I take a step away, taking my hand out of his.

When he stands up, he's not as tall as I remember. He doesn't take up as much space in this office as I thought. He seems smaller somehow, like he's a part of the world but not the only thing in it.

He moves closer to me.

"I wanted…" His hand reaches out as if he's going to brush the hair back from my face again, but he thinks better of it at the last minute, dropping his hand back to hang limply at his side. "I want to make sure you're okay."

I don't know how I missed it before. The hollowness in his tone. How he tries to gloss his words over and how that makes them slippery.

I don't say anything.

"I… I wanted to tell you I miss you," he says softly. He takes my hand again, and I let him press it to the side of his face. "You feel good. You've always felt *so* good. Mmm…" He brings my fingertips to his mouth and I feel his teeth, his tongue, scrape my flesh as he nibbles at each of them, one by one.

He presses my hand against his chest, holding it there, and bends down to me. As he runs the tip of his nose along the curve of my neck, he inhales deeply, like I am something delicious he wants to eat. Gooseflesh rises over my skin but it isn't the way it used to be. It isn't from the pleasure of his hot breath on my skin.

It's from the stench of it. Old. Stale.

"Do you want to come over for dinner tonight?" he asks, murmuring the words into my ear. There's a hint of desperation in his tone that I've never heard before. He presses his cold, dry lips to the tender skin at the curve of my neck, making his way slowly up to my jaw.

When he speaks again, his voice is husky like a groan. "I've missed your magic."

And this is where I shudder. Where I lean into him.

Where I let him close the door of his office behind me so he can whisper magic over my skin.

This is where I choose bad magic over no magic at all.

Except I don't.

I reach down into my chest, searching for the way my heart used to lift at the sight of him. The way everything in me used to cling to him, desperate for the answers I thought he had.

But I find nothing. I feel nothing.

No fairy tale.

No magic.

Nothing.

It all feels hollow. Paper-thin. Like a book no one bothered to finish.

Suddenly I can't remember why I ever thought him a prince.

He's pressing kisses to my jaw, my cheek, as if it's going to make me remember the way he kissed each one of my scars but all it makes me feel is uncomfortable. He has my hand trapped between his hand and his chest and his touch feels clammy, his hand damp with sweat.

But I don't pull away.

And then I realize I am waiting to be released. I am waiting for him to let me go. For him to take me off his shelf and bring me back to life so I can have a story beyond the one he writes for me.

But I am not a mug kept between his books. I am not cold and hard. An inanimate object he drops on the floor to shatter at will so he can admire my broken edges as he pieces me back together.

I am not a book for him to take out and read when he likes. I don't need him to give me answers. I don't need him to translate me. I don't need him to tell me which character I am.

Because I am all of them. And none of them.

I am alive.

And I have a choice to make.

I step back and look him straight in his black eyes. Not omniscient wells of knowledge that will translate all the things I don't know about myself if only I open my pages to him enough times. And not pools of black magic designed to trap me, keep me where he wants me, enshrined as a collectible in his dragon's hoard.

No.

They're just eyes.

"Kara?" he asks again, his voice nasally and pleading. "I'll make your favorite. Buy that wine we like?"

I pull my hand out of his and when I speak I don't shout, but my voice resounds in his office all the same.

"No."

I walk out.

And I don't look back.

FORTY

Once upon a time a princess met a prince.

Her body was covered in magic spells. She'd been trapped in a secret tower for years, unable to read her own body, unable to decipher the magic words she needed to get out.

He came to her rescue.

He broke her out of the tower and told her she was magic.

She believed him.

She took his hand and let him bring her into his fairy tale. She lost herself inside that fairy tale. Inside his castle walls and his magic forest. Where he was the prince and she was the princess, and everything ended happily ever after.

Until it didn't.

Until he told her she wasn't a princess.

Until she discovered he was really a dragon.

Until the fairy tale she thought she was living, the character she thought she was, was ripped into unrecognizable pieces.

Until, like her fairy tale, she disappeared.

∼

Once upon a time a girl met a boy.

Her body was covered in words. She'd been trapped in a book for years, unable to read her own body, unable to decipher the

story she was living in.
He came to her rescue.
He plucked her off the shelf and told her she was worth reading.
She believed him.
She took his hand and let him write her story. She lost herself
inside that story. Inside his bedroom walls and his lovely words.
Where he was a boy and she was a girl and everything ended
happily ever after.
Until it didn't.
Until he told her she wasn't the girl for him.
Until she discovered he wasn't the boy she thought he was.
Until the story she thought she was living, the person she
thought she was, was ripped into unrecognizable pieces.
Until, like her story, she disappeared.

∼

Once upon a time I met a guy.
My body was covered in scars. I was trapped in my secrets for
years, unable to say them, looking for someone to say them for me.
I thought he could give me answers.
I thought he could make me real.
I wanted to believe him.
I took his hand and told him all of my secrets. I lost myself
inside a world I wanted to be real. Inside my silence and his lies.
Where I was a question and he was the answer, and everything
ended happily ever after.
Until it didn't.
Until he told me he didn't want to be my answer anymore.
Until I discovered he never had the answers at all.
Until the secret I thought I was living, the secret I thought I
was, was ripped into unrecognizable pieces.
Until I wanted to disappear.

~

Once upon a time there was me.

My story started long before I met the man I once called my prince.

I started cutting when I was thirteen.

It's a secret I've kept for years.

A secret I've let myself get lost inside.

My whole life I felt like I had no idea who I was.

And I thought he knew.

I thought he had answers.

I didn't know how to find my own name.

So when he gave me one, a good one, one glowing with magic and all the stars from childhood fairytale balls, I went to him without hesitation.

And he seemed like he knew. He seemed like he knew exactly who he was.

He told me his name. Prince.

And he gave me one too. Princess.

And he kissed my scars and told me I was magic.

He gave me a story.

A fairy tale.

Once upon a time a princess met a prince.

And they lived happily ever after.

It was a story I knew.

One I'd been told over and over.

Once upon a time a princess met a prince.

There's never one without the other. Can't have a princess without a prince. Can't have a happily ever after unless you're one half of a whole.

That's the story we're all told.

But maybe it isn't true.

Maybe it never was.

Here is the story as I know it.

Here is my story as I know it.

It is at once both complicated and simple.

Last year, as a freshman, I began a romantic relationship with one of my professors. I thought he loved me. I thought I loved him.

Maybe it was all true.

Maybe none of it was.

Maybe it doesn't matter.

At the start of this semester, he ended the relationship.

Without him, I was lost.

I didn't have a name anymore.

Without a prince, I couldn't be a princess.

My cutting got worse.

And still all I wanted was to go back to him.

Because it was easy.

It was easy to be the book on his shelf. I had boundaries. I had a beginning, a middle, and an end. I was a character in a story. I was a princess. He was a prince. That's all there was.

Instead of this vast unknown.

He was a solid shape and I wanted to wrap myself around him so I didn't have to stand on my own. I let him have and take me. And he did.

I ignored all the bad.

I let him tell the story of us.

The story of me.

Because it's easier to have someone tell your story than to figure out how to tell it yourself. It's easier to have someone give you the words than it is to find them yourself. It's easier to hold out your wrists and say give me my map because then you're not lost in the middle of forever with nowhere to go. It's easier to go somewhere, anywhere, even with someone bad, because then you have somewhere.

You are someone.

So I wanted to go back to him.
Because I wanted to be someone.
And I couldn't be someone without him.
Then I read another story. The same story you've all read in this newspaper. About how this man I thought was a prince was really a dragon. About how he sexually assaulted another student. And everything I thought I knew changed again.
And still I wanted to go back to him.
Except a princess isn't supposed to want a dragon.
I couldn't possibly be a good person and still want to go back to my professor when I knew he was sexually assaulting other people.
Except I did. I still wanted to go back to him.
Because without him I was no one.
Without him, I didn't know who I was.
Without him, I didn't exist.
So I tried to end my story.
I tried to kill myself.
Because it was the only answer I had.
But I'm still here.
A good friend saved me.
And since then I've been trying to figure out how to save myself. I've been discovering I am worth saving.
And I don't have everything figured out.
But I'm trying.
I'm trying to figure out what I want to say and how to say it.
And in the midst of all the things I don't know, I know this:
I had to tell this story.
I had to tell my story.
Whatever my story is, it's important to tell it.
And maybe it's complicated and messy. Or maybe it's simple.
But here are the facts as I know them.
My professor isn't a prince. He never was. And if I do nothing else, I will stand up and say that.

For so long, all I wanted was to let him tell the story of me. To tell me I am a princess in a fairytale castle. To tell me that in spite of the scars on my skin, I am magic.

And maybe none of it is true. Or maybe all of it is.

But that isn't the point.

The point is that I was letting him tell my story.

For so long, I let him be the one talking.

Not anymore.

I'm not letting Dr. Eric Callahan tell me who I am any longer.

I'm telling my own story now.

∾

That story is coming out in this semester's final edition of the student newspaper tomorrow. Which is when Shush, Ella, and I, will also be going to the administration and telling our stories to the dean. What happens after that, I don't know.

But that's okay.

Because we'll have told the truth.

We aren't keeping his secrets anymore.

∾

Moonlight glistens off the still water of the pond, giving the familiar little clearing an ethereal glow. I walk down the hill alone in the four-a.m. stillness, stopping with my toes just short of the water.

I remember coming here at the start of this semester, after Eric had broken up with me. How I'd felt back then. Like I couldn't make it across, like one wrong move would shatter the world beneath my feet and I would drown.

Taking a deep breath of warm, almost-summer air, I glance around to make sure I'm alone. And then I slip out

386

of my sandals.

I spent today re-walking the paths from that first day, writing myself a new story. First Eric's office. In the old story, he broke up with me. In my new story, I ended things with him.

I take off my shirt and drop it on top of my sandals, baring my scars to the moonlight and to me and no one else. They still look like script I've written into my skin. Like magic spells.

I remember how Eric had first discovered them, his fingers slipping into the waistband of my jeans. How he had touched them with such reverence.

I take off my shorts, dropping them on top of my shirt.

After Eric's office I'd gone to the bathroom in the science building, the one where I'd waited for Biology to start that first day.

The words I'd written that day, unable to keep them in any longer, were still on the bathroom stall wall.

I'm sleeping with my professor.

The first domino. The words that started the rumors that took over campus before the Women's March. The rumors that had held me at a distance from Eric after he broke up with me. The rumors that had been just that last little push Shush needed to write her story in the newspaper.

I'm sleeping with my professor

I'd pulled a marker from my pocket. Carefully, I'd fixed it.

I was *sleeping with my professor.*

Past tense.

It felt good.

It *feels* good.

To fix it. To start a new story.

And now I'm here. At the pond. The one I'd been too scared to cross that first day.

I remember the way Eric had taken off my clothes the

first day I'd gone to his house, laying me on top of his bed, staring at me.

I take off my bra and underwear, until I am naked, my story plain to read. But it's all for me.

I don't need him to read me anymore.

I have a new story now.

And I'm not reading it.

I'm writing it.

I step into the water, inhaling sharply at the chill of it on my skin.

The ground is slick beneath my feet and I go carefully, making my way in deeper one step at a time. Until the water swallows my knees, my hips, my shoulders. I take a breath, and let the water close over my head.

It's quiet. So quiet.

Familiar words echo in my head through the silence.

It's all going to be okay.

∿

Earlier today I had my last session with Patricia. She referred me to another therapist in my hometown that I would see over the summer, but I still planned to see her next year when I came back to campus.

"So what do you think about your progress so far?" she asked me at the end of the session.

"What do you think about my progress so far?" I asked.

She smiled, shaking her head. "No. I want to know how *you* think you're doing. What do *you* think?"

And I just looked at her, silent.

∿

The water is cold and my lungs are starting to remind me I need air. But I'm not moving. I'm listening. To the quiet. And I'm not scared. I don't want to come up screaming. And I'm not giving up. I don't want to disappear into the dark, into the silence.

Instead I focus on the words.

It's all going to be okay.

I push off the ground, coming up for air, gasping it into my lungs. And then I start to swim, heading for the other side.

It's all going to be okay.

Over and over, with each stroke of my arms, each kick of my legs, I hear it.

It's all going to be okay.

Over and over. With each turn of my pages as I move through my story—

Eric.

Shush.

Ella.

My cutting.

My suicide attempt.

—I hear it.

It's all going to be okay.

The pond isn't very big, but still it feels like it takes a long time to swim across it. For my feet to find solid ground again. But when they do, I walk out, one step at a time, shivering slightly.

The words spin around in my head but they aren't in Eric's voice.

They're in Patricia's.

Shush's.

Ella's.

My dad's.

My mom's.

It's all going to be okay.
And one voice louder than all the rest.
Mine.
It's all going to be okay.
I push my hair out of my face and stretch my arms up to
the sky.
The moonlight makes my pale skin glow. It doesn't erase
my scars. It doesn't make my skin look like a blank first
page. But that's okay.
Because I have more stories to write.
I can keep my old stories with me. Scars and all.
And I'm smiling.
Because I feel alive.
I feel like possibility. All the possibility of a new book
opening, a new story starting.
I'm alive.
And I feel like magic.
What do you think? Patricia had said.
It's all going to be okay.
I think it's all going to be okay.

≈

"Hurry up Kara," Shush says, picking up her pace.
"We're going to be late."
"I'm coming, I'm coming."
I follow her as we weave in and out of other students
on the sidewalk, walking quickly to the café, because she's
right. We are going to be late. To the open mic Dr. Leery is
putting on for my Creative Writing class. It's part of our
final, reading our work out loud.
Shush pushes through the doors of the café and I follow
her upstairs. The place is more crowded than I've ever seen

it, with rows of chairs set up in front of the little stage. Shush immediately starts talking to someone I don't recognize and I wave at Ella, who's sitting across the room. There's so much activity and so much conversation happening around me that I can't really seem to catch my breath. There are so many unfamiliar faces, the friends and family of my classmates.

But there are plenty of familiar faces too.

"Hi honey," my mom says, pulling me tightly into a hug. My dad hugs me after her, and I smile at them both.

"Thanks for coming," I say.

"Wouldn't miss it," says my dad.

I'm about to say something else when a fist knocks into my shoulder from behind and I spin to find Jake standing there, grinning at me.

"What's up Kara?"

"Hi," I say. "I didn't think—"

"If everyone could take their seats?" Dr. Leery's voice comes over the microphone. "We can get started."

"Jake over here," says a familiar voice and I turn to find Tom sitting a couple rows back, motioning to the seat next to him. He smiles at me. "Hi Kara."

"Hey babe," says Jake, grinning widely. He leans over the students in the row between them and kisses Tom full on the mouth. Raucous applause and a few wolf whistles erupt from the students around them.

For a second I'm just stunned. I didn't know they were together. I didn't even know Tom was into guys.

And then I'm laughing.

I'm laughing so hard I can't breathe.

Tom's face is bright red when Jake finally releases him.

"Sit down idiot," he says, yanking Jake down next to him, but he's smiling as he says it, entwining his fingers with Jake's. Then he turns to me. "Break a leg Kara."

"Alright, alright," Dr. Leery says, trying to look stern and failing as the laughter in the room subsides. "If we can get started? I am Dr. Leery, and I've been teaching these wonderful creative writing students for the past four months."

I grab a seat next to Shush and Ella as Dr. Leery goes through her introductions.

"You ready?" Shush whispers to me.

I nod, pulling my papers out of my bag and clutching them in my hands, waiting for Dr. Leery to call my name.

Some days I feel okay.

I get up and there are things I want to get up for. I eat because I'm hungry. I read because there are books to explore. I spend time with my friends because I enjoy it.

I'm not forcing my way through my life.

I'm not pretending.

I'm living.

Some days I feel okay.

I say things. Give a voice to the words running around in my head.

And the world doesn't end.

My friends haven't left me. My parents still love me.

When I go outside, it doesn't feel like the ground is going to fall apart underneath my feet with each step.

Some days I feel okay.

I don't feel hollow, or even hollowed out, like a book someone tore all the pages out of.

Because I'm not a story.

Stories have beginnings and middles and ends.

I am not a story.

I am many stories.

Always evolving, always changing. Taking in new pieces, changing the scenery and the characters and the dialogue.

Asking new questions, getting new answers.

Maybe I don't know exactly who I am yet, but that's okay.

I am a work in progress.

I am the princess and the prince. I am the knight in shining armor and I am the dragon. I am the castle and the magical forest. I am everything at once.

The important part isn't what the story is.

It's who is doing the telling.

Some days I feel okay.

Some days I even feel good.

"Kara?" Dr. Leery's voice pulls me out of my head.

She's looking at me with an expectant smile and I stand up, walking slowly to the front of the room where she's standing.

"Take a breath," she says to me as she steps off the stage. "You'll be great."

I step up behind the microphone and look out at all the faces in the crowd. Dr. Leery. Tom. Jake. Ella. My parents. Shush.

Everything feels different now.

It's been two months since I last cut. And I know that me getting better will take longer. That my mental health will be something I deal with for the rest of my life.

But I also know my scars will fade.

And even though I'm nervous, part of those nerves feel different now. A little less like I'm about to fall apart and a little more like I'm about to start an adventure.

My hands are shaking and I want to say something witty, but I can't think of anything. So I just look down at the paper in my hands. The last assignment I handed in for Creative Writing.

The title in bold words at the top.

My Story

I have no idea what I'm doing. I don't know who I am and I don't know where to go from here.

But I am here.

I'm looking out at all the people who love me, who care about me.

And I know what to do next.

I know what to do right now, here in this moment.

And that's enough.

I take a deep breath—

How do you tell someone a story when you don't know how to tell them?

You just do it.

—and I start to speak.

"Once upon a time…"

AUTHOR'S NOTE

As an indie author, one of the hardest struggles I face is getting the word out about my book. I would be incredibly grateful if you could take a moment to leave a review wherever you purchased this book and anywhere else you can. Spreading the word on your own social media is so, so, so helpful. Thank you for your support.

One of the reasons I wrote this book is to raise awareness about self-harm, which impacts millions of people around the world. Even as mental health becomes more mainstream to talk about, I feel self-harm has stayed firmly in the shadows, which makes it hard for people who self-harm to talk about it and get help. It's one of the reasons it took so long for me to get the help I needed. And if I can make even the smallest difference in changing the conversation... Well, I hope it will help someone else.

But the main reason I wrote this book is for my younger self, who so badly needed a book like this.

I have found a home inside books for as long as I can remember. There's nothing quite like the feeling of reading someone else's words and thinking, *Oh, someone else has found a way to put this feeling into words when I never could.* Or *Oh, I thought I was the only one who felt this way but someone else has written about it so someone else feels this way too.* And whenever that happens, the fear that I am so strange and so broken and so alone fades away. That connection has, I swear, saved my life.

Still, it's always been so difficult to find books where the main character is struggling with self-harm, especially in a way that felt realistic to me. And I have never found a book, although I'm sure others are out there, where the main character struggles with self-harm despite having a good life. So I wrote one.

Because no matter how much connection I could find in books, I never found one with a girl like me. I wasn't abused or neglected and I never suffered a traumatic experience. I have good parents and a good family and I've always had good friends. When I was young, I did well in school and sports. When I was older, I did well at work and I found a loving partner.

But I still self-harmed.

I kept my struggle a secret for so long because I felt overwhelmingly guilty that I needed self-harm to cope when by all accounts, I had a good life.

Writing this book was the hardest thing I've ever done.

Deciding to publish this book was the bravest thing I've ever done.

Putting a piece of art out into the world to face critique is terrifying enough. But telling the world secrets I kept almost my entire life? Way, way, way worse than the one time I went sky-diving. This is the scariest thing I've ever contemplated doing, much less actually gone through with doing.

But if even one person reads it and finds it easier to get help with their struggle, I know it will be worth it.

I hope this book helps spread awareness about self-harm, but more than that, I hope one person reads it and thinks:

Oh, I'm not alone.
    Because it's true. You're not alone. And you deserve help.
You deserve to write yourself a better story.
    Be gentler with yourselves my friends.

Take care,
Erin

ACKNOWLEDGMENTS

I have been petrified to write the acknowledgments for this book since I first started drafting it a decade ago. Not because I don't have people to thank, of course I do, but because I am so worried I'll forget someone. My life has been filled with incredible people who have supported me through my doubts and my mistakes and my successes.

To my very large family on both sides of the Atlantic. Thanks for being my early readers, for your love, support, and encouragement. And for accepting all of me, even as I shared all of these difficult secrets with you and then with the world.

To my mom and dad, thanks for telling me I could be whatever I wanted, and supporting my decision when I switched from wanting to work for NASA to wanting to be a writer.

To my number one social media hype person, you slay every day.

To Pamela, who worked with me through the initial extremely rough drafts of this novel, and whose quiet and unwavering encouragement helped nurture me into the writer I am today.

To Jennifer, my friend and mentor. Thank you for always being willing to share your wisdom and for helping me learn to stand tall. I look forward to hikes and pints with you for years to come.

To John, my incredible writing coach and editor, without whom this book would most likely still be sitting unread and rejected. Thanks for helping me find my confidence and believing in me enough to push me to be better.

To the lads, who always make me laugh. Thanks for your very particular and outrageous flavor of support.

To my other two musketeers, I would not be the person I am today without you. Thanks for being there with me through thick and thin.

To Stephen, who has loved me through all my struggles and supported me every step of the way as I decided to undertake this very scary thing. Thank you, love, for always making me nachos and reminding me to rest.

To all the people whose name might not be on this list, thank you. I am so grateful for your love and support and encouragement as I have gone through not only writing this very difficult story, but also talking to the world about struggles I kept secret for so long. Every follow, every like, every comment, every emoji, every kind word have meant so much to me.

And to you, my dear reader. Thank you for being the reason I wrote this story and the reason I will write so many more.

Words cannot express how grateful I am for the people in my life, and I would know, because I'm a writer and I have tried.

I love you all, and I hope the best for each and every one of you.

Take care of yourselves.

ABOUT THE AUTHOR

Erin Lodes currently lives between Ireland and Michigan. She hopes one day to be a full time author but until then, manages to fit writing in around a challenging but fulfilling day job. When she's not writing or reading you can find her walking her dog Charlie, doing a puzzle, or watching her favorite TV shows for the millionth time.

All her social media can be found on her LinkTree by scanning the QR code below.

RESOURCES

There is no shame in asking for help. It's the best thing I ever did.

To Write Love On Her Arms: twloha.com

United States CrisisTextLine.org/help-for-self-harm Text CONNECT to 741741 for free 24/7 help

MentalHealth.org.uk/explore-mental-health/publications/ truth-about-self-harm

International Helplines: twloha.com/find-help/ international-resources/

You can find all these links on my LinkTree by scanning the QR code on the previous page.